Contemporary Strategic Concerns

Making India's Presence Felt

Contemporary Strategic Concerns

Making India's Presence Felt

Edited by

Dr Sitakanta Mishra
Dr Banita Mahanandia
Dr Gyanaranjan Swain

GYAN

Published by

Gyan Publishing House
5, Ansari Road
Daryaganj, New Delhi-110002
Phone: 011-47034999, 9811692060
E-mail: books@gyanbooks.com

Distribution Network
www.gyanbooks.com
India, USA, Canada, UK, Australia, France

ISBN: 978-93-7133-186-9 (HB)
First Published, 2025

Printed at: Gyan Press, Delhi.

Contemporary Strategic Concerns

Making India's Presence Felt

Edited by: Dr Sitakanta Mishra, Dr Banita Mahanandia, Dr Gyanaranjan Swain

Contents

Introduction: Making India's Presence Felt 7
– Sitakanta Mishra, Banita Mahanandia, Gyanaranjan Swain

1. **A Roadmap for India's National Security Strategy: Priorities and Challenges** 15
– Neeraj Singh Manhas

2. **Russia-Ukraine Crisis: How Did the World Respond?** 31
– Rajaram Panda

3. **Sino-Russia Cooperation to Challenge US Hegemony: Concerns for India** 51
– Singh Subhalaxmi Baidhar, Prasanna Kumar Panda

4. **Reimagining Kosli Identity through Human Security Approach** 67
– Shankar Chhatria

5. **Issue of Migration in Indo-Bangladesh Relations: Challenges for Human Security** 83
– Duryodhan Nahak

6. **India-Vietnam Partnership and the China Factor: Assessing Human Security in the Indian Ocean Region** 99
– Navonil Dey

7. **The Future of the Indian Ocean in the New Cold War Era: Certainties and Imponderables** 121
– Shreya Das

8. **India's Dynamic Foreign Policy: Indo-Pacific Strategy and Balancing Role in Quad** 141
– Naresh Kumar Behera

9. India's Role in QUAD 157
– Gopika Pavithran

10. The QUAD and India-China Relation: An Indian Perspective 165
– Kalpesh Bag

11. Securing the Tide: The Grand Design of Aspiring India for the Indian Ocean 185
– Subham Tripathy

12. Unravelling Ethnic Gulf in Manipur: A Land at Crossroads 201
– Keshab Chandra Ratha

13. Human Trafficking: An Overlooked Security Threat to India 213
– Priyanka Masant

14. India and the Road to G20 Presidency: Evolution, Trajectory and The Way Forward 223
– Mohammed Badrul Alam & Reyaz Ahmad Ganaie

15. India's G20 Presidency: Strengthening Multilateralism for the 21st Century 239
– Neeraj Singh Manhas

16. The Competitive Edge of G-20 in Multilateral Negotiations to Further Inclusive Global Digital Economy 255
– Nisarg Jani

17. Nuclear Energy is a Non-negotiable Choice: A G-20 Approach 273
– Reshmi Kazi

About the Editors 291

About the Contributors 293

Introduction:
Making India's Presence Felt

India as a non-aligned country takes meritorious stand, or actively participates as the situation warrants, in every issue or event occurring in any part of the world. As a responsible member of the community of nations, and as an unavoidable 'rising power', it is poised to play a significant role in every contemporary concern that affects the world. This is of course nothing new. During the previous decades since 1947, even when it was not at today's level of prowess, New Delhi partnered with the world to allay many global concerns. It has often shouldered global responsibilities when new geo-political ground realities threaten world peace and harmony. Therefore, many consider it a 'compassionate global power' "with a worldview that fosters global peace, harmony, and the well-being of humanity as a whole."

India's presence in the world has always been felt, especially during crises. Way back during the Cold War, both the US and USSR were entangled in an ideological tussle to dominate the world, which led the world almost towards Armageddon. This was a prolonged global crisis when the Afro-Asian countries (Third World) were afraid of getting sucked into this rivalry and were in search of leadership to bail them out. India, with its powerful idea of non-alignment, offered a unique solution that helped in containing and defusing the Cold War crisis. In many other crises, India has extended leadership, such as the Indonesian freedom struggle of 1947, the Korean crisis of 1950, the Suez Canal crisis of 1956, Operation Cactus in response to the coup in Maldives in 1988, LTTE crisis in Sri Lanka and India's air operation 1989-90, several air evacuations of nationals from war zones, humanitarian assistance and disaster relief operation during 2004 Tsunami in Southeast Asia. In the recent past, India showcased crisis-time leadership during the COVID-19 pandemic when all major powers were inward-looking; India managed to sync its domestic requirements and global responsibilities. Besides humanitarian assistance, "India delivered over 65 million doses of vaccines to 100 countries" and emerged as the 'pharmacy of the world'. All these prove that India is capable of providing crisis-time global leadership.

Today, the world is grappled with many strategic concerns for which collaborative efforts are warranted to resolve them. Some of these concerns even intricately affect India as well. Be it in the domain of superpower rivalry, military conflicts over territory, illegal migration, human trafficking, human security, ethnic violence, energy security, or multilateralism, the global arena is marred with full of spark points, potential to drag all of us towards Armageddon. This volume is an endeavour to ponder over some of those pressing concerns thriving in different parts of the world where India's role or views matter.

About the Volume: The volume is also partly an outcome of a national seminar (ICSSR sponsored) on "Debating National Security in India: A Human Security Perspective" organised by the School of Political Science, Gangadhar Meher University, Sambalpur, Odisha, India during December 22-23, 2022. Selected research papers of the seminar have found their place in this volume, and many other chapters are invited from experts on the issue area. Essentially, one agreed upon theme of the seminar set the tone for this volume, i.e., India is one of the leading countries in the world which has set very high benchmarks in many ways. The maturity of its political system, resilience of its economic framework, age-old social fabric, its 'emerging power' status, etc. make it a country of great interest for policymakers, researchers and scholars around the world. But while many of India's threats and conflicts are strategized and discussed within the confines of security and strategic studies within the conventional international relations perspectives, many less visible challenges emerge, impacting significantly India's unity and integrity. The attempt therefore is to probe how to make sense of the roots of those strategic concerns and amicably address them.

The volume incorporates a range of contemporary concerns: 1. national security encompassing comprehensive national security and human security; 2. Foreign policy including bilateral and multilateralism; 3. Global concerns involving energy security, migration, multilateral grouping, etc. In each of these themes, scholars have contributed chapters making the contents a logical flow. On some pressing concerns, multiple chapters by authors have been accommodated, largely to cover all aspects of the issue area. For example, on the human security issue area, four authors have deliberated on various aspects like illegal migration, bilateral cooperation, linguistic-ethnic identity, and the Indian Ocean Region. Similarly, on the national security domain, the security issues involving the Indian Ocean discourse have been deliberated by multiple authors. On multilateral groupings like G20, which was led by India in 2023, multiple authors have inquired upon its origin, function, strategy, and future. The Ukraine-Russia war that has become protracted and how the world responded is closely investigated by Rajaram Panda. It is a new churning of the global geopolitics and he rightly predicts that the three key channels that could be affected by the ongoing conflict are commodity and food price shocks, financial repercussions from the sanctions, and security challenges in a scenario of an escalating or wider military conflict.

The chapter by Shankar Chhatria entitled "Reimagining Kosli Identity through Human Security Approach", discusses the federal structure of India that allow for a unified but culturally diverse country by combining equality for the individual with equality for various communities. However, language movement across the nation constituted a significant danger to India's internal security. In this chapter, the author discusses the "Kosali identity" in Western Odisha, which was neglected by successive governments of Odisha in terms of infrastructure, public institutions and political representation. This study focuses on factors influencing regionalism in Western Odisha and Kosal movement with the lens of human security approach.

Shreya Das in her chapter "The Future of the Indian Ocean in the New Cold War Era: Certainties and Imponderables", focuses on the future of Indian Ocean region which depends on the objectives, policies and concerns of various nations in the region. After the demise of UUSR in the cold war, a multipolar international order developed in which China emerged as major global power. The US has a serious conflict of interests with China. This conflict has increased hostilities and geopolitical competition in the Indian Ocean region. Many experts refer it as emergence of new cold war. On the other side QUAD which is an informal alliance between the US, Australia, Japan, India cooperates to promote their mutual interest in the region. This act is criticized by the China that four countries aimed at containing China. Therefore, the challenge posed by India to China's regional objectives also provides an important context to the geopolitics in the Indian Ocean region.

Navonil Dey in "India-Vietnam Partnership and the China Factor: Assessing Human Security in the Indian Ocean Region" highlights the maritime border of India is not secured because of the presence of Chinese Navy in the region is constantly challenging the security and stability of the sub-continent. The study would try to focus on India's strategy to maintain the status quo as a peace-loving nation on one hand, and its cooperation with the ASEAN countries especially with Vietnam to counter Chinese influence in the region, on the other. The study would also focus on the Environment and Political Security aspects of Human Security and how they are connected with India's engagement in the Indian Ocean Region.

Naresh Kumar Behera, in his chapter "India's Dynamic Foreign Policy: Indo-Pacific Strategy and Balancing Role in Quad," he focuses on India's changed foreign policy which is now more proactive and dynamic in an ever-changing modern world. Role of India in Quad for the development of global order. This chapter studies India's joining of the Quad through its Indo-Pacific strategy for a wider Indian Ocean vision. Further, the study also highlights India and the United States' global strategic partnership to a greater extent.

Gopika Pavithran in her chapter on India's Role in Quad discusses how the Quad objective is to make the Indo-Pacific region a free and prosperous space. China, the regional power, has shown a diplomatic resistance against this forum. Quad aims to counter Chinese domination in this strategically important region. In India's view, growing belligerence compelled them to accelerate the pace of the Quad. India has also gone beyond the Quad and has deepened its bilateral ties with the Quad members. Every member state has done the same for protecting their national interest. So, they have announced their intention to launch a supply chain resilience initiative. China is the major threat for India. India's bilateral relations with 'like-minded' countries with the backdrop of the Quad can be strengthened further through information sharing agreements, arms exchange agreements, defence ties, and much more.

Subham Tripathy in the chapter "Securing the Tide: The Grand Design of Aspiring India for the Indian Ocean" focuses on how China is increasing its footprint in the Indian Ocean. It also tries to unfold the answer to how and why does the growing Chinese presence challenge India's sphere of Influence in the Indian Ocean? India's grand strategic vision to counter Chinese influence in its backyard and secure its position as the key security provider to the countries in the Indian Ocean Rim.

Singh Subhalaxmi Baidhar and Prasanna Kumar Panda in their chapter "Sino-Russia Co-Operation to Challenge U.S. Hegemony; A Growing Concern for India's National Security" focus on the emergence of China as an economic superpower, which has been proved as a silver lining for Russia to counter U.S hegemony. Although China and Russia have been working together more closely in the last ten years, particularly in the wake of the pandemic, in the areas of trade, security, infrastructure, energy, and vaccination campaigns, as well as to outlast US dominance, India has been deeply concerned about the possibility of deeper Sino-Russian ties and what that would mean for the country's national security, especially in light of the Ukraine crisis.

Keshab Chandra Ratha in chapter "Unravelling Ethnic Gulf in Manipur: A Land at Crossroads" highlights the Manipur issue on the division of the majority Meitei community and other indigenous populations, which currently seems unbridgeable. Major thrust of the chapter is on cultural geography of Manipur, Chinese connection to Manipur, ethnicization and poor governance, trust deficit, the spirit of partisanship, growing religious fundamentalism, false narratives and disinformation by establishing the fact that a process of inter-ethnic dialogue to work out a roadmap for long-term ethnic reconciliation by involving all stakeholders is the need of the hour.

Priyanka Masant in chapter "Human Trafficking: An Overlooked Security Threat to India" discusses threats, which is a force or action that disrupts the stability, peace, and harmony of individuals and nations alike. Among these threats, trafficking in human beings stands as a pervasive issue that jeopardizes national stability and security. Indian national security is significantly threatened by human trafficking, which affects the country's legal, economic and social structures. The chapter intended to investigate and establish the linkages between trafficking and national security, and the imperative role of the policies, as well as a collaborative approach to combat this widespread threat.

In recent times, India's global leadership was visible with its G20 presidency. Nisarg Jani, a young scholar with a focus on technology and international relations, looks into the G-20 edge in multilateral negotiations to further the Inclusive global digital economy. He brings out how the Indian presidency of the G-20 was well accepted within the international community because of its spirit of people-centeredness which was termed as "Jan Bhagidari." Plethora of meetings were held all across India where delegates from all around the world witnessed the richness of Indian hospitality and cultural diversity. The Indian spirit of "One Earth, One Family" was effectively reflected in the proceedings of digital governance where the focus was on balancing data sovereignty with global efficiency. He highlights how the Indian policymakers hold a conviction that G-20 has acted like a bridge between G-7 and emerging economies, as can be seen from the growing membership of the BRICS grouping, which along with the G-7 is a part of G-20.

On the other hand, Professor Reshmi Kazi focuses on a single theme of energy security through multilateral fora. In her chapter "Nuclear Energy is a Non-negotiable Choice: A G-20 Approach", advocates for an urgent need for the international community to collectively develop related energy technologies that are low carbon intensive and cause least social and environmental impacts. Despite the decisiveness of the situation, the recently concluded Group-20 (G-20) Summit 2023 held in India, overlooked nuclear energy as an important carbon-free energy source. Her chapter explores the global need for a clean energy transition; why should nuclear energy be regarded as a viable alternative to facilitate the energy transition to clean and carbon-free energy resource for sustainable economic development? She explores how international groupings like the G-20, as a collective community, can help the expansion of including nuclear energy as part of a globally acceptable governance framework for sustainable energy security and climate neutrality? How can the G-20's deliberations help nuclear energy achieve "equal footing for collaborative action" as part of its agenda?

Last but not the least, Neeraj Singh Manhas in the chapter "A Roadmap for India's National Security Strategy: Priorities and

Challenges" examines India's approach to safeguarding its national interests and securing its sovereignty. The author views that as India gets integrated with the rest of the world, the range of security challenges it will face will increase. One of the most significant of these challenges, as the author argues, is the growing hostilities with China and Pakistan. The author outlines a roadmap for the development of a comprehensive National Security Strategy which should involve a coordinated and integrated approach among all stakeholders.

Concluding Remarks: In the process of compiling this volume, we have accumulated many intellectual debts. To count them individually would be stupendous. All the contributors have meticulously argued their assigned area of concern and the reviewers have stringently brought to fore the possible areas of improvements for shaping the volume into a presentable form. We sincerely hope the volume will generate further intellectual deliberations. The intent is to bring to fore India's views, opinions, strategies, and outlook on every global concern, like the way a major power does so, to make India's presence felt in every corner of the world.

Sitakanta Mishra
Banita Mahandaia
Gyanaranjan Swain

1

A Roadmap for India's National Security Strategy: Priorities and Challenges

– Neeraj Singh Manhas

Introduction

India's National Security Strategy (NSS) is a comprehensive framework that outlines India's approach to safeguarding its national interests and securing its sovereignty. It provides a roadmap for the country's security policy, including the identification of key threats and challenges, and the development of strategies to counter them. The NSS encompasses a wide range of areas, including defence, intelligence, diplomacy, economics, and technology. India since independence, has focused on the socio-economic development as its priority is understandable given its large and growing population.

However, as the country becomes more integrated with the rest of the world, it is also facing a range of security challenges.[1] One of the most significant of these challenges is the growing hostilities with China and Pakistan. Both countries have a long history of conflict, and the situation has been exacerbated in recent years by cross-border terrorism and the disputed region of Kashmir with Pakistan and an unsolved border dispute at the Line of Actual Control (LAC), with China. To deal with this challenge, India has shifted towards a strategy of war prevention, seeking to deter China and Pakistan from engaging in any further military action. This has involved a range of measures, including strengthening its military capabilities, building closer ties with other countries, and engaging in diplomatic efforts to resolve the underlying issues.

At the same time, India is contending with a wide variety of precarious situations about international security. They include the spread of nuclear weapons, the importance of economic power in international politics, relations with the United States and Russia, unrest in Central Asia and Afghanistan, terrorism on a global scale, and an ongoing feud with China and Pakistan. The conditions surrounding India's national security are complicated and are changing quickly. It will need to negotiate a range of difficulties and opportunities to secure its sustained success and security as it continues to grow and engage more closely with the rest of the globe.[2]

Geography Impacts Political Conditions and Foreign Policy

The Indian Subcontinent is surrounded by the Himalayas, the Arabian Sea, the Indian Ocean, and the Bay of Bengal. Mountains and seas have long been seen as guardians of borders by the Indians. India's natural security zone, many analysts believe, is South Asia, from the Himalayas to the Indian Ocean.

Its image as a worldwide behemoth stems from its size and location. History and culture have shaped Indian strategic thinking. This is because any protection measure taken in the country must be regarding the geography it occupies and the sort of culture that has been prevalent in India. India's history implies it will aspire to become a superpower in its own right. A conservative attitude toward life, a protective mentality, and a caste-dominated and hierarchical society explains the country's historically slow pace of social progress. Indians' worldview mirrors their hierarchical culture. A primarily Brahmin worldview, India believes in a world system centred on riches and power. This used to be one of the primary concerns for Independent India. However, it cannot be denied that over some time, all of this has changed to bring India into the fight to become one of the world's major powers. It also cannot be denied that the population of India, its resources, its rich culture, and the capabilities of its nationals have acted as its saving grace and have tremendously helped it climb heights.[3]

The late-19th century rediscovery of Indian history informed Indian strategic thinking. Indian nationalists searched for precedents of Indian unity but discovered only fleeting periods of unity. The first three Mauryan empires were a time of Indian unity, strength, and glory (Chandra Gupta, Bindusara, and Asoka). Further instances from history shaped India's behaviour as the country has a rich historical landscape and lessons from way earlier would be highly beneficial to modern-day issues. It can also not be denied that India has a lot to learn from some of the major strategists of history, particularly in the above-mentioned empires. As a result, India sees itself as both old and modern and started to acknowledge its rich history.

Current Challenges to India's Regional Dominance

India's position is impacted by its interactions with South Asian countries. On account of its huge geographical area, economic power, military force, and strategic placement over the Indian Ocean, its relationship with other South Asian nations had a huge significance. The Belt and Road Initiative (BRI) has upset the hegemonic balance, allowing other, weaker regional governments to challenge China's dominant influence. China has been involved in South Asian regional diplomacy while preserving its Western suppliers. According to Bangladesh and Sri Lanka, the BRI has made India more adaptive to change and accountable for its actions. India is concerned about expanding Pakistan-China ties.[4]

The BRI crosses Pakistan-held Kashmir, endangering Indian sovereignty. Several conflicts along China's and India's long borders cause mutual displeasure. Even if the US and China want peace and stability in the area, Pakistan and India refuse to cooperate. Pakistan's foreign policy tries to reduce animosity. Terrorism emanating from Pakistani territory has frequently hampered efforts to address simmering tensions and India continues to remain on guard regarding the same. The BRI and Chinese intervention have had no substantial impact on India-Pakistan ties. India has long been critical of Pakistan, but China's involvement in Pakistan worries India. The repeal of Article 370 from the Indian Constitution allowed India more administrative control over the territory, increasing Pakistan's animosity. Further, incidents in Jammu and Kashmir, alleged terrorist ties all continue to cause a hurdle in the India-Pakistan relationship. These incidents have strained relations, with no obvious settlement in sight.

Relations between India and Sri Lanka have been strained since India sent a peacekeeping force there in the 1980s. The countries have maintained a strained relationship as a result of the conflicts between the Liberation Tigers of Tamil Eelam (LTTE) and India. Due to uncontrollable circumstances in Sri Lanka, India was forced to withdraw its forces within two years, causing a division. India's efforts to achieve its goals in Sri Lanka have caused unrest. Due to India's forced withdrawal from the Hambantota Port project, China gained access to Sri Lanka's economy.[5]

The Hambantota accord boosted Sri Lanka-China relations, and China has spent approximately $15 billion in Sri Lanka, mostly after 2013. Those ties have deteriorated with India since 2015 after the outgoing President blamed India for his defeat. India, on the other hand, has been sceptical of the new government. India has given Sri Lanka investments like the Eastern Container Terminal, built with the assistance of Japan, and a $450 million pledge.

Unlike Nepal, Bangladesh, and Pakistan, India-Sri Lanka ties have never culminated in any major or protracted conflict. The only source of displeasure has been India's grim outlook, which continues to exert significant influence over Sri Lanka's foreign policy. After India objected to submarines entering the port in 2014, Sri Lankan MPs advised China not to do so in 2018. Indian investments are also welcomed in Sri Lanka. However, either due to domestic political issues, such as the current Tamil conflict, or carelessness, their relationship has been strained.[6]

Bhutan-India ties have become stronger over time. Bhutan joined the Bangladesh–Bhutan–India–Nepal initiative, which India proposed. In partnership with Japan, India proposes to link Bhutan to Dan Nand in Vietnam, combining the Act East strategy and the Free and Open Indo-Pacific policy. The current Indian government supports Bhutan's aspirations and is trying to make it a more prominent factor in India's foreign policy. For the mutual purpose of protecting their borders from China, India-Bhutan relations have been good and enthusiastic throughout.

Indian relations with the Maldives improved after a new president was elected in 2018. In response to COVID-19, India and the Maldives inked bilateral agreements on infrastructure, a $1.4 billion line of credit and currency swap, and medical equipment. As indicated by President Yameen's decision to terminate economic projects and redirect them to China, the Maldives' relationship with India has deteriorated. China dominated Maldives' infrastructural projects during Yameen's leadership.[7]

With the help of Cambodian politicians, China has dominated Cambodia's real estate market, bringing in Chinese builders and changing the ethnic mix of the region. The Maldives have so far avoided this scenario with Indian assistance. Fearing China's expanding influence, the new leadership has turned to India. India cannot afford to miss this chance and should keep its pledge to President Solih.

China's military is rapidly developing. President Xi Jinping says China's military must be modernised by 2035. "World-class" military power capable of "winning wars" by 2049, is what they want to achieve. It's a big job, but they are on track. The Stockholm International Peace Research Institute, which annually assesses global stockpiles, claims China has increased its warhead count. Despite China's denials of testing hypersonic missiles, Western experts say two launches last summer indicate the military is well on its way. No one knows what China's working on. India has been closely monitoring all Chinese PLA activities, according to Former Chief of Army Staff Gen MM Naravane.[8]

Importance of National Security Strategy in India

India's desire to enhance its international standing and become a major player in world affairs is understandable given its size, population, and economic potential. As one of the fastest-growing economies in the world, India is poised to make significant contributions to global trade, investment, and innovation.

India's location in South Asia is both a challenge and an opportunity. On one hand, the region is beset by political instability, conflict, and poverty. On the other hand, South Asia is a vast market with enormous potential for growth and development. India's economic rise has the potential to transform the region, creating new opportunities for trade, investment, and cooperation.[9]

India's strategic importance is also due to its location on the Indian Ocean, which is becoming increasingly important in global affairs. As a major maritime power, India has a crucial role to play in ensuring the security of the sea lanes of communication that are essential for global trade and commerce.

India's emergence as a great power will require sophisticated strategic thinking and a willingness to engage with the international community. As a diverse and democratic country, India has the potential to be a model for other developing nations. However, India must also address the challenges of poverty, corruption, and inequality if it is to fully realise its potential.

The NSS is important for several reasons. First, it will help to prioritise and coordinate India's national security efforts across different sectors and government agencies. By providing a unified and integrated approach, the NSS can help to ensure that resources are allocated effectively and that security policy is consistent and coherent.[10]

Second, the NSS helps to identify and assess the threats and challenges that India faces, both domestically and internationally. This can include traditional security threats, such as military aggression and terrorism, as well as non-traditional threats, such as cyber-attacks, pandemics, and climate change. By understanding these threats, India can develop strategies to mitigate and counter them.

Third, a National Security Strategy provides a framework for coordination and collaboration among various government agencies, military forces, and other stakeholders. It ensures that all relevant actors are working towards the same objectives and that resources are being allocated efficiently and effectively.

Finally, It can help to build public trust and support for the government's security policies. By providing a transparent and comprehensive approach to national security, citizens can better understand the rationale behind government decisions and be more willing to support them.[11]

National Security Policy

India's national security policy objectives, as summarized by the Indian Prime Minister in 1995, highlight the importance of defending national territory, maintaining internal security, promoting harmonious relationships with other regional countries, and contributing to international stability through out-of-area operations. However, as noted, India faces significant challenges in meeting these objectives due to a lack of preparedness and coordination.

The combat systems used by the Indian armed forces are on the verge of becoming obsolete, and there is a lack of defined processes for decision-making, planning, and coordination among the country's three branches of the armed forces regarding matters of national security. As many argue, India has historically taken a lackadaisical approach towards defence expenditures by not considering it as a core priority, besides having the structure of the armed forces bureaucratic and inflexible.[12]

India has made attempts in recent years to solve some of these structural challenges as it has become more aware in recent years of the necessity for strategic defence and has made these efforts. Nonetheless, there is a never-ending discussion going on in India regarding the most effective approach to resolving these issues and making certain that India is better equipped to accomplish its national security objectives.

India's Military Strength

According to studies, the US military expenditure is $732 billion per year, outspending all the other countries. China has $261 billion, followed by India with $71 billion. Modernisation has increased financial resources available to the military. Payroll expenditures are increasing, especially for a manpower-intensive Indian army.[13] The army received 56% of the budget for 2020-2021, or $38 billion, with only 18%, or roughly $7 billion, allocated for capital expenditures, such as modern weapons and spares. $7 billion nowadays does not get a country very far in military development. The Modi government's core modernisation initiative aims to unify the Army, Navy, and Air Force's capabilities.[14]

To better respond to future crises, the present 17 single-service units will be grouped into five "theatre commands." With 1.45 lakh active military forces, India ranks fourth in the GFP annual defence assessment for 2022. 140 nations were considered. The GFP list was created using the PwrIndx rating, which is based on a long-term offensive or defensive military conflict. India has a PI of 0.0979. The country's overall aircraft strength is 2,182, including fixed-wing and rotorcraft platforms from all armed branches. India has 12,000 armoured vehicles and 4,614 tanks. India is a leader in missile research and development, but it falls behind the US, China, and Russia in terms of range. Many surface-launched systems exist.[15]

The Strategic Forces Command utilises Agni and Prithvi. Agni is India's only rival for an ICBM, which is only available to a few countries. Prithvi is a 350 km long strategic surface-to-surface missile. India tested defying satellites in April 2019. The Prithvi Defence Vehicle Mk 2 intercepted a low-orbit satellite. India now ranks fourth in terms of capability, after the US, Russia, and China.[16]

Since then, India has improved its ranking to fourth, behind the US, Russia and China. Sources say India developed its cryogenic engine and tested it in a 23-second flight. The Chinese submarine fleet consists of about 70 submarines, including 7 nuclear ballistic missile submarines (SSBN), 12 nuclear attack submarines (SSN), and over 50 diesel attack submarines. The fleet is three times larger than the Indian Navy's (20).[17]

India's Military Requirements

The requirements for India's military are wide, with the primary emphasis being on being ready for large-scale regional wars, whether they be conventional or unconventional, including the possibility of the use of weapons of mass destruction. The Indian Armed Forces are capable of conducting both defensive and offensive operations against land-, air-, and sea-based missile attacks, as well as executing sea denial and sea control missions against Chinese and Pakistani incursions. In addition, they can defend against land-, air-, and sea-based missile attacks using land-, air-, and sea-based missiles.

The growing body of discourse within the canon of military writing points to an increased reliance on long-range air power as well as a change in the balance of conventional military force towards the Navy and Air Force. India has recently developed a new war-fighting doctrine, and one of its core tenets is that the country's armed forces require significant modernisation to be ready for cyberwar in the 21st century. The emphasis is placed on more nimble and mobile fighting groups that are meant to degrade the combat capabilities of the adversary.[18] These groups make use of intelligent weapons to neutralise enemy offensive forces before they are within visual range. The goal is to avoid being an escalator for nuclear war by moving away from the employment of enormous tank and artillery armies and placing more of an emphasis on the destruction of enemy combat capabilities rather than capturing land. This will need a shift in strategy.

India's Defence Budget

The budget estimates for the fiscal year 2020-2021 indicate that the anticipated expenditure on defence will be Rs.3,62,345.62 Crore (US$ 49.6 billion), which is an increase of Rs.24,792.62 Crore (US$ 3.4 billion) over the previous year's estimates. When combined with defence pensions, the current appropriations reach Rs.4.78 Lakh Crore (US$ 65.5 billion), up from Rs.4.71 Lakh Crore (US$ 64.5 billion) in the previous fiscal year—representing an increase of 1.4% from the previous year to the current year.[19]

When pensions are taken into account, these allocations represent around 2.15% of GDP. When pensions are not taken into account, these allocations represent approximately 1.63% of India's projected GDP. Capital has been allocated to the DRDO at a rate that is 8% higher (Rs.11375.50 Crore, or US$ 1.6 billion more) than it was previously, and capital has been allocated to Border Roads at a rate that is 7.5% higher (Rs.6004.08 Crore, or US$ 0.8 billion).[20]

It is important to note that defence expenditure is an essential component of a country's national security and is allocated based on various factors such as geopolitical situation, economic conditions, and strategic requirements. But the main question is the determination of an adequate and optimum yearly defence budget allocation requires a careful analysis of the strategic environment, the country's security needs, and its economic capacity, and it should be based on a rational and well-informed assessment of these factors.

Priority Areas for India's NSS

(a) Countering cross-border terrorism and insurgencies

India has faced numerous incidents of cross-border terrorism and insurgencies, which have destabilized the country's internal security and contributed to political instability. Addressing this threat is crucial for India's security, and the NSS should prioritize measures such as increasing border security, improving intelligence gathering, and enhancing coordination with neighbouring countries.

(b) Safeguarding territorial integrity and border security

India shares borders with several countries, and territorial disputes have been a constant source of tension. Therefore, it is important for India to safeguard its territorial integrity and border security. The NSS should focus on strengthening border infrastructure, deploying advanced surveillance technologies, and enhancing the capacity of border security forces to counter any potential threats.

(c) Enhancing maritime security and naval capabilities

India is a maritime nation with a long coastline, and its security is also dependent on the security of its seas. India faces threats such as piracy, terrorism, and smuggling in its waters. The NSS should prioritize the development of a robust maritime security strategy and enhance its naval capabilities, including the acquisition of advanced maritime technologies.

(d) Improving cybersecurity and protecting critical infrastructure

Cybersecurity threats are becoming increasingly sophisticated and pose a significant risk to India's national security. The NSS should prioritize measures such as strengthening cybersecurity laws and regulations, developing a cybersecurity framework, and improving the protection of critical infrastructure such as power grids and transportation systems.

(e) Strengthening the economy and reducing vulnerabilities to economic threats

India's economy is a significant factor in its security, and it is important to safeguard it against economic threats. The NSS should prioritize measures such as diversifying the economy, reducing dependence on external sources, enhancing economic competitiveness, and improving infrastructure to attract foreign investment.

(f) Addressing social and political instability

Social and political instability can have far-reaching consequences for India's security. The NSS should prioritize measures such as promoting social cohesion, addressing ethnic and religious tensions, and improving governance to address issues such as corruption and inequality. It is also important to enhance political stability to prevent internal security threats.

India's NSS should prioritise a comprehensive approach to security that includes all of these key areas. By addressing these priorities, India can enhance its security and safeguard its national interests. It is also important for the NSS to adopt a long-term perspective, considering the dynamic nature of security threats and the need for constant adaptation and innovation to meet emerging challenges.

Challenges and Obstacles to Developing a Comprehensive NSS

Developing a comprehensive National Security Strategy (NSS) is a complex process for India, and several challenges and obstacles may arise during its development. One of the key challenges is coordination and communication among the various government agencies responsible for different aspects of national security. Lack of communication and coordination may lead to inefficiencies and the failure to address critical security threats. Resource constraints and competing priorities are other challenges that India may encounter in developing the NSS, and balancing short-term and long-term priorities is crucial. Political and bureaucratic hurdles may also delay the development of the NSS, making it less effective or even derailing it altogether.[21]

To address these challenges, India can take several steps, including ensuring effective coordination and communication among government agencies and stakeholders, prioritising and allocating resources efficiently, involving political leaders and other stakeholders in the development of the NSS, and striking a balance between short-term and long-term priorities. Establishing a flexible and adaptable NSS that can address both immediate and emerging security threats is essential. Regular review and updating of the NSS will ensure that it remains relevant and effective.

The development of a comprehensive NSS is critical for India's security, and various challenges and obstacles may arise in the process. However, effective coordination and communication, prioritization of resources, overcoming political and bureaucratic obstacles, and balancing short-term and long-term priorities can help India develop an effective NSS to safeguard its national security.[22]

Opportunities and Innovations for India's NSS

India has a multitude of opportunities and innovations that it can utilise to improve its national security strategy (NSS). One potential avenue for enhancing security capabilities involves leveraging the thriving technology industry in India. This includes investing in cybersecurity, developing new border security technologies, and utilising artificial intelligence and machine learning for intelligence analysis. Additionally, strengthening partnerships and cooperation with regional neighbours and partners can enhance NSS and establish a secure regional security architecture. Investing in human capital and training for security personnel is also essential to develop a highly skilled workforce that can address various security challenges, such as cybersecurity, counterterrorism, and intelligence gathering.[23] India can integrate public-private partnerships and civil society organisations to enhance its NSS. This includes collaborating with private companies to develop new security technologies and partnering with civil society groups to address issues such as radicalisation and social unrest. By incorporating these opportunities and innovations into its NSS, India can significantly enhance its national security.[24]

The potential benefits of incorporating opportunities and innovations into India's NSS are vast. By improving its cybersecurity capabilities, India can protect critical infrastructure and sensitive data from cyber-attacks. Additionally, enhanced intelligence gathering and analysis capabilities can enable India to anticipate and respond to emerging threats proactively. Improving border security can prevent the infiltration of terrorists and other threats, thereby enhancing national security. Strengthening the regional security architecture can promote stability and reduce the risk of conflict, which can have positive implications for the entire region. A highly skilled security workforce can respond to a wide range of security challenges, making India more resilient to various threats.[25] Finally, increased collaboration and cooperation with regional partners and civil society organisations can help to address security challenges more effectively. Overall, these opportunities and innovations have the potential to significantly enhance India's NSS and improve its overall security posture.

Conclusion

National Security Strategy (NSS) is an essential tool for any country in today's complex and rapidly evolving security environment. India, being a major player in the international arena, faces multifaceted security challenges, and the absence of a comprehensive NSS limits its ability to respond effectively to emerging threats.[26] Therefore, the development of a comprehensive NSS is of utmost importance for India's national security, which should involve a coordinated and integrated approach among all stakeholders.

The chapter has highlighted the key points of the importance of a comprehensive NSS for India and the recommendations to ensure its effectiveness. These include enhancing coordination and communication among stakeholders, investing in human capital and training, leveraging technology and innovation, and strengthening partnerships with other countries and international organizations.[27] India's comprehensive NSS will provide a clear roadmap for its security priorities, resource allocation, and institutional reforms. It will also enhance its credibility as a responsible and capable actor in the global security architecture. Therefore, it is imperative that India takes swift action to develop and implement its NSS to ensure its security and prosperity in the long run.[28]

ENDNOTES

1. A. Z. Hilali, India's Strategic Thinking and Its National Security Policy, *Asian Survey*, Vol. XLI, No. 5, 2001; https://www.jstor.org/stable/10.1525/as.2001.41.5.737 pp. 737-764.
2. Virain Mohan, Changing Political Dynamics in South Asia: The Belt and Road Initiative and Its Effects on Indian Regional Hegemony; *Journal of Indo-Pacific Affairs,* Air University Press, August 25, 2021; https://www.airuniversity.af.edu/JIPA/Display/Article/2743694/changing-political-dynamics-in-south-asia-the-belt-and-road-initiative-and-its/
3. A look at how strong is India's military strength for 2022, *Money Control News*, January 17, 2022;https://www.moneycontrol.com/news/photos/india/a-look-at-how-strong-is-indias-military-strength-for-2022-7948781.html
4. Krishn Kaushik, explained: India's missile capability, and where it stands in relation to its neighbours, *The Indian Express*, December 21, 2021; https://indianexpress.com/article/explained/explained-indias-missile-capability-7680821/
5. Kartik Bommakanti, Indian Military Platform Modernisation: Uncertainties, Challenges, and Progress, Issue Briefs and Special Reports, ORF, September 29, 2021; https://www.orfonline.org/research/indian-military-platform-modernisation/

6. Peri, Dinakar (7 July 2021). "N.N. Vohra pitches for publicly known national security policy". *The Hindu*; https://www.thehindu.com/news/national/nn-vohra-pitches-for-publicly-known-national-security-policy/article35195550.ece
7. PK Khup Hangzo, (10 April 2020) Rethinking National Security in an Age of Pandemics, VIF, https://www.vifindia.org/article/2020/april/10/rethinking-national-security-in-an-age-of-pandemics
8. Lt Gen (Retd) AS Lamba, Book Review: The New Arthashastra: A Security Strategy for India, Institute of Peace and Conflict Studies, http://www.ipcs.org/ipcs_books_selreviews.php?recNo=282
9. Gupta, Arvind, (20 October 2011), "A National Security Strategy Document for India". Manohar Parrikar Institute for Defence Studies and Analyses;

   https://idsa.in/idsacomments/ANationalSecurityStrategyDocumentforIndia_arvindgupta_201011
10. Saran, Shyam (4 June 2019). "Need for a Comprehensive National Security Strategy". Centre for Policy Research. Retrieved 20March 2023;

    https://cprindia.org/wp-content/uploads/2022/03/Policy-Challenges-2019-2024.pdf
11. Menon, Raja (8 February 2021). "India Must Chart Out a National Security Strategy for a Changing Geopolitical World". *The Wire*. Retrieved 20 March 2023;

    https://thewire.in/security/india-must-chart-out-a-national-security-strategy-for-a-changing-geopolitical-world
12. Sethi, Deepak (26 August 2020). "China Impasse the Product of India's Lack of National Security Strategy, Accountability". *The Wire*. Retrieved 20 March 2023;

    https://thewire.in/security/india-must-chart-out-a-national-security-strategy-for-a-changing-geopolitical-world
13. Pandit, Rajat (2 May 2018). "New defence panel to focus on national security, reforms in 1st meeting". The Times of India. Archived from the original on 2 January 2019. Retrieved 20 March 2023; https://timesofindia.indiatimes.com/india/new-defence-panel-to-focus-on-national-security-reforms-in-1st-meeting/articleshow/63993291.cms
14. Sunil Khilnani et al., Nonalignment 2.0: A Foreign and Strategic Policy for India in the Twenty First Century, Centre for Policy Research, New Delhi, February, 2012, http://www.cprindia.org/sites/default/files/NonAlignment%202.0_1.pdf.
15. C. Raja Mohan and Ajai Sahni, India's Security Challenges at Home and Abroad, National Bureau of Asian Research, Special Report 39, May 2012, p. 2.

    https://www.nbr.org/publication/indias-security-challenges-at-home-and-abroad/
16. Christine Fair, "Prospects for effective internal security reforms in India", *Commonwealth & Comparative Politics*, Vol. 50, No. 2, April 2012, pp. 145 –170.

    https://www.christinefair.net/pubs/India_CCP_Fair.pdf
17. Sumit Ganguly, "India's Foreign Policy Grows up", *World Policy Journal*, Vol. 20, No. 4, Winter 2003–04, http://www.worldpolicy.org/journal/articles/wpj03-4/%20ganguly.html. Accessed on 20 March 2023.

18. Nitin Pai, "The Paradox of Proximity: India's Approach to Fragility in the Neighbourhood", Centre for International Cooperation, New York University, April 2011,

https://old.takshashila.org.in/policy-briefs-and-notes-2011-12/ Accessed on 20 March 2023

19. Ashok Malik, "India's New World: Civil Society in the Making of Foreign Policy", May 2011,http://lowyinstitute.cachefly.net/files/pubfiles/Malik_and_Medcalf,_%20India's_new_world_web.pdf. Accessed on 20 March 2023.

20. A. G. Noorani, "Nehru's China policy", *Frontline*, Vol. 17, No. 15, 22 July – 4 August 2000, http://www.frontlineonnet.com/fl1715/17150780.htm. Accessed on 20 March23

21. Robert Trumbull, "Indians Dispute the Dalai Lama", *New York Times*, 9 September 1959, https://query.nytimes.com/mem/page.html?res=F10D1EF8355B107B93CB+A91782D85F4D8585F9.&legacy=true&status=nf Accessed on 20 March 2023.

22. Rajesh Rajagopalan, "India's Strategic Choices: China and the Balance of Power in Asia," Carnegie India, www.carnegieindia.org, date accessed: 16/03/2018,

https://carnegieindia.org/2017/09/14/india-s-strategic-choices-china-and-balance-of-power-in-asia-pub-73108

23. Lieutenant General Philip Campose (Retd.), *A National Security Strategy for India: The Way Forward* (New Delhi: KW Publishers, 2018), p. 154.

http://kwpub.in/Home/product/9789387324305/a-national-security-strategy-for-india-the-way-forward

24. Major General P K Chakravorty (Retd.), "Indian Army: Modernization and Current Status, *India Strategic*, www.indiastrategic.in, date accessed: 16/03/2018,

http://www.indiastrategic.in/topstories3648_Indian_Army_Modernisation_and_Current_Status.htm.

25. Lieutenant General Prakash Katoch, "India's Sub-Conventional Warfare Deficit," *Indian Defence Review*, www.indiandefencereview.com, date accessed: 20/03/2023,

http://www.indiandefencereview.com/spotlights/indias-sub-conventional-warfare-deficit/

26. Group Captain GD Sharma, VSM (Retd.), "Exploiting Indian Military Capacity in Outer Space," Centre For Joint Warfare Studies, (India, Xtreme Office Aids Pvt. Ltd.), 2016. https://cenjows.in/wp-content/uploads/2022/03/Layout_Exploiting-Indian-Military.pdf

27. Arindrajit Basu, "India Needs a Credible Deterrence Strategy for Cyberspace," The Wire, www.thewire.in, date accessed: 20/03/2023, https://thewire.in/tech/india-needs-credible-deterrence-strategy-cyberspace

28. Lieutenant General Prakash Katoch, "Military Diplomacy: Time to Bridge the Void," I*ndian Defence Review*, www.indiandefencereview.com, date accessed: 20/03/2023,

http://www.%20indiandefencereview.com/news/military-diplomacy-time-to-bridge-the-void/

2

Russia-Ukraine Crisis: How Did the World Respond?

– **Rajaram Panda**

The ongoing geopolitical conflict following Russia's invasion of Ukraine has enhanced the scope of further worsening rather than moving towards a thaw. As the conflict drags on, economic impact will build more, beyond Ukraine. The key three channels that could be affected by the ongoing conflict are commodity and food price shocks, financial repercussions from the sanctions, and security challenges in a scenario of an escalating or wider military conflict.

A new churning in the world's geopolitics is taking place following Russia's invasion of Ukraine. The world has responded strongly, with the US leading in imposing crippling sanctions against Russia. Russian President Vladimir V. Putin has warned the West to stay out. Even when the Russian military continues to make inroads, Putin upped the ante by keeping his nuclear assets on alert. The world finds itself suddenly on the brink of an unparalleled crisis. Powered with veto power, Russia prevented the UNSC resolution in condemning the Russian move. India, China and UAE abstained from voting, saying that dialogue is the only means to resolve the crisis.

India's stance stems from two visible reasons. Russia is a time-tested friend of India and has stood by it at times of crises. Besides, Russia is a major source of military procurement by India, which India cannot overlook. Secondly, nearly 20,000 Indian students, mostly undertaking medical courses, were trapped in the crisis and their safety and safe return was a priority for the government. The death of an Indian student on 1 March 2022 led India to augment its evacuation process. Several related issues led to the Ukraine crisis. These need close scrutiny to understand the issue dispassionately and objectively. But before doing that, an understanding of the background of the crisis between Russia and Ukraine that reached dangerous proportions shall put this study in perspective.

Background

The root cause behind Russia's invasion of Ukraine is Russia considers Ukraine within its natural sphere of influence and felt unease as Ukraine was seen drifting closer to the West. The possibility of Ukraine joining the NATO or the European Union unnerved Putin as NATO would be on the border of Russia, exposing its security vulnerabilities. At present Ukraine is part of the neither, but the very fact of a possibility of that happening worried Putin. Ukraine is dependent upon both the US and Europe for financial and military aid. Putin felt that Ukraine's potential membership of the NATO posed an existential threat to Russia.[1]

The tensions between Russia and Ukraine started in 2014 when Russian military entered Ukraine's territory when Ukraine's President supported by Russia was replaced by a pro-Western candidate. Russia saw this as a provocation and annexed Crimea, triggering a separatist movement in the east. Though a ceasefire was reached the following year, fighting continued. Putin maintained the military's presence near the Ukraine border for months. On 21 February 2022, Russia signed decrees recognising two pro-Russia breakaway regions in eastern Ukraine. Two days later, Putin declared the start of a "special military operation", justifying that he responded to the plea for assistance from the leaders of the Russian-backed separatist territories of Donetsk and Luhansk. Putin justified his action to stop ethnic cleansing carried out by the Ukrainian forces. This has precipitated a crisis of global proportion.

Ukraine President Volodymyr Zelensky's response was swift. The same day, he declared a 30-day state of emergency to halt further damage to government institutions by cyberattacks. This was followed by the declaration of martial law. Ukraine's President and foreign minister appealed to the world leaders to prevail upon Putin from causing further damage to Ukraine's sovereignty and territorial integrity.

Before analysing what transpired after Russia invaded Ukraine and the world's reactions of the action, it might be instructive to analyse the import of the remarks by Russia's Foreign Minister Sergey Lavrov wherein he warned about the danger of a future war that could be World War III and nuclear wherein the NATO, the European Union and the United Nations shall be pitted against Russia over its invasion of Ukraine.[2] Lavrov warned that the next World War would involve nuclear weapons and be destructive. He further warned that what if Ukraine acquired nuclear weapons, the two may lead to that eventual conflict with perilous consequences. Lavrov was only echoing Putin's threats of the use of nuclear force if the NATO forces got directly involved in defending Ukraine. Putin ordered Russian nuclear deterrent forces on alert, which placed several European officials on edge.

This brings us to the debate on the larger question, would Putin have attacked Ukraine had it kept its nuclear stockpile after the Budapest accord in 1994?[3] It may be recalled when the USSR collapsed in 1991, Ukraine inherited 176 strategic and more than 2,500 tactical nuclear missiles. At that point of time, Ukraine had the third largest arsenal of nuclear weapons in the world after the US and Russia. The control systems, the so-called black suitcase with the start button, were however with the Russian President Boris Yeltsin at that time. Since Ukraine's coffers were empty and it would have cost $65 billion to manufacture and maintain them, it could not have maintained those weapons and readily agreed to give up. The Ukrainian missiles were either transported to Russia or destroyed. As compensation, Ukraine received financial assistance from the US, cheap energy supplies from Russia, and security guarantees that were enshrined in the Budapest Memorandum. It soon transpired that the Budapest Memorandum was not an agreement on security guarantees, but only committed to respect the sovereignty and territorial integrity of Ukraine. It did not matter that Russia's action violated Ukraine's sovereignty and territorial integrity.

Response of the World

The world reacted as swiftly as Putin's military action on Ukraine, with the US and the EU leading the condemnation of

Russia's aggression and imposing economic sanctions against Russia. Germany halted certification of a gas pipeline linking it with Russia. Like India, China refused to call the attack an "invasion" and called for dialogue. As Russia controls vast global resources such as natural gas, oil, wheat, palladium and nickel in particular, the conflict left almost immediately with far-reaching consequences. Energy and food prices quickly spiked, spooking investors. Global banks too came up with sanctions crippling Russia's banking infrastructure and choking Russia's banking business transactions with the outside world.

Sanctions and Worsening Situation

Even when fighting continued to rage and Europe's biggest ground war in more than 75 years with Russian missiles pounding Ukraine's second-largest city and troops pressing closer to the capital Kyiv and more than a million Ukrainians fleeing the country, the leaders of both Russia and Ukraine agreed to return to the dialogue process. But the first round failed. A second round of peace talks was also held after Ukrainian delegates demanded an immediate ceasefire and withdrawal of Russian forces during initial talks on the border of Belarus. This too failed and no ceasefire was reached.

The US was sceptical over Russia's intentions as it felt diplomacy at the barrel of a gun was no diplomacy. What the US, its European allies and Ukraine wanted was substantive and genuine diplomacy. Regretfully, that did not happen and Russian incursions continued. What Russia wanted was an agreement that was in the interest of both sides. In reality, it meant Russia's conditions must prevail.[4] The sanctions-imposing countries collectively agreed to coordinate efforts to impose severe costs and consequences to hold Russia accountable. While the EU announced to send fighter jets to Ukraine, Australia committed to an unspecified delivery of lethal military equipment.

As expected, Russia viewed the decisions of the EU and Australia to arm Ukraine as hostile behaviour and an "extremely dangerous and destabilizing factor". In a swift response to the moves of the US, its allies and Europe, Putin went on an overdrive and asked his defence minister to put nuclear forces in a "special regime of combat duty". This was an overreaction that Putin could have avoided. To molly-coddle, the US Ambassador to the UN Linda Thomas-Greenfield remarked that Russia was "under no threat from NATO, a defensive alliance that will not fight in Ukraine". He urged Putin to tone down his dangerous rhetoric regarding nuclear weapons and avoid making provocative and escalatory statements. White House press secretary Jen Psaki cautioned that there could be risk of miscalculation that is best avoided.

The influential daily of Japan, the *Asahi Shimbun,* quickly commented in an editorial that the world is on the brink of an unparalleled crisis with Putin's nuclear threat. Being the only victim of the nuclear bomb in history, Japan is very sensitive to the mention of the word 'nuclear', though this nomenclature is already in an overhaul process. That is not easy but the editorial's remarks reflected the popular sentiment of the Japanese people. It saw the mention of the threat to use nuclear arms as the "ultimate inhuman weapon".[5]

Japan's Economic Stake in Russia

Japan, an ally of the US, too, joined the sanctions bandwagon. Japan has the festering territorial disputes over the Northern Islands (Kurile islands chain) north of Hokkaido and this has led to the troubled relationship since the end of World War II. While the nuclear-sharing debate was triggered by former Prime Minister Abe Shinzo as a response to Putin's nuclear threat, Japanese firms started mulling over exiting from Russia as sanctions started biting. The Japanese move came after rapid exit of Western companies from Russian ventures in response to the military invasion of Ukraine.[6] Earlier Shell Plc of Britain announced that it was pulling out of energy enterprises in Russia, including the Sakhalin II liquefied natural gas project. Japan is an energy deficient country and depends on imports for the bulk of its energy needs. Japan decided to go ahead with the European nations and the US. Though two Japanese trading companies, Mitsui & Co. and Mitsubishi Co. have stakes in the Sakhalin II project, which is a major source of LNG for Japan, the companies decided to cooperate with the international community, including Group of Seven nations, from the standpoint of energy security. ExxonMobil of the US also announced on 1 March it was pulling out of the Sakhalin I project in Russia.

Two leading Japanese trading houses, Itochu Corp., Marubeni Corp., and government-affiliated oil companies had set up the Sakhalin Oil and Gas Development Co. (SODECO). In total, Japan holds a 30 per cent stake in Sakhalin I. Japan's automobile industry too has a strong presence in Russia. Mitsubishi Motor Corp. has a plant in western Russia through a joint venture with European automaker Stellantis. Toyota Motor Corp, and Nissan Motor Co. too have plants in Russia that are currently operating. These companies have started facing difficulties in shipping parts from Japan and Thailand to the Russian facility, and are considering whether they continue operations or pull-out stakes. Mitsubishi manufactured around 21,000 vehicles in 2021 in the Russian facility and this could be dented because of problems on the availability of parts.

As economic sanctions imposed by the West have excluded major Russian banks from the international settlement network known as SWIFT, Japanese companies that sell products in Russia would now face the problem of receiving payment. There are other Japanese companies engaged in other business activities in Russia and their interests are heavily affected. For example, Komatsu Ltd., construction machinery manufacturer, accounted for 10 per cent of annual sales of its products to the former Soviet Union region. That could be hit now. As a fallout of the worsening situation, Japanese companies engaged in corporate social responsibility would not ponder if such activities could continue in the changed situation.

The sanctions soon began to bite Russia. Its economy soon started fraying, the currency collapsed and debt mounted. A potential default could cost investors billions and shut the country out of most funding markets. Facing the situation of paying back $117 million in interest on dollar bonds, it now faces the possibility of default of about $150 billion in foreign currency debt owed by both the government and Russian companies.[7]

End of Switzerland's Policy of Neutrality?

When the global efforts were directed to punish and isolate Russia, continued and targeted Russia's finances, Putin remained unperturbed. The mood of the world can be best judged when traditionally neutral Switzerland announced it would forgo its commitment to "Swiss neutrality" and joined the growing coalition of nations imposing sanctions and demanded that Russia should withdraw its troops immediately. Though Putin claimed that civilians were not targeted, the collateral damage in terms of civilian casualties could not be prevented.

The world was a bit puzzled on Switzerland's stance, why it decided to veer away from its traditional neutrality policy. By joining the coalition of nations imposing sanctions on Russia, Switzerland broke its 200-year-long neutrality policy. Why was this so? It was probably because Switzerland thought that the world was drifting towards a completely new situation where a World War III scenario could be envisioned.[8] Days later Switzerland announced its position, Russian foreign minister Sergei Lavrov issued a stern warning that if the West does not stay away from meddling in Ukrainian affairs, the possibility of a World War III could not be prevented from becoming "nuclear and destructive". Such pronouncement would look scary and alarming to anyone, particularly those countries that prioritise dialogue and diplomacy as the preferred route. Besides joining the sanctions bandwagon, Switzerland closed its airspace to Russian aeroplanes, curtailing entry to the Swiss with Russian connections and imposing financial sanctions on Putin, Prime Minister Mikhail Mishustin and Foreign Minister Sergey Lavrov.

The tiny Alpine nation seen as the world's paradise, maintained its neutrality policy since 1815 as the basic principle of Swiss foreign policy. It is not a part of the NATO and joined the UN only in 2002 after the majority of its population endorsed it. But it pursued a policy of armed neutrality, putting into place compulsory military service that still continues to maintain military readiness in event of an invasion.

Interestingly, though Switzerland saw this time in Russia's military operation in Ukraine as an unprecedented attack on a sovereign European country and therefore chose to risk its policy of neutrality, it did not take a similar stance when Russia annexed Crimea in 2014. When Russia announced military operations, thousands of Swiss people participated in demonstrations in Zurich, Bern and Basel questioning why their government was not supporting the EU sanctions. The coronavirus pandemic with its global spread also could have played a pivotal role in rejigging how the Swiss saw themselves in the globalised world.

Would Sanctions Bite Putin as the West Expects?

Though the West by imposing sanctions of various kinds aims to freeze Putin's assets as punishment, it is believed that his hidden wealth is over $100 billion.[9] Some other sources believe that Putin's assets could be over $200 billion. This could sustain Putin to withstand the sanctions. Putin's assets are believed to be so widespread within Russia and outside that it will be difficult for the West to bring those under the sanctions as getting proofs could be difficult. However, such sanction measures could be seen as a politically important signal.

But Russia's strength, besides its military and nuclear assets, is much more than Putin's purported personal assets and thus sanctions would have little impact on Russia. On the contrary, the West is heavily dependent on Russia's energy and if Russia stops supplying to the needs of West's energy needs, the economies of the West could be crippled, biting more than the sanctions on Russia. If the West imposes sanctions on Russian energy, those would damage their economies.[10]

Though the US is the world's biggest producer of oil, its dependence on imports remains high as domestic demand for consumption continues to rise. In February 1977, then President Jimmy Carter had warned about the over dependence on foreign oil. That warning comes real now as Russia's invasion of Ukraine spurred an oil crisis with rising fuel costs. Russia, a top oil and gas producer, would not hesitate to use its energy supplies as a weapon if it suits its national interests. Here, one cannot miss the inter-linkages of energy and geopolitics. Under the given situation, can the US and the West afford to impose sanctions on Russian energy as such measures would hurt their economies? It would be difficult to measure the consequences on the West if Russia decides to turn off the taps to pressure the West. Managing energy security and promoting a transition to cleaner energy to control climate change linked with Russian gas and oil is something beyond calculation. So, the task is huge.

Despite Carter's policy to diversify the sources of energy decades ago, true energy independence has not been achieved by any country in the world. Dependence on imports from energy producing countries continues. There exists no mechanism to prevent price disruption as energy can be stored only for a limited period and therefore exposed to price volatility in any crisis situation as demonstrated by the Russia-Ukraine crisis.

For the record, Russia produces one out of every 10 barrels of oil the world consumes and up to a third of Europe's natural gas supplies. Russia is the second-largest crude producer in the world, behind the US and ahead of Saudi Arabia, but sometimes that order shifts.

Putin is aware that the petroleum card gives him strategic leverage well beyond Russia's nuclear arsenal. In the 1970s, the Organization of the Petroleum Exporting Countries played a similar card. The actors are different this time, but the cudgel is essentially the same. Countries such as those in Western Europe and Japan, which are dependent on imported oil and gas, could stand to lose exports of manufactured goods if their economies slow as energy prices rise. The energy matrix in the geopolitical context puts Russia in a strategic advantage. Seen only from this angle, Putin is unlikely to be a loser.

The West might consider reducing their energy purchases from Russia to hurt the Russian economy. The G-7 nations – the US, UK, Canada, France, Germany, Italy and Japan – are toying with such an idea. Though Russia produces close to 11 million barrels per day of crude oil, it consumes roughly half of this output and exports the rest. Of these, roughly 2.5 million barrels per day is shipped to European countries, including Germany, Italy, the Netherlands, Poland, Finland, Lithuania, Greece, Romania and Bulgaria. Some of these exports go through the Druzhba Pipeline through Belarus and the rest by ships from various ports.[11]

In this complex matrix, where does China position itself is another question that demands analysis. Though this China angle shall be discussed in detail in another section of this article, it would be instructive to mention here that China is another buyer of Russian oil and this important factor does shape China's policy in the larger Indo-Pacific context. Like the EU countries, China too imports 1.6 million barrels per day of Russian crude oil. Half of this is supplied via a special direct pipeline, the Siberia Pacific Ocean pipeline. This also services other customers via port, including Japan and South Korea. If the West reduced imports of oil from Russia, other supplier countries such as Norway and Saudi Arabia might step in to meet the shortfall. But Russia has other options. Some Asian countries such as Thailand and India could bail out Russia by increasing their intake of oil imports. Moreover, Russia has special supply arrangements with countries such as Cuba and Venezuela.

It is here India can step in to bail out Russia by increasing its imports. India already bought Russian crude cargoes that were already at sea at a sharp discount and Russia can find other buyers with little stake with the current Russia-Ukraine crisis with reduced prices.

That would help oil the Russian economy. Given the impending rise in global oil prices stemming from the current situation, the US and the West might urge India and China to redirect some quantity of Russian oil to Europe to ease the pressure and to offset direct purchase from Russia. The maintenance of the Strategic Petroleum Reserve by countries such as India and Japan could make this possible. It remains unclear if India and China would cooperate, but one could expect both countries would be on board in the interest of keeping crude oil prices under control in the larger interest of the global economy.

India's Dependence on Russia and Compulsions

Where does India position itself in its foreign policy narrative given its historical friendly relationship with Russia, seen as a reliable ally, while maintaining its strategic autonomy in any crisis? It abstained from the US-sponsored UNSC voting condemning Russia's military action against Ukraine. India decided to maintain its national interests and thought it was the correct decision to stay away. India also joined 35 countries in the 193 member UN General Assembly by abstaining from voting on a resolution deploring in its strongest terms Russia's actions in Ukraine and demanding that Russia "immediately, completely and unconditionally" withdraw all of its military forces from the territory of Ukraine within its internationally recognised border.

India's abstention was in line with what the government described as its consistent position that allows it to reach out to both sides to find the middle ground and foster dialogue and diplomacy. Explaining India's position, Indian ambassador T.S. Tirumurti subtly sent a message to Russia that the UN Charter, international law and principles of sovereignty and territorial integrity must be respected.[12] India's decision to abstain did not mean support for Moscow but reflected India's reliance on its Cold War ally for energy, weapons and support in conflict with neighbours.[13] But at the same time, questions are being raised if India can revisit its policy of overdependence on Russia for its military needs.

Prime Minister Narendra Modi spoke with Putin on the telephone and appealed for an "immediate cessation of violence" and return to the dialogue process with the NATO group. In the past, Russia stood by India by using its veto power in the UNSC whenever the Kashmir issue was put to vote and therefore cannot afford to go against the interests of its time-tested friend. Interestingly, Pakistani Prime Minister Imran Khan landed in Moscow the day Russia launched its military operation against Ukraine and felt 'excited'. Both Pakistan and China have territorial disputes with India. By abstaining from the UNSC resolution, China was seen to be on the Russian side. Though this could be a matter of worry for India, India is confident that Moscow would navigate its policies in such a manner that Beijing's hard stance against India on the border issue could be managed. Seen from a larger perspective, India's stance at the UNSC and General Assembly might not be ideal but was a better option in the circumstances. While maintaining its strategic autonomy in its foreign policy, India has to balance between the US with which it has warmed relations recently, and the Western world and Russia. Russia shall always continue to enjoy India's priority when it comes to global strategic issues.

This brings us to the discussion on another critical issue on the India-Russia relations, namely India's continued reliance on Russian weapons. That has remained and shall continue to remain for quite some time as the bedrock in the India-Russia relationship. On the trade front too, both sides have set a target of $30 billion in bilateral trade by the end of 2025.

Russia has remained as the main supplier of defence procurements for India. This single issue underlines the depth of India-Russia friendship and commitment to stand by each other. The latest in this journey was that in October 2018 India signed a $ 5 billion deal with Russia to buy five units of the S-400 surface-to-air missile defence system, despite a warning from the then Trump administration that going ahead with the contract may invite US sanctions. When Modi and Putin met in 2021, both leaders signed an agreement to extend their military technology cooperation for the next decade.

India's acquisition of the S-400 missile systems is critical in countering China, though it remains as an irritant in its relations with the US. The S-400 is a sophisticated surface-to-air defense system and India expects these would give it strategic deterrence against rivals China and Pakistan. Though the Modi government has put stress on Atmanirbhara or self-reliance including that on strengthening India's defence capability, that is a long-term goal and unlikely to be achieved in the near term. This means reliance on imports of weapons and technology shall continue. India has also diversified sources of procurement such as from the US and France to reduce dependence on Russia. During the Trump presidency, India concluded with the US defence deals worth over $3 billion. Similarly, it is procuring the Rafale system from France. India had ordered 36 Rafale fighter aircraft from France in September 2016, seen as a major capability booster for the IAF. The induction of 36 aircraft into the IAF would be a major capability booster for the IAF. The twin-engine Rafale jets are capable of carrying out a variety of missions: ground and sea attack, air defense and air superiority, reconnaissance, and nuclear strike deterrence. The Rafales carrying the long-range Meteor air-to-air missiles are considered to have an edge over fighter planes with Pakistan and China. The planes equipped with the Hammer missiles have enhanced India's capability to carry out air-to-ground strikes.

This being so, as the Ukraine crisis deepens, the real problem for India is how it navigates international sanctions against Russia. The missile system deal with Moscow put India at risk of US sanctions, after Washington asked its partners to stay away from Russian military equipment. It is to be seen if India can break out of its dependence on the Russian weapons. The US and others are expected to understand India's compulsions as it would be difficult to alienate India. The realism that countries balance principles with real politicking and diplomacy could bail out India from being understood.

The spate of sanctions imposed by the US and its NATO partners on Russia could adversely impact India at multiple levels, particularly about materiel supplies for which New Delhi is hugely dependent upon Moscow.[14] There is a fear that India's military faces the grim and worrying prospect of interrupted and interminably delayed Russian defence kit.

India has developed in collaboration with Russia in the production of BrahMos supersonic cruise missile and successfully negotiated a $375 million export deal of the BrahMos with the Philippines and now fears the US and European sanctions could jeopardise this.[15] If embargoed, it could seriously threaten India's first major overseas contract to boost materiel exports fivefold to $5 billion by 2025. India has always pursued an independent foreign policy and its defence acquisitions are guided by its national interests.[16]

In view of the changing dynamics in global politics with shifting alliances and new configuration of power relations, the debate arises whether India should abandon its decades-old policy of strategic autonomy and take positions on global issues. If that could be the case, India might reconsider its dependence on Russia.[17]

Impact of Russia's Action on Ukraine in Germany

Russia's military operations in Ukraine influenced other countries' long-standing foreign policy stances. Germany initiated the process of shedding its doctrine of pacifism behind its foreign policy since World War II. This speaks volumes to the gravity of Putin's actions. Criticised for its initial placid response to Kremlin's aggressive posturing and then invasion, Germany was awakened to the possibility that in the event of a Russian victory in Ukraine, its position in the world could be challenged. This persuaded Chancellor Olaf Scholz to take a swift position and a harsher stance against Russia.[18]

Amid pressure from allies and horrors at Russia's attack on Ukraine, Germany initiated a virtual U-turn and announced to strengthen its military. It took an invasion of a sovereign country nearby and threats of nuclear attacks for Germany to shake its decades-long faith in a military-averse foreign policy that was born of the crimes of the Third Reich. As Chancellor Scholz remarked in an address to a special session of Parliament, 24 February 2022 marked a "historic turning point" in the continent when Putin ordered Russian forces to launch an unprovoked attack on Ukraine.[19]

Scholz announced that Germany would increase its military spending to more than 2 per cent of the country's economic output. He announced the release of an immediate one-off 100 euros or $113 billion to invest in the country's woefully underequipped armed forces. He too announced to speed up construction of two terminals for receiving LNG, part of efforts to ease the country's reliance on Russian energy.

The event in Ukraine shocked countries with pacifist minds and drove them to a rethink. Germany was the first to abandon more than 30 years of trying to balance its Western alliances with strong economic ties with Russia. Scholz's steps marked a fundamental shift in not only the country's foreign and defence policies, but its relationship with Russia.

Russia's military operations in Ukraine influenced other countries' long-standing foreign policy stances, with some reviewing their stances. In Japan, nuclear-sharing discussion sparked a domestic debate. Another European nation, Germany, too initiated a process of shedding its doctrine of pacifism behind its foreign policy since World War II.

For Germany, the Russia-Ukraine crisis was "a turning point" on how Berlin sees itself in the world. Criticised for its initial placid response to Kremlin's aggressive posturing and then invasion, Germany was awakened to the possibility that in the event of a Russian victory in Ukraine, its position in the world could be challenged. This persuaded Chancellor Olaf Scholtz to take a swift position and a harsher stance against Russia.[20] Within a week, Europe saw a remarkable shift in Germany's stance on foreign policy.

Amid pressure from allies and horrors of Russia's attack on Ukraine, Germany initiated a virtual U-turn and announced to strengthen its military. It took an invasion of a sovereign country nearby and threats of nuclear attacks for Germany to shake its decades-long faith in a military-averse foreign policy that was born of the crimes of the Third Reich. As Chancellor Scholz remarked in an address to a special session of Parliament, 24 February 2022 marked Zeitenwende, a "historic turning point" in the continent when Putin ordered Russian forces to launch an unprovoked attack on Ukraine.[21]

Scholz announced that Germany would increase its military spending to more than two per cent of the country's economic output. He announced the release of a one-off 100 billion euros or $113 billion to invest in the country's woefully underequipped Bundeswehr, Germany's armed forces. He too announced to speed up construction of two terminals for receiving LNG, part of efforts to ease the country's reliance on Russian energy.

Scholz's commitment to increase defence spending was not something sudden or stemmed from the crisis in Ukraine. Way back in 2014, the two per cent cap was the goal set for NATO member states within a decade but a crisis of Ukrainian proportion spurred Scholz to activate the proposal. Former US president Donald Trump had urged Germany and other NATO members to increase their defence at least to 2 per cent of the GDP. Trump had criticised former Chancellor Angela

Merkel for Germany's failure to meet NATO targets that marked the transatlantic relationship. The US spends almost 3 per cent of its GDP on the defence. Trump always used to blame Germany that it was not doing enough to strengthen the NATO alliance. Germany just needed a spark to act and this came from the Ukraine crisis.

What is significant that Scholz now wants the enhanced military spending to be anchored into the country's Constitution, which he feels would be in the long-term interest of Germany's security. The financial bazooka for the Bundeswehr to be written in the German Constitution as announced by Scholz included three major departures from Germany's traditional foreign policy postures: pulling a volte-face in decisions relating to banning Russia from SWIFT, the Nord Stream 2 pipeline, and the supply of arms to Ukraine.

As a part of the sanction measures, the US, UK and some EU members expelled several key Russian banks from the Society for Worldwide Interbank Financial Telecommunication (SWIFT). SWIFT is an international finance system that allows countries to move their money around the world and by expelling Russia from this, it was aimed to strangulate its banking operations with the outside world. Germany and other EU countries are major importers of Russian gas and raw materials. The global interbank payment system – SWIFT – is used to pay for such imports and by expelling Russia from the system would mean that Germany will no longer be supplied with gas or raw materials.[22]

Japan's Economic Stake in Russia

Japan, which was hesitant to impose sanctions on Russia in 2014, strongly condemned the invasion. Opinions surfaced if strengthening its military could be an option. Japan has the festering territorial disputes over the Kurile islands chain, north of Hokkaido, and this has led to the troubled relationship since the end of World War II. Japanese firms started mulling over exiting from Russia as sanctions started biting. The Japanese move came after rapid exit of Western companies from Russian ventures in response to the military invasion of Ukraine.[23] Earlier Shell Plc of Britain announced that it was pulling out of energy enterprises in Russia, including the Sakhalin II liquefied natural gas project. Japan is an energy deficient country and depends on imports for the bulk of its energy needs. Japan decided to go ahead with the European nations and the US. Though two Japanese trading companies, Mitsui & Co. and Mitsubishi Co. have stakes in the Sakhalin II project, which is a major source of LNG for Japan, the companies decided to cooperate with the international community, including Group of Seven nations, from the standpoint of energy security. ExxonMobil of the US also announced on 1 March it was pulling out of the Sakhalin I project in Russia.

Two leading Japanese trading houses Itochu Corp., Marubeni Corp., and government-affiliated oil companies had set up the Sakhalin Oil and Gas Development Co. (SODECO). In total, Japan holds a 30 per cent stake in Sakhalin I. Japan's automobile industry too has a strong presence in Russia. Mitsubishi Motor Corp. has a plant in western Russia through a joint venture with European automaker Stellantis. Toyota Motor Corp., and Nissan Motor Co. too have plants in Russia that are currently operating. These companies have started facing difficulties in shipping parts from Japan and Thailand to the Russian facility, and are considering if they should continue operations or pull out stakes. Mitsubishi manufactured around 21,000 vehicles in 2021 in the Russian facility and this could be dented because of problems on the availability of parts.

As economic sanctions imposed by the West excluded major Russian banks from the international settlement network known as SWIFT, Japanese companies that sell products in Russia would now face the problem of receiving payment. There are other Japanese companies engaged in other business activities in Russia and their interests are heavily affected. For example, Komatsu Ltd., construction machinery manufacturer, accounted for 10 per cent of annual sales of its products to the former Soviet Union region. That could be hit now.

In 2021, Russia was Japan's second biggest supplier of thermal coal, making up 12.48 per cent of its thermal coal imports. Russia was Japan's fifth biggest supplier of crude oil and liquefied natural gas (LNG) in 2021, accounting for 3.65 and 8.84 per cent of its total imports respectively. Japan accounted for 4.1 per cent of Russia's crude oil exports and 7.2 per cent of its natural gas exports.[24] Though Japan has sufficient reserves of oil and LNG, the disruption of Russian supplies shall have a significant impact on energy supplies, at least in the short-term. International oil prices have already risen and their impact on companies and households not only on Japan but on many countries, including India, shall be felt.[25]

Interestingly, in the past on such occasions Japan had adopted rather a softer stance. The return of the four Kurile Islands presently under Russian occupation since the end of World War II remains a contentious issue between Japan and Russia, and therefore did not want to unnecessarily complicate bilateral ties and choose to give priority to dialogue and diplomatic negotiations to resolve the issue. This time on the Ukraine issue, Japan chose a tougher stance along with the West.

Japan sensed the gravity of the crisis as governments, citizens, organisations, and businesses around the world shared the crisis from the same viewpoints. By coming together and condemning the Russian move, Japan stood with the world as one by sending a sharp message to Putin for his misadventure and by imposing crippling sanctions.[26]

As the Ukrainians stood firm to defend their sovereignty and territorial integrity, the world came to their rescue with Germany, France, the US, Australia and others providing defence equipment to strengthen the hands of Ukraine. Japan was also provided with defence equipment, such as bullet proof vests, gloves, tents and helmets.[27] This is besides the $100 million (11.5 billion yen) in loans that Japan pledged to Ukraine to support its efforts to fight against Russia. An additional $100 million was pledged for humanitarian assistance. Respecting the spirit of Article 9 of the Constitution, Japan had eschewed exports of any defence equipment.

Japan's Response to Nuclear Threat

When Putin announced to keep its nuclear assets on alert, putting his nuclear forces on "special combat readiness" to ensure the Russian military be able to unleash its nuclear arsenal at a moment's notice, the threat looked real. Russia's foreign minister upped the ante further by saying that there could be devastating consequences if a nuclear conflict takes place. Being the only victim of the nuclear bomb in history, Japan was alarmed. Japan saw the world on the brink of unparalleled crisis with Putin's nuclear threat. The influential *Asahi Shimbun* observed in an editorial that the use of nuclear arms would be the ultimate inhumane act and the international community must express in the strongest possible terms its utter abhorrence to Russia's such pronouncement and threat.[28]

As expected, Putin's threat of nuclear use triggered a disastrous chain of serious reactions. This opened the floodgates of nuclear weapons-owning countries to think seriously if the use of nuclear weapons can be an option in a conflict situation. Putin's threat also could tempt near-nuclear countries or countries capable of going nuclear in a short term if those see this nuclear armament as the only option for defense.

In view of the deteriorating scenario in the Northeast Asian region, this nuclear debate has been going on for quite some time in Japan and South Korea as doubts increase on the continued US nuclear deterrence and because of pressure from the US to increase security burden. Abe found an ideal opportunity on Russia's military action on Ukraine to float the idea of "nuclear sharing", which would allow Japan to host US nuclear weapons for use in a security crisis.[29]

As expected, Prime Minister Fumio Kishida flatly rejected Abe's idea, saying that in view of Japan's position to adhere to the three Non-Nuclear Principles, nuclear-sharing idea cannot be acceptable. Kishida argued that nuclear-sharing would mean that the US shall be allowed to deploy its nuclear weapons in Japan even in peacetime and maintain an arrangement in which the country can load nuclear weapons onto its own fighter jets in the event of emergencies. So, the issue is very complicated.

ENDNOTES

1. Jayant Prasad, "To avoid a cold Turkey", *Times of India*, 10 March 2022.
2. Christopher Hutton, "Russian foreign minister warns that World War III will be nuclear", 2 March 2022, https://www.washingtonexaminer.com/news/russian-foreign-minister-warns-that-world-war-iii-will-be-nuclear. Also see, Shekhar Gupta, "Would Putin Have Attacked Had Ukraine Kept Its N-Bombs?", 9 March 2022, https://www.rediff.com/news/column/shekhar-gupta-would-putin-have-attacked-had-ukraine-kept-its-n-bombs/20220309.htm
3. In 1994, Ukraine gave up its nuclear weapons in exchange for security guarantees from Russia and the West. Today, Ukraine feels betrayed. The document was signed on 5 December, 1994 at the summit of the Organization for Security and Cooperation in Europe (OSCE). Ukraine, a nuclear power at that time, voluntarily gave up its nuclear weapons in exchange for security guarantees. The US, Great Britain and Russia welcomed the decision of the Kyiv regime at that time to accede to the non-proliferation agreement and pledged, among other things, to respect the independence and "existing borders" of Ukraine. The Soviet Union, Belarus and Kazakhstan signed similar memoranda on the same day.

4. Carla Babb, "Ukraine, Russia Prep for 2nd Round of Talks as Kyiv Demands Cease-Fire", 28 February 2022, https://www.globalsecurity.org/wmd/library/news/ukraine/2022/ukraine-220228-voa01.htm?_m=3n%2e002a%2e3266%2eon0ao069c5%2e30z2
5. "World on brink of unparalleled crisis with Putin's nuclear threat", *The Asahi Shimbun*, editorial, 1 March 2022, https://www.asahi.com/ajw/articles/14560543
6. "Japanese firms mull exodus from Russia as sanctions bite", *The Asahi Shimbun*, 2 March 2022, https://www.asahi.com/ajw/articles/14561726
7. "Russia is heading towards $150 bn default nightmare", *The Times of India,* 17 March 2022.
8. Navmi Krishna, "Russia-Ukraine war: Why Switzerland veering from its traditional policy", *Indian Express*, 3 March 2022, https://indianexpress.com/article/explained/russia-ukraine-war-switzerland-policy-7798603/
9. Mike Mclntire and Michael Forsythe, "Putin Faces Sanctions, but His Assets Remain an Enigma", *The New York Times*, 26 February 2022, https://www.nytimes.com/2022/02/26/world/europe/putin-sanctions-money-assets.html
10. Clifford Krauss, "Ukraine and the Mirage of Energy Independence*", New York Times, 25 February 2022,* https://www.nytimes.com/2022/02/25/business/ukraine-russia-us-oil-gas.html
11. Amy Myers Jaffe, "Can wealthy nations stop buying Russian oil?", *Asia Times*, 2 March 2022, https://asiatimes.com/2022/03/can-wealthy-nations-stop-buying-russian-oil/
12. *Times of India*, 3 March 2022
13. Ashok Sharma and Aijaz HUssain, "India Walks Tightrope Over Calls for Russia's Isolation",

27 February 2022, https://clarionindia.net/india-walks-tightrope-over-calls-for-russias-isolation/

14. Rahul Bedi, "New Sanctions on Russia Spell Trouble for India's Defence Procurement", 23 February 2022, https://thewire.in/security/new-sanctions-on-russia-spell-trouble-for-indias-defence-procurement

15 "Philippines inks $375M deal to buy BrahMos supersonic missiles from India", 28 January 2022, https://www.globalsecurity.org/military/library/news/2022/01/mil-220128-rfa01.htm?_m=3n%2e002a%2e3240%2eon0ao069c5%2e303v

16. "India's defence procurement guided by national security interests: MEA on S-400 deal", 26 November 2021, https://www.newindianexpress.com/nation/2021/nov/26/indias-defence-procurement-guided-by-national-security-interests-mea-on-s-400-deal-2388548.html
17. Avinash Paliwal, "India should reconsider its Russian dependence", https://www.msn.com/en-in/news/opinion/india-should-reconsider-its-russia-dependence/ar-AAUldXl
18. Mira Patel, "Explained: What's made Germany shed its pacifism after the invasion of Ukraine?", *Indian Express*, 3 March 2022, https://indianexpress.com/article/explained/whats-made-german-shed-its-pacifism-after-the-invasion-of-ukraine-7797948/

19. Melissa Eddy, "In Foreign Policy U-Turn, Germany Ups Military Spending and Arms Ukraine" *New York Times,* 27 February 2022, https://www.nytimes.com/2022/02/27/world/europe/germany-ukraine-russia.html
20. Mira Patel, "Explained: What's made Germany shed its pacifism after the invasion of Ukraine?", *Indian Express*, 3 March 2022, https://indianexpress.com/article/explained/whats-made-german-shed-its-pacifism-after-the-invasion-of-ukraine-7797948/
21. Melissa Eddy, "In Foreign Policy U-Turn, Germany Ups Military Spending and Arms Ukraine" *New York Times,* 27 February 2022, https://www.nytimes.com/2022/02/27/world/europe/germany-ukraine-russia.html
22. Saadhya Mohan, "Germany's Three Major Policy Reversals Over Russia-Ukraine War", 28 February 2022, https://www.thequint.com/news/world/germany-three-major-policy-reversals-over-russia-ukraine-war-crisis-putin-scholz#read-more
23. "Japanese firms mull exodus from Russia as sanctions bite", *The Asahi Shimbun*, 2 March 2022, https://www.asahi.com/ajw/articles/14561726
24. "Factbox: Asian buyers of Russian oil, gas and coal", 22 February 2022, https://www.reuters.com/business/energy/asian-buyers-russian-oil-gas-coal-2022-02-22/
25. "Japan imposes sanctions on Russia over actions in Ukraine", 23 February 2022, https://www.reuters.com/world/japan-imposes-sanctions-russia-over-actions-ukraine-2022-02-23/
26. "Standing as one, world can send sharp message to Putin", *Asahi Shimbun*, editorial, 3 March 2022, https://www.asahi.com/ajw/articles/14562098
27. "Japan moving to supply Ukraine with defense equipment", *Asahi Shimbun*, 4 March 2022, https://www.asahi.com/ajw/articles/14563974
28. "World on brink of unparalleled crisis with Putin's nuclear threat", *Asahi Shimbun*, editorial, 1 March 2022, https://www.asahi.com/ajw/articles/14560543
29. "Abe suggests Japan start 'nuclear sharing' discussion" *Asahi Shimbun*, 28 February 2022, https://www.asahi.com/ajw/articles/14560003

3

Sino-Russia Cooperation to Challenge US Hegemony: Concerns for India

– Singh Subhalaxmi Baidhar, Prasanna Kumar Panda

Introduction

Since the USSR's establishment, the People's Republic of China and the USSR have had a boundary dispute that has hampered the achievement of common foreign policy goals. The misalignment of their foreign policy gave the American nation a distinct edge during the long Cold War. Since the end of the Cold War, the United States has continued to dominate the global economy and geopolitical landscape. Since then, Russia has been struggling to maintain its sphere of influence against the U.S. The emergence of China as an economic superpower has been a silver lining for Russia to counter the U.S. The conventional wisdom that Russia and China would never ally no longer stands valid. The Soviet Union under Leonid Brezhnev and Mao Zedong appeared to be engaged in a fierce battle that happened a long time ago. In their stated hostility to American dominance in international affairs, the two nations stand united. Advocating for a world with several powers, they pledge to oppose any perceived danger of the United States encroaching on their domains. Despite many hindrances, the camaraderie between Moscow and Beijing has developed through various common platforms like SCO, BRICS, ARCTIC COUNCIL, and the Asia Pacific Cooperation Summit.

The recent decade has seen developing cooperation between Russia and China in the Trade, Security, Infrastructure, and Energy sectors to outlast U.S. hegemony in Eastern Europe, the Middle East, and the African regions. Russia has successfully bagged two multi-billion-dollar Su-35 and S-400 deals with China despite the U.S. CAATSA sanctions. In the South China Sea, Both Russia and China are conducting bilateral exercises against the U.S. freedom of navigation operations. They voted almost in unison in the United Nations Security Council to counter the U.S. in the recent past like the Iran nuclear deal and the Syria issue. The axis of convenience between Russia and China is posing a direct threat to the eternal U.S. hegemony in the world order. A litany of barriers, historical mistrust, and economic and military asymmetries are being kept aside to pursue common objectives to deter U.S. supremacy. A potential replacement for the unipolar world that the United States monopolizes is the expanding partnership between Beijing and Moscow. Aside from this, it is also clear that one of India's biggest difficulties in the coming years will undoubtedly be the cooperation of Russia with China. China is "consolidating" its total national power and developing strong military capabilities with Russia's assistance. After it is finished, China is probably going to make more of a show about its claims, especially in India, its immediate neighbour.

Evolution of Sino-Russia Relations in the Post-Soviet Era

President Boris Yeltsin of Russia first adopted an overtly pro-Western stance as the Soviet Union fell apart in 1991. In the first year of its establishment, however, the policies of the newly formed Russian state gradually became somewhat more balanced. Following President Yeltsin and Foreign Minister Kozyrev's travels to Beijing in 1992, the Russian military was evacuated from Mongolia. A deal to remove combatants and offensive weaponry from regions up to 100 miles from the border was made in December. Similarly, 200,000 troops were redeployed in the Russian Far East. Additionally, in 1992, Yeltsin declared that foreign policy would now be "balanced between East and West" at the summit with Chinese leaders. Through the formation of an alliance with China, Yeltsin was able to assert that Russia was counterbalancing US hegemony, which appears to have been the result of internal nationalist pressure and their strong electoral support. At their seven summits between December 1992 and December 1999, Boris Yeltsin and Jiang Zemin spoke of a year-over-year improvement in bilateral ties.

Jiang Zemin was indeed the first Chinese president to visit Russia since Mao Zedong and Josef Stalin did it in 1993.1994 saw the establishment of a Russian-Chinese "constructive partnership," although significant changes did not occur until 1996. Yeltsin signed a "strategic partnership" with Zemin in April of that year, and as the July presidential elections approached, he strengthened ties with China to lessen the influence of Communist rival Gennady Zyuganov. Reorganising the Russian government's ministerial ranks aided in promoting a foreign policy that was friendlier to China. In January 1996, the Russian Federation's Foreign Minister, Evgenii Primakov, took over from the openly pro-Western Andrei Kozyrev, and this opened the door for a significant re-engagement with long-standing allies including China, North Korea, and India. With Primakov's 1998 plan to establish a strategic triangle linking China, Russia, and India, this Asian involvement was also going to be formalized. Nonetheless, during the mid-1990s, economic connections stagnated despite the stronger political ties. The goal of $20 billion in bilateral trade volume by the end of the decade, which was set in 1994, appeared a long way off, and commerce between China and Russia even fell in 1993.

This was because of the tightening of visa regulations brought about by the large-scale migration wave, which ultimately caused a 40% decline in trade in the first half of 2004. Although it continued to hover around $5–7 billion for the remainder of the decade, bilateral trade had slightly recovered by 1995. As it turned out, bilateral trade reached a mere $6 billion under Yeltsin's presidency. Russia was unable to establish its worldwide standing as a result of the free fall of the Russian economy, which saw a GDP decrease of 13% in 1991, 19% in 1992, 12% in 1993, and 15% in 1994. During this time, Russia, in the words of Lowell Dittmer, went from being a "bipolar nemesis to diplomatic non-entity." Concurrently, China saw fast development rates, with its GDP rising by 9.2 percent in 1991, 14.2 percent in 1992, 13.5 percent in 1993, and 12.6 percent in 1994.

The incursion of Western powers into the former Soviet space also corresponded with Russia's economic downfall. Russia developed a growing sense of caution about the growing influence of the West as six former Soviet governments joined the Council of Europe and NATO wanted to add three more East-European members. Following the US-led NATO intervention in Kosovo in 1999—which took place without a UN Security Council mandate—China and Russia started to express increasing fears about the US's unilateral actions. The US's "accidental bombing" of the Chinese embassy in Belgrade did not defuse the already high tensions. The rise of Islamic extremism in Central Asia and Chechnya during this same period was another factor that pushed Beijing and Moscow closer together. As worldwide condemnation of Moscow's crackdown and use of oppressive measures in Chechnya mounted, especially from the West, China's support of Russia's right to non-interference in domestic affairs proved vital.

In light of the international criticism, it faced after the events at Tiananmen Square, China, for its part, could connect to this. It is appropriate to view the relationships formed in the mid- to late-1990s using this framework. An accurate evaluation of Sino-Russian relations thus points to a more reactive rather than a proactive nature, with the two countries emerging more as adaptable answers to Western policies than as an unbreakable necessity for one another, even though these are difficult to distinguish analytically because they reinforce one another.

The Putin Era

Putin's goal upon taking office on December 31, 1999, was to seize back control of the state machinery, which included the Far East, the Russian Federation's periphery, and Russia's "near abroad," which included the Caucasus and Central Asia. Furthermore, Putin's initially pro-Western policies have altered the strong China-Russian relations that were established under Yeltsin. Beijing was also not pleased with Russia's participation in the war on terror and its 2001 consent to a US military deployment in Central Asia. Putin's re-engagement with Washington was equally problematic for his domestic base, which included both the elite and the common public. And just when it seemed that things could not get any worse, Putin backed NATO's expansion into the Baltics, allowed the US to leave the ABM pact, and tacitly approved of US forces stationed in Georgia. These actions alarmed the Russian people, the Duma, and, to a lesser degree, the Chinese. China was relieved of some of its worries when Chinese President

Jiang Zemin and Russian President Vladimir Putin signed the Treaty of Good Neighbourliness and Friendly Cooperation on July 16, 2001.

Since the era of Mao and Stalin, no deal has been signed with as much scope as the 20-year strategic and economic cooperation agreement. But on July 18, just two days later, Russian President Vladimir Putin didn't seem to be considering any other options besides China interaction. Especially considering that the two-day prior treaty signed with China stated explicitly that "the contracting parties shall not embark on any such action, including the conclusion of such treaty with a third country which compromises the sovereignty, security, and territorial integrity of the other contracting party." China can hardly have placed much faith in the significance of this accord in light of Putin's remarks. However, the Chinese maintain that relations between China and Russia are still developing. Among other things, the late November 2002 article "China-Russia Relations Remain Better than Russian-US Ties" in People's Daily, the mouthpiece of the CCP, served as evidence of this.

The Siberian Pipeline Conflict and Putin's Augmentation of Presidential Powers: In addition to working to build relationships with both the East and the West, Vladimir Putin was successful in undermining the federal Duma (the parliament) to increase his authority and presidential powers in the areas of foreign and security policy. Putin demonstrated this most visibly in his foreign policy towards China and Japan, particularly in his choice to support Japan over Russia in the Siberian pipeline project, a move that was received with opposition at the time from the majority of Russian decision-makers. This was against the terms of the July 2001 agreement, which stated that the Siberian pipeline would be constructed from the Russian town of Nakhodka to the Chinese town of Daqing. Up to 20 million tonnes of oil, or 12% of China's total oil consumption, were intended to be transported by the 2,400-kilometer pipeline. The agreement was ultimately struck in late May 2003 when the Chinese National Petroleum Business (CNPC), a state-owned oil business in China, and the head of Yukos, Mikhail Khodorkovsky, agreed.

An agreement was also signed about the general development of oil exports, with Yukos promising to raise oil deliveries to 20 million tonnes per year between 2006 and 2010 and then to 30 million tonnes between 2011 and 2030. The majority of Russian domestic actors that were worried, including the Energy Ministry, Prime Minister Mikhail Kasyanov, and the pro-China faction within the Russian Foreign Ministry, endorsed the agreement. However, Putin began promoting the pipeline's extension to Japan in place of narrowing it down to just China. To be honest, there was another motivation for this, a generous counter-offer from Japan, in addition to the desire to avoid going through China.

Concurrently, there was a vigorous campaign against the oligarchs and private enterprises operating in the Russian energy sector. The notable events were the arrest of Yukos CEO Khodorkovsky, the seizure of the company's assets, and the suspension of the pipeline development to China. PM of China Wen Jiabao made an official visit to Moscow in September 2004 to rescue the crucial agreement inked with Yukos. Although he could not convince the Russians to approve a rise in oil exports, he was successful in persuading them to build the pipeline. Chinese banks further gave Russia a $6 billion loan to buy Yukos' assets in return for energy contracts, guaranteeing a steady supply of Russian oil. In October of that same year, Putin finally chose the route to Japan, but with a branch line that continued to China. Subsequently, Putin returned to the Chinese option but did not provide any information regarding when the project would be completed. Without a doubt, this has harmed bilateral relations, even though China has tried to downplay this dissatisfaction with diplomatic rhetoric.

Beijing Reengages with Moscow in 2003–2004: At the same time, Russian foreign policy began to shift towards a more China-focused foreign policy overall, beginning in 2003–2004, even though it was evident that Moscow's indecision was working against Chinese objectives. The Russian government decided to focus on achieving a balance between Russia and China rather than joining forces with the US. China and Russia fiercely opposed this infringement of Iraqi sovereignty at the same time that the US launched Operation Iraqi Freedom.

The Shanghai Cooperation Organization's (China, Russia, Kyrgyzstan, Kazakhstan, Tajikistan, and Uzbekistan) further institutionalisation was one of the signs of these strengthening Sino-Russian relations. Aside from the Iraq War, the main reason for Moscow's abrupt strategic change is probably the fact that, despite being forced to make many intolerable concessions, Russia saw no real advantages from the closer ties with the United States that it had established following September 11, 2001. This may have to do mostly with permitting US presence in Russia's neighbourhood. Although Moscow still holds this opinion, it neglected the advantages that Russia derived from the US's stabilization of Afghanistan. Public opinion, the Duma, the Defence Ministry, and other ministries where Soviet nostalgia still exists were all quite against this. One of the reasons Putin began looking into possible areas of overlap with China's interests was pressure from these groups. Perhaps also playing a role in this was the strengthening of the Russian Federation as a result of higher oil and gas exports coupled with a relatively high price level.

Russia's energy business has had to draw in international investors even with the growth of its oil revenues. The main instance of this came in 2004 when a $6 billion loan from Chinese banks enabled Rosneft to purchase Yuganskneftegaz, a former Yukos company. In 2006, Sinopec, the national oil corporation of China, completed a similar transaction whereby it acquired TNK-BP's $3 billion stake, or 96.9 percent, in Russian Udmurtneft. As soon as the purchase was completed, it had to sell 51 percent of the shares to Rosneft.

Beijing has 49 percent of the shares in the later purchase, thus the significance of this should not be overstated even if it is the first direct access for a Chinese business to Russian assets. Apart from Russia's urgent need for foreign investments to develop new energy discoveries and maintain its energy infrastructure, the nation must also contribute to keep the strategic alliance from disintegrating. According to Russia's Energy Strategy 2001-2020, estimated expenditures of 450-600 billion euros will be required for an aging capital stock to attain the projected growth of 4 to 5 percent throughout this time frame. As a result, the Russian oil sector desperately needs Chinese hard money right now.

When everything is taken into account, it is impossible to dispute the improvement in bilateral ties during the 2000s. In addition to enjoying a thriving bilateral trade, China and Russia have resolved the majority of their unresolved border disputes and conducted a sizable military drill known as Peace Mission 2005. Additionally, in 2005, the two nations signed the China-Russia Joint Statement on 21st Century World Order, which emphasised their shared interests, commonalities, and good intents. Over $30 billion in bilateral trade was done in the same year, a 37% increase from the year before. The Politburo of the

Chinese Communist Party and the Security Council of Russia have established a high-level structure for bilateral security talks. China and Russia also adopted a statement in March 2006 titled "Russia, China support energy diversification," which outlined increased strategic cooperation in this field.

The Sinopec and Rosneft shareholder agreement of Udmurtneft was reached as recently as November, which signifies a positive development in Sino-Russian energy relations. But, given that Moscow still holds the majority stake, the significance of this should not be exaggerated.

Sino-Russia Relations in the Era of Unipolar World Order to Challenge US Hegemony

Russia and China both eventually returned their relations to normalcy during the last years of Soviet authority. They committed to establishing mutually beneficial and equal relations, refraining from hostilities, observing each other's domestic affairs without intervention, and respecting the sovereignty and territorial integrity to foster peaceful coexistence. Chinese-Russian ties continued under the tenet of "no alliance, no conflict, and no targeting any third country" even after the Soviet Union collapsed two years later (Ying, 2016).

The concept of the Normative Model of Democratic Peace Theory can be connected to this circumstance in some way. "The normative model suggests that norms of cooperation and compromise keep their conflicts of interest from turning into violent confrontations, which is why democracies do not fight each other" (Russett, 1993). As a result of their shared ideology, governmental system, and social mores—as well as their consistent pursuit of collaboration and partnership—China and The Soviet Union managed to give up the idea of starting a full-scale war during their difficult fifteen years of diplomatic ties. Each nation was aware of its true allies and adversaries; it was clear to them who could betray them in their hour of need or provide an opening for suggestions that would lead to wealth and the establishment of new states. Fighting one other would increase the might of the West, especially the USA, which might lead to one of them losing in the end. Therefore, China and the Soviet Union made a sensible choice that produced a favourable result by reaching a compromise.

The most fruitful years for two-state bilateral ties that could lead to the establishment of an official anti-West coalition in the contemporary world were the 1990s. China became Russia's top trading partner as a result of progressively stronger and better relations between the two countries. The main pillars of relations were investment, bilateral trade, the sale of guns and other weapons, and, most importantly, the trade of gas and oil. Due to the US embargo on China, there was a significant demand for Russian gas and oil.

As time went on, the degree of bilateral economic ties increased more quickly. To put this expansion into perspective, "keep in mind that, while China and Russia's annual bilateral trade was only about $5 billion in the early 1990s, it nearly reached $100 billion by 2014" (Ying, 2016). The turning point in the economic relations between China and the United States came with the signing of the $400 billion deal in 2014 to deliver natural gas over thirty years. According to Paton and Guo (2014), "as U.S. President Barack Obama arrived in the Chinese capital for the Asia-Pacific Economic Cooperation summit, Russian President Vladimir Putin and Chinese President Xi Jinping signed the preliminary gas-supply agreement in Beijing."

This proved to be a significant advancement in the formation of an anti-Western coalition. China becomes more reliant on European customers and Russia becomes less dependent on them as a result of this agreement. At the same time, China gains from this agreement as it enters into a pact with a strong hegemonic state that will guarantee China's security. A really severe move against the United States is these kinds of close economic links. Natural gas and oil are the main sources of the cold war in the twenty-first century. Even though the United States hasn't traded oil with any nation since the 1900s, 2015 will go down in history as the year the United States began trading oil. Anti-West alliances are beginning to show their effects as the United States begins to take unprecedented actions. Due to their mutually beneficial economic relationships, both states have been able to rise together and create an alliance.

Their political collaboration as well as their economic links influenced their strategic goals against the USA. Russia and China frequently agreed on decisions together and, in particular, exercised their veto power simultaneously in the Security Council, as demonstrated by their vetoes of the 2014 action in Syria and the 2008 sanctions against Zimbabwe. The contrasting policies of the two states have a direct effect on US power globally. The persistent problems in Asia and the South China Sea are causing the USA and China to distance themselves from one another, in addition to the fact that UN decisions must be made. In these interactions, Taiwan's case is quite significant. Even though Taiwan has US support, China opposes Taiwan's independence and seeks to prevent China from furthering its interests in Asia. "With an Asia Pacific strategic focus, Obama launched a number of foreign policy initiatives. Later, in an effort to strengthen US multifaceted engagement in the region, it was dubbed the "US strategic pivot" or "rebalancing" towards Asia. Feng (2015) said.

Initially, the Chinese government took great offence at Washington's advocacy of the Trans-Pacific Partnership (TTP) among Asian nations, which did not include China. Taiwan's purchase of armaments and weaponry through sales and other channels poses a second threat to China's security in Asia. However, China and Russia are also making progress in these areas of collaboration. "On new international financial institutions, like the BRICS foreign exchange reserve pool, the Asian Infrastructure Investment Bank, and the New Development Bank BRICS, they are collaborating." The Foreign Affairs Council.

In West-Asian relations, the Taiwan question continues to be one of the key examples. There may be advantages for both governments from Russia's engagement in the Taiwan issue. The USA gained greater authority on this matter when China demonstrated its neutrality during the Ukrainian Crisis. China will expect recognition for the Ukrainian Crisis from Russia if it supports China in the Taiwan dispute. Due to this, the Sino-Russian alliance's fight against the West will advance with this kind of dual partnership.

There are numerous ways to define the motivation behind this alliance's founding. Realistically, China works with Russia to ensure its survival. One could argue against this remark by pointing out that China would also survive if it collaborated with the West, but geopolitical considerations are crucial in this kind of scenario. The borders between China and Russia are open from the Siberian side, and a significant migratory population of Chinese people reside there. There, fishing is a well-developed industry, and Chinese people can simply relocate from Siberia to more central regions of Russia to expand their companies.

Concurrently, Russia has developed increasingly attractive offers for Chinese nationals to draw them away from ties to the United States and the West. Thanks to the Treaty of Good Neighbourly Friendship and Cooperation, which the two countries signed in 2001, the 4,300-kilometer boundary was ultimately established in 2004 and 2005—albeit inside a 20-year treaty framework (Scott, 2007, p 146).

The liberal perspective holds that the two states' stronger links stem from their shared political ideologies, the convenience of trade that comes with being close to each other, and the significant influence that military backing has on such ties. In general, China finds it more comfortable to cooperate with Russia than to maintain tight ties with the United States.

The reason for this is that whenever a state works with the United States of America, the latter attempts to subjugate that state entirely, accelerate the process of Americanization, and—above all—make that state under its authority. In addition, the United States of America employs these states whenever it is suitable to do so to keep out of any conflicts or wars. The Great World Wars serve as an example. During those conflicts, the United governments did not actively engage with any state; rather, it only provided them with military or economic support and ultimately became one of the governments involved in determining global peace.

One of the strongest partnerships in history has the potential to be formed between China and Russia. These governments have the potential to overthrow the US and Western powers in the world, which might lead to the opening of doors for numerous emerging or impoverished nations. States in Eastern Europe that join the EU in an attempt to move westward almost always suffer politically and economically under pressure from the more developed EU members. However, Eastern European and Asian states can receive equal power, opportunities, and independence thanks to Sino-Russian cooperation.

Sino-Russia alliance, a National Security Threat to India

There is a wide range of challenges to the Indian state in the nuclear, conventional, and sub-conventional (terrorism and insurgency) realms. India faces contested borders and conflicting territory claims with China and Pakistan along its land borders. The de facto boundary with Pakistan known as the Line of Control (LoC) and the unmarked boundary with China known as the Line of Actual Control (LAC) have been sources of contention for many years. Although they are in the conventional realm, both states provide military risks to India both in the maritime and continental domains.

The People's Liberation Army Navy's frequent surface and subsurface naval deployments bear witness to the fact that today, for the first time in the tumultuous strategic history of Sino-Indian ties, China has, with Russia's help, strengthened its position as an actor in the Indian Ocean Region (IOR). The establishment of permanent Chinese facilities coupled with supply and logistics hubs will reduce the Indian Navy's strategic and geographic advantages, according to the IOR. At the moment, China and Pakistan collaborate on their naval activities to a great extent.

China uses Gwadar, a deepwater port in Pakistan, for its nuclear submarines (SSBNs and SSNs), while Karachi serves as the nation's primary logistics hub. Sino-Pak naval cooperation is unparalleled in its engagement of China's fleet with Russia in the Persian and Indian Gulf. However, the People's Liberation Army Navy (PLAN) receives its supply from other places inside the Gulf Cooperation Council (GCC), including the ports of Salalah in Oman and Aden in Yemen. China has maintained its first overseas naval station in Djibouti since 2017.

China currently sees formal diplomatic agreements more as a way to secure "places" in the Indian Ocean than as a way to secure "bases" where PLAN warships can replenish food, fuel, and fresh water. As a result of Colombo's inability to pay back Chinese loans, Beijing was granted a 99-year lease under which it currently owns 70% of the port of Hambantota in southern Sri Lanka. Adding to this list of "places" is this port. Nonetheless, New Delhi faces greater military challenges from the Sino-Russian strategic alliance. Beyond this collaboration, there have been other fronts in which China and Pakistan have been more cooperative, such as enhanced military interoperability in the areas of theory, force structure, and operational planning. With growing equipment compatibility, interoperability also applies to military hardware.

China supplies Pakistan's navy with frigates, for example, and both nations' navies use similar warcraft. Together with the People's Liberation Army Air Force, the Pakistan Air Force trains, pilots Chinese-built aircraft, and takes part in joint drills. Pakistan has secure communication capabilities and access to China's BeiDou satellite navigation system thanks to fibre optic lines that travel beside the Karakoram Highway. Beijing has established alliances with other FOR governments as well, though not to the same extent as its ties with Pakistan. China's Yunnan region has a border with Myanmar, sometimes known as Burma, which acts as a gateway into the Indian Ocean. Beijing may now pursue a more aggressive policy in the FOR because Pakistan and Myanmar both provide solid execution capabilities.

Beijing can now more readily deploy its military thanks to the Xi regime's establishment of five integrated theatre commands in 2015 and improved defence cooperation with Russia. A progressive change in the nation's objectives has also resulted from these reforms. These developments have strengthened the offensive capabilities of the Chinese military and allowed it to progress faster.

The military obstacles presented by China thus represent important military capabilities and operational postures as well as significant defence cooperation between Russia, China, and Pakistan. They demand in return that the Indian armed forces have distinct command structures that incorporate tri-service collaboration and capability. The preponderance of the sub-conventional threat to the Indian state comes from Pakistan, even though insurgencies in northeastern India also have a military cost. India confronts a serious nuclear danger from Pakistan and China, with whom it has long maintained close ties in the fields of nuclear technology and missile delivery, in addition to conventional and sub-conventional challenges.

Conclusion

China, France, Germany, India, and Russia, the second-tier great powers, have given up on the conventional "hard balancing" approach that is based on opposing alliances and systemic arms buildups, ever since the Cold War ended. The primary explanation for this is that they do not fear surrendering their security and sovereignty to the

USA, the current hegemon, which is a prerequisite for any balancing to take place. Those who possess nuclear weapons see the US less as a predatory state and more as a limited hegemon, whose power is limited by internal politics, democratic institutions in the US, and other influences.

The United States' growing unilateralism and propensity to militarily engage in sovereign states to overthrow regimes that follow anti-US policies (like those in Iraq) after September 11 worry the other major countries in the secondary rankings, leaving the United Kingdom alone. Using strategies like jumping on board, buck-passing, and free-riding, the states ranked second on the importance scale limit federal power while preserving their security and influence. They have also started "soft balancing," which is forming small-scale diplomatic ententes or coalitions. Due to their inability to find a path out of the alliance and their willingness to join them in this endeavour, second-class nations like China and Russia have developed the ability to counterbalance American influence. It can be presumed that the steps taken to construct an anti-West alliance will likely be unprecedented in the globe and lead to the establishment of a system characterized by greater equality and less hegemony among hegemonic governments.

REFERENCES

Andrew Kuchins, "Russian Perspectives on China: Strategic Ambivalence," in *The Future of China-Russia Relations*, ed. James Bellacqua (Lexington: University Press of Kentucky, 2010), 33.

Bakshi, Jyotsna. 2002. "Post-Cold War Sino-Russian Relations: An Indian Perspective." *Strategic Analysis*. Vol. 26 (No. 1).

Bolt. Paul. J, (2014): 'Sino-Russian Relations in a Changing World Order' in *Strategic Studies Quarterly*, Vol. 8, No. 4, pp. 47-69.

Buries, Mark. 1999. *Chinese Policy Towards Russia and the Central Asian Republics. Santa Monica*, CA: RAND.

Dahl, Erik. 2006, March 8. "Interview With China's NDRC Vice Director Zhang Guobao." *Interfax-China*.

Dittmer, Lowell. 2001. "The Sino-Russian Strategic Partnership." *Journal of Contemporary China*. Vol. 10 (No. 28).

Donaldson, Robert H. 2003. "The Arms Trade in Russian Chinese Relations: Identity, Domestic Politics, and Geopolitical Reasoning." *International Studies Quarterly*. Vol. 47, p. 712.

Hars. V. Panth, (2019) India's national security challenges and dilemmas in *International Affairs*, vol. 1, pp. 12-44.

Dmitri Trenin, "True Partners? How Russia and China See Each Other," Centre for European Reform, February 2012, 12.

Kotkin. Stephen, (2009): 'The Unbalanced Triangle: What Chinese-Russian Relations Mean for the United States' in *Foreign Affairs*, Vol. 88, No. 5, pp. 130-138

Leszek Burzynski, "Overshadowed by China: The Russia-China Strategic Partnership in the Asia-Pacific Region," in *Future of China-Russia Relations*, 278—80.

Lo, Bobo. 2004. "The Long Sunset of Strategic Partnership: Russia's Evolving China Policy." *International Affairs*. Vol. 80 (No. 2).

Mette Skak, "Russia's New 'Monroe Doctrine,'" in Russian Foreign Policy in the 21st Century, ed. Roger E. Kanet (Basingstoke, UK: Palgrave Macmillan, 2011), 138—54;

Norling. Nicklas, (2007): 'China and Russia: Partners with Tensions' in *Policy Perspectives*, Vol. 4, No. 1, pp. 33-48.

Rozman, Gilbert. 1998. "Sino-Russian Relations: Will the Strategic Partnership Endure?", *Demokratiza-tsiya*. Vol. 6 (No. 2).

Foreign Affairs, (2019): 'Are Russia and China Really Forming an Alliance?' Accessed on 19 June 2019, Available At https://www.foreignaffairs.com/articles/china/2019-04-04/are-russia-and-china-really-forming-alliance

Foreign Affairs, (2019): 'A Russian-Chinese Partnership Is a Threat to U.S. Interests' Accessed on 19 June 2019, Available At https://www.foreignaffairs.com/articles/china/2019-05-14/russian-chinese-partnership-threat-us-interests

Sergei Blagov, "Russia Seeks Closer Energy Partnership with China," *Eurasia Daily Monitor* 10, no. 42, (6 March 2013), http://www.jamestown.org/single/Jno_cacheU&tx_tt news%5Bswords%5D=8fd5 89394 Id69d0be3f378 57626 lae3e&tx_ttnews%5Ball_

M. Taylor Fravel, Strong Borders, Secure Nation: Cooperation and Conflict in China's Territorial Disputes (Princeton, NJ: Princeton University Press, 2008), 201—17.

James Kynge, "Ukraine a Setback in China's Eastern Europe Strategy," Financial Times, TJ February 2014, http://blogs.ft.com/beyond-brics/20l4/02/27/ukraine-a-setback-in-chinas-eastern-europe-strategy/?European Council on Foreign Affairs, (2016): 'CHINA AND RUSSIA: GAMING THE WEST?' Accessed on 19 June 2019, Available at https://www.ecfr.eu/publications/summary/china and russia gaming_the_west7166

Weitz. Richard, (2012): 'SUPERPOWER SYMBIOSIS: The Russia-China Axis' in *World Affairs*, Vol. 175, No. 4, pp. 71-78

Weede, Erich. 2003. "China and Russia: On the Rise and Decline of Two Nations." *International Interactions*. Vol. 29 (No. 4).

Wishnick, Elisabeth. 2001. "Russia and China: Brothers Again?", *Asian Survey*. Vol. 41 (No. 5).

4

Reimagining Kosli Identity through Human Security Approach

– **Shankar Chhatria**

Introduction

India is best known for its unity in diversity. In the early years of independence, national leaders and constitutional framers discussed a federal structure that would allow for a unified but culturally diverse nation-state. They started with an understanding, combining equality for the individual with equality for various communities.[1] Besides, India is a multilingual country that has many highly developed languages with a wealth of expression, grammar and literature. Each language has its unique script. However, they are not all equally developed. Some languages lack both a native script and written literature. Furthermore, a large number of these languages can be placed into one linguistic family because they are closely linked to one another.[2] Language movements across the nation constituted a significant danger to India's internal security. Western Odisha was originally a part of the historic Kosal Kingdom, which had its unique history, culture, and notable traits. This "Kosali identity" has become the defining feature of the call for a separate Kosal state. Not only do the people of western Odisha have a shared origin, but they also share the same fate: being undeveloped and backward.[3]

Regionalism is deeply rooted in the socio-political body of the state. The successive governments of Odisha have neglected the Kosal region in terms of infrastructure, public institutions and political representation. However, regionalism is often manifested in an intensely virulent form in academic institutions. It is very important to note that politicians and academics work hand in hand encouraging regionalism in Odisha. Now it has given a political colour; it would not be an exaggeration to say that regionalism forms an important input of the socialization process and a child, from the very beginning. This paper analyzes factors influencing regionalism in Western Odisha and the Kosal movement with the lens of the human security approach. Here the researcher argues that linguistic identity or Kosli nationalism in Western Odisha is not the only determining factor, but the disparities and inequalities are influential factors behind the Kosal Movement. The author suggests that human security in the Kosal region can be maintained by the decentralization of authority and further democratization of public institutions.

This paper is designed into six sections. The first section begins with a brief introduction and methods used in this study. In the second section, the researcher defines the meaning of human security. Then it explores the visions of the founding fathers of the Indian Constitution and the assertion of the state for autonomy. The fourth section analyzes regional disparities and the factors behind the growth of Kosli identity in Western Odisha. Here the researcher highlights specific factors such as cultural, political, and socio-economic factors. Then the next section analyzes human security threats faced by the people of Western Odisha. Lastly, it concludes with a view of Indian secularism as well as the responsibility of the federal government and citizens.

Concept of Human Security

Human security is a universal concept. It applies to everyone, rich or poor, in all countries. The components of human security depend on one another. It is concerned with how individuals interact with their environment, how much access they have to socio-economic opportunities, how freely they exercise their many options and whether they live in peace or conflict. In 1994, the UNDP Report defined human security as "safety from chronic threats such as hunger, disease and repression, protection from sudden and hurtful disruptions in the patterns of daily life whether in jobs, in homes, or communities". The seven dimensions of human security (Figure 1), such as personal, environmental, economic, political, community, health, and food security were taken into consideration in the report while developing this definition. The following general definition of human security was provided by Kofi Annan in his report to the United Nations:

> "Human Security, in its broadest sense, embraces far more than the absence of violent conflicts. It encompasses human rights, good governance, access to education and health care, and ensuring that each individual has opportunities and choices to fulfill his or her own potential. Every step in this direction is also a step towards reducing poverty, achieving economic growth, and preventing conflict. Freedom from want, freedom from fear, and the freedom of future generations to inherit a healthy natural environment- these are the inter-related building blocks of human and therefore, national security".[4]

Figure 1: Human Security

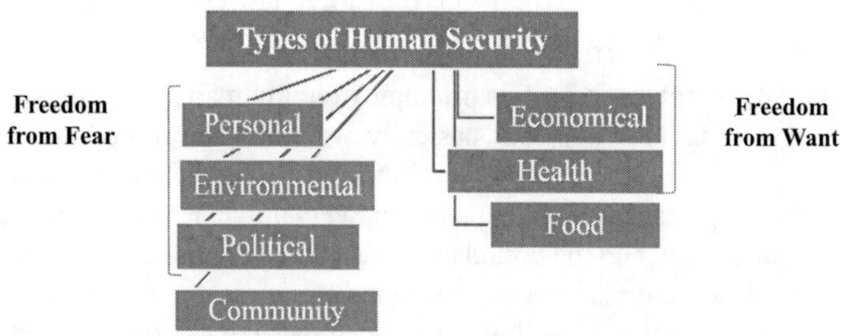

Source: Horizontal multi-level hierarchy art compiled by the researcher

Regionalism and National Integration: A Bird's Eye View

Unity in diversity is a unique feature of India. National leaders and constitutional drafters discussed a federal structure that would allow for a unified but culturally diverse nation-state in the early years of independence. They agreed to combine equality for the individual with equality for various communities at the outset. A federal constitution is designed to guarantee ensured parity among the federating entities and equitable representation of each section for national integration. Policy alternatives for this include sectoral reservations and proportional representation. However, a polity is said to be more stable and integrated when it has a variety of power centres, facilitating maximum participation in the polity; minority welfare and identity protection through legal, constitutional, and political means; constitutional recognition of "unity in diversity" or "diversity in unity" as a value; reduction of inequality (social and economic) through the assertion of affirmative action by the state; promotion of grassroots democracy; and accountability. In a nutshell, integration is encouraged and federal stability is preserved through the federal features of civil society, a democratic political system, and a republican federal constitution.

The Indian Constitution encourages the idea of a strong centre around which state-formation policies and substance have been developed. If the Indian government did, at least in the first few decades following Independence, accede to the different pluralist demands from reservation to regionalization of institutional political processes. It did so as an exception, not the rule. Jawaharlal Nehru's remarks on the States Reorganization Bill, 1956, made during his speech in the Lok Sabha on August 10, 1956, probably sum up the policy of the Indian state well. He said:

> "We do not stand for this principle of unilingualism. We may have a unilingual state... but basically we stand for something from that... language is important, but... there is a difference between the importance of a language, the encouragement of a language and all that, and the boundaries of a state. Language should not be confused with the boundaries of a state. It may be that sometimes the boundaries may be linguistic. We have no objection. It is good thing. But to think that it is a vital issue, that a state should be bounded by a certain linguistic area is, I think, a basically wrong approach.... It does not matter very much, in my humble opinion, where the boundary of a state is. It is a matter for careful consideration. There are sentiments about it. Let us consider sentiments. Let us consider the question, the economic aspect of it, the strategic aspect of it, the cultural aspect or whatever you like... the first, and absolutely first, consideration is the unity of India and the homogeneity of India....The second point would be the economic advantage to India or to that particular place. These are two basic things; other things follow...."

The assertion of state rights and calls for decentralization and autonomy are frequently seen as challenges to territorial integrity, while regionalism and regional movements are sometimes portrayed as disintegrating processes. The regionalization and federalization processes are two crucial and mutually reinforcing steps in the formation of democracy and a federal state, but policymakers ignore this reality. Federalization shapes units structurally to live together for a shared goal, but regionalization permits diversity to maintain its identity and to participate institutionally in the process of nation-building. Additionally, the centralist approach to national unity and its imposing centre fails to see how the region, regional identity, and regional movements all work together to create a whole.[5]

Regional Disparities and Identity in Western Odisha

Map 1: Map of Odisha with District Boundary

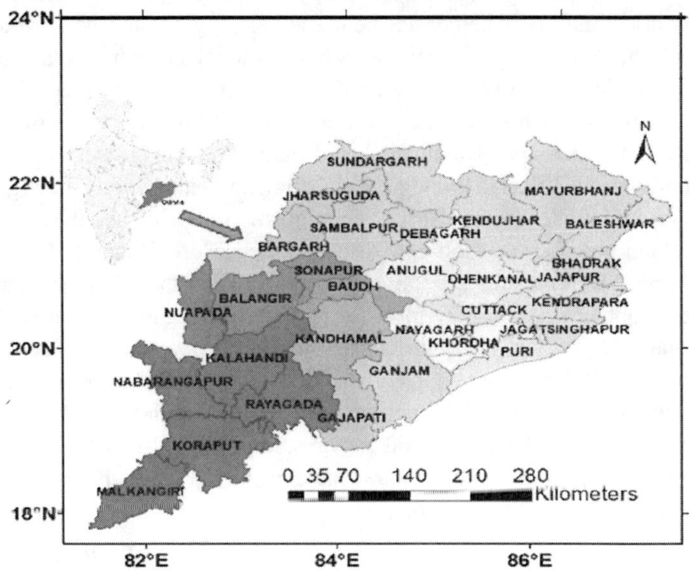

Source: ResearchGate, accessed on 13 December 2022

A key factor in the harmonic expansion of the federal state is balanced regional growth. India, however, shows a regionally diverse economic picture in terms of socio-economic indicators of economic growth, such as per-capita income, the percentage of the population living below the poverty line, the population employed in agriculture and industry, the literacy rate, the infant mortality rate, life expectancy at birth, physical and social infrastructure (in terms of availability and accessibility of education and health care), and the percentage of the population in urban areas. It is significant to remember that certain areas are very economically advanced while others are less so. Even within each district, certain areas are more advanced and others are virtually in the stone age. We are aware that regional imbalances may be caused by uneven natural resources, as well as by the neglect of certain regions and the preference for others when it comes to investments and development initiatives.[6]

Odisha has a diversified geography and is divided into several unique areas (Map 1), each of which has its levels of wealth, forms of economic activity, population density, racial and ethnic makeup, and political culture. The coastal belt, southern region, and western area are the three geographically separate regional groupings that make up modern-day Odisha. Undivided districts along the coastal belt included Balasore, Cuttack, and Puri; in the south, there are undivided districts in Koraput, Kandhamal, and Ganjam; and in the west, there are undivided districts in Balangir, Kalahandi, Sambalpur, and Sundargarh. Following the 1992 district reorganization in Odisha, the coastal region now includes the new districts of Balasore, Bhadrak, Cuttack, Jajpur, Kendrapara, Jagatsinghpur, Puri, Khordha, and Nayagarh; the southern region now includes Koraput, Rayagada, Nawarangpur, Malkangiri, Ganjam, and Gajapati; and the western region now includes Balangir, Sonepur, Kalahandi, Nuapoada, Boudh, Kandhamal. Sambalpur, Bargarh, Jharsuguda, Deogarh and Sundargarh. Regarding historical knowledge, cultural customs, linguistic differences, political advantages, and socioeconomic advancement, these three regional units differ from one another.

Historically, districts in the inland regions of Odisha were governed by princes, while those on the coastal regions were governed by the British. The uneven political evolution of the state was influenced by two areas. The interior of Odisha lags behind the coastal area both in terms of economic growth and political modernization. Comparatively, the coastal region has a denser population and is commercially and culturally developed. Along with having a high percentage of literacy rate, the population in these locations is also more politically aware. Naturally, this leads to the assembly allocating more members to the coastal region and even to the development of strong leadership. However, the western and southern regions are wealthier than the coastal districts in terms of natural resources and industrial potential. In recent years, the urban areas in the western districts of Odisha have intensified their campaigns to promote locals to the position of power.

Although the western area is larger, it only makes up 26.53% of the state's population, which was 36804660 as of the 2011 Census; in contrast, the relatively smaller coastal region makes up 47.82% of the population. While just 23.95% of SC and ST people live in the coastal districts, 48.47% of the population in the western districts is SC and ST. A key aspect of regional poverty in Odisha is revealed by the greater concentration of backward people in the western and southern districts. The low agricultural intensity in the western and southern regions is an indication of generally low agricultural growth there since intense farming depends on a range of variables, including irrigation, climate, topography, etc. The income discrepancy also indicates the robust economic regionalism in Odisha, which in turn reflects the state's racial/ethnic distribution and the various physical characteristics of its many areas.[7]

Cultural Factor

Regionalism is strongly supported by its distinctive cultural traits in western Odisha. Tribal culture has affected the people of western Odisha, as evidenced by their dialect, eating habits, beliefs, customs, traditions, dance, theatre, music, fairs, and festivals. This particular culture is very useful in defining the regional identity in western Odisha.[8] One's personality is shaped by the language they use, which also helps to define their identity and bind them to a certain group of people. Understanding language is an inquiry into human beings and the qualities that determine their origin, existence and potential.[9] Sambalpuri/Kosli dialect and language are distinct from the traditional Odia speech spoken by natives of coastal Odisha. Sambalpuri is regarded as a dialect or regional variant of the Odia language in formal and everyday speech, but to the inhabitants of western districts of Odisha, it is a distinct language all on its own. Even though the residents of Coastal and Western districts of Odisha are both Odias, they feel very differently from one another and the residents of South Odisha. Furthermore, urban Odisha, where the majority of businessmen, educated and employed people reside, is notably different. Compared to the rural areas of the state, they are wealthier and have a wider range of economic and cultural influences.

Political factor

The political cleavage is another important element that boosts regionalism in Odisha. Politics in Odisha were first divided along regional lines by political groups like the Ganatantra Parishad (GP) and subsequently the Swatantra Party. The GP/Swatantra was connected with the interests of western Odisha, whereas the Congress was considered a party predominantly aligned with the interests of coastal Odisha. The elections for the Odisha Legislative Assembly very much mirrored this regional polarization of politics. The Congress and its breakaway organizations, such as the Jana Congress and Utkal Congress, won the most seats from coastal districts between 1952 and 1974 while doing exceptionally well in the western area. The Congress politicians from the coastal area, however, controlled the administration and politics in Odisha during the 1980s under J.B. Patnaik, while those from the western region were virtually ignored. Regional factionalism developed within the Congress as a result of its favouritism of coastal Odisha. The consecutive administrations led by Biju Patnaik, J.B. Patnaik, and Naveen Patnaik, respectively, saw a substantial extension of the same internal gridlock.

The western region consistently has less representation in government and decision-making organizations than the coastal area. Odia leaders from the coast have mostly controlled the office of chief minister in Odisha. Only R. N. Singh Deo and Hemananda Biswal, two individuals from the western area, briefly held the position of the chief minister. Of the State's Council of Ministers, the western area has, once again, been underrepresented, except for the sporadic coalition governments in 1959, 1967, and 1971. The proportion of the western area in the State bureaucracy, courts, and police is still relatively low. In Odisha, cultural and social differences can be attributed to regional variations. The Odisha Legislative Assembly is where these regional disparities in politics are most visibly reflected. Additionally, sub-nationalism is becoming a significant element affecting how individuals vote. This has had an important effect on the growth of distinctive sub-regional political personalities.

Socio-Economic Factor

Along with political fragmentation, socio-economic divisions had a big impact on the growth of regionalism in western Odisha. With a few notable exceptions, the majority of the western region has had very little socio-economic progress since the colonial era. Even though the situation has improved, the level of socioeconomic development in western Odisha is still relatively low in contrast to coastal Odisha in the post-independent age. Both "autonomist" and "separatist" regional mobilization have grown significantly in western Odisha; the former argues for increased regional autonomy and equitable development, while the latter encourages the establishment of a separate provincial state named Kosal for western Odisha. The initial justification for the claim was the regional identity and economic backwardness. But more recently, a particular regional nationalism known as "Kosli nationalism" has served as the foundation for the aspiration for an independent state. The Kosal movement represents an internal threat to the integrity of Odisha and the cohesion of Odia nationalism.

Sub-regional political behaviour has been significantly shaped by non-political causes. Odisha is one of India's most underdeveloped states. When intra-regional differences are taken into consideration, the poverty of development assumes a very major role. Considering education is a crucial component of development, it is found that 50.97% of women and 74.95% of males are literate. Malkangiri has the lowest percentage of literacy among the districts (31.26%). The districts with the lowest rates of female illiteracy are Nabarangpur (21.02%) and Malkangiri (21.28%). The district of Khurda, which includes Bhubaneswar, has the highest literacy rate at 80.19%. The greatest rate of female literacy (71.06%) is likewise seen in this district. The fact that the state capital was included in the statistics undoubtedly had an impact on Khurda district's high literacy rates. Khurda's neighbouring district, Jagatsinghpur, has a literacy rate of 79.61%. Compared to 65.38% the national average, the literacy rate of 63.61% of Odisha is comparable. However, there are significant regional differences among the various locations and towns.[10]

Thus, it has been observed that political polarization, socio-cultural divisions, and economic disparities all provide to the development of regional consciousness in Odisha. Western Odisha has been experiencing many human security threats due to such imbalances and inequalities in the state. Also, it is probably the reason behind the claim for a separate Kosal State.

Human Security Threats in Western Odisha

The Rajan Committee Report identified Odisha along with Assam, Bihar, Chhattisgarh, Jharkhand, Madhya Pradesh, Meghalaya, Rajasthan and Uttar Pradesh as the "Least Developed" States in India.[11] The Rajan Committee was formed to design a Special Action Plan for rural infrastructure development in the 100 most backwards areas in the country. The eight districts that make up the KBK region, Kalahandi, Balangir, Koraput, Nuapada, Sonepur, Malkangiri, Nawarangpur and Rayagada, are among the poorest in the state of Odisha.[12] Although poverty in KBK districts was one of the biggest challenges, the majority of dangers to human security result from inequalities. Inequalities may exist in the social, political, economic, health, and other domains. Income inequality is the most harmful type of disparity. Educational inequality, unequal access to healthcare, unequal access to clean water, and many other inequities are all caused by income inequality. This is undoubtedly a cause for concern.[13]

Poverty, Unemployment and Migration

Problems of chronic poverty are associated with human suffering, vulnerability, deprivation of basic needs, abrogation of human rights and degraded citizenship. Since chronically poor people are the least likely to gain from present national and international development initiatives, chronic poverty is to be characterized as the transfer of poverty over generations. The term "chronically poor" refers to someone whose income is unstable. Indigenous and nomadic peoples are among the caste, racial, and ethnic groups that experience discrimination, disadvantage, and marginalization. The chronically poor are multidimensionally disadvantaged along with capacity deficient. Their low levels of material possessions and socio-political marginalization keep them in poverty. In other words, poverty for those who experience it regularly entails more than just having a very low income. It also encompasses a wide range of deprivations, including physical insecurity, socio-political discrimination, starvation, illiteracy, unsafe drinking water and lack of access to primary healthcare.

Though there are many different and effective ways for people to earn their living, migration is a key element and method for many poor people. Therefore, a thorough investigation of migration and the chronically poor is impossible when migration is viewed as largely a means of economic survival for those directly engaged. The diversity of definitions and viewpoints on these topics is reflected in the complexity and breadth of the definitions used to describe migrants, migration, and poverty, as well as the various ways in which these concepts are combined to conceptualize and analyze the relationship between migration and poverty.

Despite widespread depictions of "the poor" as a homogeneous group in development theory, policy, and practice, the poor are a diverse population with varying access to resources, power, and control. Their unique vulnerabilities shape their lives in different ways, and as a result, there are a wide variety of alternatives, options, and paths they might choose. Even while the migration is still a key component of family livelihood plans, some people utilize it as a response to their poverty. As a result, it cannot be expected that everyone among the poor would always have the opportunity to immigrate. By using migration as a livelihood strategy, people and communities run the risk of continuing to be chronically impoverished.[14]

Most migrant workers in Odisha come from scheduled, backward, or tribal castes, and a sizable portion of them work as agricultural labourers who do not own land. In a few cases, people with restricted land did not have the resources necessary to develop the same, and as a result, the barren land was left uncultivated for years. Consequently, they perform agricultural labour on the properties owned by wealthy zamindars or landlords in their villages or nearby villages. They find it difficult to survive because of the seasonal nature of their occupation and the minimum wages. Thus, it appears that the primary driving force behind the debt that causes such labourers to migrate in great numbers in search of work is the inadequacy of their income to pay living expenses even at a subsistence level. In addition, the tribal people in the study region move beyond the districts and states for six months with their women and children to survive. This is due to deforestation, pressure on the land, recurrent droughts, poverty, and unemployment.

Many socioeconomic indexes classify the KBK region in Orissa as being backward and one of the poorest regions in the country. In Orissa, the tribes have remained at the bottom of the socioeconomic scale and have suffered from social, economic, and educational disadvantages. Tribes have been forcibly displaced as a result of the KBK region's low-income levels, widespread unemployment, underemployment, and poverty. These migrant tribal people face bondage, social isolation, and identity crises in addition to being exposed to dishonest contractors.

Because of their remote location, makeshift economy, persistent poverty, and illiteracy, they were left defenseless against outside influences and eventually fell victim to all forms of exploitation. There is also evidence that indicates the tribal people of KBK migrate outside the state in search of employment and livelihoods in construction projects, brick kilns, and other manual labour due to deforestation, restrictions placed by the government on the use of forests, pressure on land, recurrent droughts, unemployment, and chronic poverty. It must be remembered that there is nothing wrong with migration, which is the movement of people in search of certain cherished goals like a better job, better pay, and better quality of life. However, the issue becomes extremely serious when such migration results in human suffering and exploitation.[15]

Health

In general, the health condition is assessed in terms of the infant mortality rate, life expectancy at birth, crude birth rate, crude death rate, and fertility rate. Health has numerous facets, therefore rather than choose just one as the best indicator of health condition at this point, it could be necessary to refer to a number of them. Life expectancy is the most cited health indicator. It appeals because it possesses a fundamental skill that is essential to one's well-being. WHO defines "health as a condition of the whole physical, mental, and social well-being, as opposed to the absence of illness or infirmity". Health status statistics, birth and death rates are better indications of the country's changing demographics. Health indicators of the population include life expectancy and the infant mortality rate. These four indicators are interdependent across time, as may be shown by examining their relationships with one another.[16]

It is found that the infrastructure development image among the districts of Orissa is elusive and severely unbalanced. State health centres only exist on paper in the tribal highland districts. Even the paramedical staff, such as the auxiliary nurse midwife (ANM), does not prefer to stay there to provide the necessary medical services to the impoverished and helpless tribal population. Local media routinely state that tribal areas have higher rates of infant mortality, general morbidity rate, and death than more developed coastal areas like Cuttack, Puri, Baleswar, etc.

Climate Change

The most important development issue of our time is climate change. Human potential is affected by climate change and variability. It also deprives individuals and communities of their capacity to defend and improve their standard of living. Since the distribution and production of natural resources are regulated by climatic dynamics, climate change will have major effects on people whose livelihoods depend more on them. The Fourth Assessment Report of the Inter-Governmental Panel on Climate Change (IPCC) asserts that because the consequences of climate change are unevenly dispersed across time and place and disproportionately harm the poor, they are likely to result in further disparities. As a result, climate change will offer significant problems for the poor who rely on climate-sensitive industries for their survival, and even minor climate shocks might result in significant and irreversible losses that lead to destitution and poverty.

Only three districts in Odisha were at risk for drought in the 1950s. The five districts that make up western Orissa were all prone to drought by the 1980s. Among the 30 districts, 25 districts experienced drought throughout the 1990s. In Orissa, rainfall days are decreasing by one day every five years, according to research by Mohapatra and Mohanty (2006) which examined the geographical and temporal variability of summer monsoon rainfall throughout the region. According to data acquired from the government's rainfall statistics, rainfall has increased in the coastal districts of Baleshwar, Puri, and Ganjam while significantly decreasing in the western and southern regions of Orissa.[17]

Conclusion

It is clear to observe how the residents of Western Odisha are imagining themselves as a "political community" by establishing nationality in the region and demanding a separate Kosal state. In addition, one may observe volumes of Kosli literature and the spectrum of folk songs, folk dances, and folk plays are fairly notable. The western Odisha region, which was until recently mocked for its poverty, backwardness, and underdevelopment, is currently being reimagined by activists of the movement, folklorists, authors and researchers. Therefore, it is time to examine how various Kosli identifiers, such as literary, linguistic, and cultural representations, are increasingly being used by the forerunners of the Kosal movement to unite all of the locals on a single platform under the guise of pan-Kosli identity despite their internal differences.[18]

A salient message of this paper is that human security of Western Odisha may be greatly improved by civil society, the network of non-governmental groups, organizations, and movements that enable individuals to handle their problems.[19] Secondly, district-level planning should be viewed as planning for an essential component of a national system rather than a particular sector or region of the economy. It ought to aid in both its own growth and the growth of the country as a whole.[20]

In overall terms, true secularism is necessary for India's prosperity by preventing internal tensions and violent outbreaks in a multilingual, multireligious, and multicultural society. The main responsibility of the federal government is to locate these gaps in the complex society that is riven by competing interests. Without the regulation of violence, many of the ideals that nations and people want to uphold may be upset, particularly in an era when lethal small arms and nuclear weapons have spread to several countries and subnational organizations. People and the state have severe concerns about the administration, breakdown, and maintenance of the law-and-order apparatus. The most crucial factor that demands effort is addressing the innate absence of responsibility. It should not be assumed that the state alone is in charge of preserving law and order. All organizations and individuals are equally accountable for helping to resolve internal conflicts.[21]

ENDNOTES

1. On this see Miklian, J. (2015). Peacebuilding, Diversity and Human Security. *Projects/ 1638*. PRIO. Retrieved December 13, 2022, from https://www.prio.org/projects/1638
2. Kishore, S. (1987). *National Integration in India.* New Delhi: Sterling Publishers Private Limited.
3. The Kosli-Sambalpuri language is growing every day. Volumes of literature are already accessible in practically every literary form, including poetry, prose, essays, critiques, autobiographies, and they continue to grow every day. These works cover both historical and contemporary issues. For more details see Kumar, T. (2018, March). Rethinking Kosli Identity: Language, Literature and Culture of Western Odisha. *Social Trends,* 5, 37-63.
4. More so than during the cold war era, insecurity is not only ubiquitous but is also reaffirming its worrisome undertones. There are currently dangers that are extremely dissimilar from a military invasion of a country's territory. Therefore, the definition of "national security" needs to be changed. Gandhi, N. (2010). *National Security: Emerging Dimension and Threats.* New Delhi: Pentagon Security International.
5. For an in-depth study of federalization and regionalization, see B. D. Dua, & M. P. Singh, *Indian Federalism in the New Millennium* (pp. 85-108). Manohar.
6. Bandyopadhyay, D. K. (2020) in Regional Disparities in India: Issues Related to Inter-State Variations argued that regional imbalance can result from a complex interplay of factors. For this, see A. K. Thakur, & D. Kumar, *Disparities in India: A Development Perspective* (pp. 45-75). New Delhi: Deep and Deep.
7. Bhuyan, D. D. (2021). *Odisha Government and Politics: Institutions and Processes.* Cuttack: A. K. Mishra Publishers PVT. LTD provides a comprehensive analysis of the state's political system, including its legislative, executive, and judicial institutions, as well as the role of political parties, civil society, and media in the state's political process.
8. Ibid.
9. Syracuse University. (2022, December 13). *Language Matters*. Retrieved from Syracuse University College of Arts and Sciences: https://thecollege.syr.edu/research/language-matters/
10. Bhuyan, D. D. (2021). *Odisha Government and Politics: Institutions and Processes.* Cuttack: A. K. Mishra Publishers PVT. LTD.
11. Ministry of Finance. (2013). *Report of the Committee for Evolving a Composite Development Indexes of States.* New Delhi: Ministry of Finance Government of India. According to the statement of Finance Minister, based on data from the NSSO's per capita consumption survey, the poverty ratio, and a variety of other metrics, the Committee has developed a multidimensional index of backwardness that is consistent with the Twelfth Plan's multidimensional definition of poverty. According to the Committee's recommendations, states should be categorized as "Least developed" if their Index score is 0.6 or higher, "Less Developed" if their score is between 0.4 and 0.6, and "Relatively Developed" if their score is 0.4 or lower.

12. Sahu, P. R. (2017, November 20). India Today. *The State of the State Odisha*. India Today. Retrieved December 17, 2022. For details follow, http://www.ihdindia.org/pdf/Att3.pdf
13. Rajkumar, P. P. (2013). National Security: Different Strokes. In M. B. Pillai, *India's National Security: Concerns and Strategies* (pp. 23-35). New Delhi: New Century Publications. In this the author argued that if poverty is not addressed, it can lead to social unrest and instability, which can in turn threaten India's security and stability.
14. For an interesting study of Migration issues, see Tripathy, S. N. (2011). Chronic Poverty and Distress Migration. In B. K. Mohanty, *Economic Development in India: Issues and Challenges* (pp. 203-220). New Century Publications.
15. Ibid.
16. Kumar, D. (2020). Regional Pattern of Disparities and Levels of Living in India. In A. K. Thakur, & D. Kumar, *Disparities in India: A Development Perspective* (pp. 78-115). Deep and Deep.
17. Mishra, A., Upadhyay, H., & Lingaraj, G. J. (2011). Climate Change and Agri-Livelihood. In B. K. Mohanty, *Economic Development in India: Issues and Challenges* (pp. 226-246). New Delhi: New Century Publications. They emphasises the need to adopt climate-smart acriculture practices, which involve the use of innovative techniques and technologies to increase agricultural productivity while minimizing the impact of the environment.
18. Kumar, T. (2018, March). Rethinking Kosli Identity: Language, Literature and Culture of Western Odisha. *Social Trends, 5*, 37-63.
19. Gandhi, N. (2010). *National Security: Emerging Dimension and Threats*. New Delhi: Pentagon Security International.
20. District Planning Committees (DPCs) were established in India in the 1990s as part of a decentralization effort to promote local communities. These committees were meant to be participatory and inclusive, Degaonkar, C. K. (1997). *District Planning in India.* Jaipur: Pointer Publishers.
21. For the additional information about economic security and economic development, see Verma, N. M. (2001). *Dynamics of National Security-Essential Dimensions and Perspectives.* Mumbai: Jaico Publishing House. This work has been influential in shaping policy debates and has contributed to the development of India's national security strategy.

5

Issue of Migration in Indo-Bangladesh Relations: Challenges for Human Security

–**Duryodhan Nahak**

Introduction

In the contemporary era, the history of migration, both legal and illegal, throughout the 20th and 21st centuries, indicates that the movement of individuals has been genuinely worldwide. This is evident from the significant migration of people from underdeveloped nations to the more developed ones, either by crossing international borders or oceans. However, towards the end of the 20th century and the commencement of the 21st century, a new migration phenomenon emerged within developing countries. This new phenomenon of migration became prominent, not only because of the substantial number of individuals involved but also due to the conflicts that arose in the underdeveloped world as a result.

Foreign-born individuals who have broken a valid admission prerequisite or who are simply staying in India are against the law and are considered illegal immigrants. They are principally people who infiltrate the nation covertly by avoiding a screening by the border control agency. Due to its status as the most developed country in South Asia and its geostrategic location, India has become a desirable safe-haven for persecuted refugees and illegal migrants. While migrants from other neighboring countries of India are typically taken care of, the issue of illegal immigration from Bangladesh has largely gone unchecked. This is because India and Bangladesh share the longest border in the world, which stretches for 4,096 kilometers, much of which is porous and unfenced, making it susceptible to in-migration. The problem of illegal migration from Bangladesh into India is not a recent phenomenon. And unlike typical migration patterns that are primarily motivated by economic opportunities, the movement of Bangladeshis to India is heavily influenced by complex political dynamics and religious factors unique to the region's historical and cultural context.

The story of the immigration goes back to the times when India, Pakistan, and Bangladesh were one country governed by the Britishers as British India. The partition of 1947 by the British resulted in the division of the former Bengal province into two distinct entities: West Bengal, which became part of India, and East Bengal, which was incorporated into Pakistan. Subsequently, in 1971, East Bengal seceded from Pakistan and emerged as the sovereign nation of Bangladesh. Since the late 19th century, both Muslim and Hindu refugees have been migrating in significant numbers for a variety of reasons across regions. Nearly 4.7 million Hindus and Sikhs migrated to India between 1946 and 1965, whereas 6.5 million Muslims migrated to West Pakistan (now Bangladesh).[1]

The illegal influx of entry into India was fueled by ethnic conflict, socioeconomic chaos, and civil unrest. These influxes of immigration had their origins in the separation of the subcontinent into India and Pakistan (with Bangladesh as the erstwhile East Pakistan) in 1947 and then into Pakistan and Bangladesh in 1971. For instance, at least 10 million Bangladeshis relocated to West Bengal and the north-eastern provinces of India in 1971 when deaths occurred following the Mukti Bahini (the liberation brigade) War of Freedom for autonomy from Pakistan.[2] The estimated number of illegal immigrants ranges from 12 million to 13 million, and they have reportedly settled in the northeastern states of India and even as far away as Delhi or Mumbai[3]. Adding to the complexity of the situation, Bangladeshi nationals are difficult to differentiate from locals due to their ethnic, linguistic, cultural, physical, and social similarities with the people of the northeastern region. The issue of illegal immigration from Bangladesh into India has led to a divergence in interests between the two countries, resulting in a significant decline in their bilateral relations. This deterioration in ties between India and Bangladesh has far-reaching consequences, not just for the two states but also for South Asia and the global community. It is imperative to address this issue as it has implications for regional security, economic stability, and human rights.

Problems Behind It

Such uncontrolled and unfettered migration patterns provide India with a challenging issue that has significant implications for its economic resources and national security. Due to the political parties' interest in the vote banks, the majority of these immigrants have Aadhaar cards and ration cards. Since the majority of these immigrants arrive in India due to unemployment and poverty, they constitute a huge security concern to India by engaging in terrorism, bonded labor, fake money rackets, drug trafficking, prostitution, and smuggling. Additionally, it brought about a shift in society and a plethora of problems, including racial, political, social, and economic tensions and conflicts in many of India's cities, as hunger, poverty, and security threats recognise no border[4].

The administration of India has taken several aggressive steps to reduce illegal cross-border movement and activity. However, there hasn't been much success in these measures dealing with immigration. The Illegal Migrants Determination by Tribunal (IMDT) was established in 1985 to detect immigrants, particularly in Assam. The Indian Supreme Court invalidated it in 2005 because it was inadequate to handle the immigration issue. The decision to fence off the whole border with Bangladesh in two stages was reached by the Indian government in 1986. India also endorsed the plan to put floodlights along the border for a distance of more than 2840 kilometers.

Although relations between India and Bangladesh are improving, the issue of illegal immigration continues to be a serious concern in Bangladesh and is expected to hurt those relations. India should convince Bangladesh that there is a problem with illegal immigration, and both countries should try to create an environment where this problem can be resolved amicably, and innovative solutions, such as work permits, may be taken into account. so that Bangladeshis might come, work, and then go. India should also leave open the option of utilizing any advice or other assistance offered by the UNHCR to handle Bangladeshi refugees, particularly for repatriation or third-country settlement.

According to estimates from the United Nations Department of Economic and Social Affairs (UNDESA), Bangladesh is the sixth largest country in the world in terms of emigration, with approximately 7.4 million Bangladeshis living abroad, which constitutes 4.5% of the total population as of mid-2021. The majority of these emigrants, approximately 88%, reside in other Asian countries, with the Middle East being the most popular destination for male emigrants. India is the top destination country for Bangladeshi emigrants, followed by Saudi Arabia, the United Arab Emirates, Malaysia, and Kuwait. Around 67% of Bangladeshi emigrants are male, and women tend to migrate to India, North America, and Europe in slightly higher numbers than men. The districts with the highest number of male emigrants are Cumilla, Chattogram, and Brahmanbaria in the Chattogram division, while female emigrants mostly come from the Dhaka district and the Chattogram division. The shared Bengali linguistic and cultural heritage serves as a primary unifying factor between Bangladeshis and the Bengali population in India, particularly in West Bengal. This common cultural foundation fosters a sense of connection and kinship across national borders and facilitates the illegal migration.

The primary reasons for emigration are economic, and climate change is also becoming an increasingly important factor. Among the reasons for migration are unemployment, following a relative who is migrating, and having access to a community abroad. Economic reasons and family issues are the most commonly reported push factors for emigration, according to multiple surveys conducted by the International Organization for Migration (IOM) in various districts in Bangladesh, particularly in the Dhaka and Chattogram divisions. The choice of destination country is mostly influenced by the presence of friends and relatives in the host country.

Background

Migration from what is now Bangladesh had begun in the later part of the 19th century[5]. In the pre-independence era, migration within India from one region to another was not considered international migration. However, after the partition of India in 1947 into India and Pakistan on religious grounds, the movement of people between the two countries became illegal. Despite this, the migration of people from East Bengal (now Bangladesh) to India in search of economic opportunities continued, especially after the influx of Hindu refugees escaping communal riots and religious persecution[6]. This migration trend was reflected in the census data of bordering states like Assam, Tripura, and West Bengal, which showed a higher population growth rate due to migration. The Registrar General of Census estimated in 1963 that around 2,20,691 "infiltrates" had entered Assam.[7] The 1971 War of Liberation in East Pakistan and the subsequent genocide led to a massive inflow of refugees into India, with an estimated 10 million people from East Pakistan crossing the border.

This trend intensified due to the influx of Hindu refugees who were fleeing communal violence and religious persecution. Even after the partition of India and Pakistan, the migration of people from East Bengal into India continued, especially into Assam, Tripura, and West Bengal[8]. The census data of these bordering states indicate a steady increase in population growth, which is believed to be due to large-scale migration from Bangladesh. For instance, the Muslim population in Assam increased from 24.68 per cent in 1951 to 28.43 per cent in 1991 to 34.2 per cent in 2011, with an increase in Muslim population in the bordering districts of Goalpara, Nowgong and Cachar. The state of Tripura also witnessed massive inflow of people from East Pakistan, with a majority of them being Hindus[9]. As a result, the state's population grew from 6.39 lakhs to 11.42 lakhs in the first decade after independence, registering a growth of 78.71 per cent, which was the highest in the country. The deportation of migrants from Assam in the 1960s did not deter them, as most of them re-entered India. This trend is also evident in the census figures of 1971 for Assam, which showed an increase of 820,000 Muslims, with 424,000 more than that accounted for through natural increase.

Reasons Behind the Migration

A large number of individuals move from Bangladesh for financial reasons in quest of better opportunities for livelihood and economic benefits in the receiving country. The cause is a dearth of jobs in Bangladesh, as well as a low standard of living. Family reunion and the joining of friends, relatives, and neighbours are sometimes important components of the ongoing migration process, as are the cheap costs of cross-border travel.[10] In Bangladesh, natural calamities such as floods, cyclones, and droughts occur annually and cause significant damage to the lives, properties, and economy of the country.[11] These events also lead to migration from Bangladesh, as they destroy crops and habitats of the impoverished population. The occurrence of these natural disasters is further compounded by the uneven development in the region. According to official estimates, approximately 18-20 million people are displaced by floods in Bangladesh every year. Consequently, these individuals are forced to migrate to safer areas such as India, where they can secure comparatively stable living conditions and food security.

Political factors such as state-sponsored terrorism, religious fundamentalism, minority group insecurity, and deteriorating law and order as reasons for migration. News reports also support these claims. The problem has been further compounded by the politicization of migration[12]. Migrants are often used as pawns by politicians. Bangladeshi migrants work in India's informal sector as rag pickers, agricultural laborers, rickshaw pullers, domestic helpers, construction workers, and other similar jobs[13]. Some political parties capitalized on the migrant population by providing them with ration cards and other facilities that were only meant for Indian nationals, such as land distribution. Additionally, some parties sought to exploit the problem for their political agenda by giving it a communal color.

Recently, the Supreme Court of India admitted a petition alleging the presence of 40 lakh illegal immigrants in the voter's list in Assam and issued notices to the central and state governments, and the Election Commission of India. The petition filed by Assam Public Works (APW) seeks the deletion of the names of illegal immigrants from the voter's lists and freezing of the list until the names of the foreigners are deleted. The petitioner also demanded that Assembly polls, scheduled for 2011, be kept in abeyance until the voter's list is corrected. However, in another judgment in 2008, the Delhi High Court rejected a petition filed by a Bangladeshi national challenging her deportation order. The court's decision emphasized that undocumented immigrants from Bangladesh present a substantial threat to India's internal security, thereby upholding the government's stance on the matter.

During the hearing of a Public Interest Petition filed by O.P. Saxena, a lawyer representing the All-India Lawyers Forum for Civil Liberties

(AILFCL), the Supreme Court bench comprising the Chief Justice and two other Justices expressed concern that Bangladeshi migrants were negatively impacting the economy and posing a security threat to the country. The bench criticized the Union Government for its indifference towards resolving the issue and recommended that the government take exemplary steps to tackle illegal migration, including deportation. In his petition, Saxena alleged that more than 10 million Bangladeshi migrants had illegally entered India, causing a significant strain on the resources of West Bengal and poor North-eastern states. The petition sought a direction from the Court to the Union Government to identify these migrants and deport them with the assistance of agencies such as the National Human Rights Commission (NHRC).

Statistics Behind the Migration

There are no reliable government data to determine the precise number of illegal migrants in India, even though illegal migration from Bangladesh has continued unabatedly throughout the years. The Government of India frequently argues that since illegal immigrants enter the nation covertly, it is hard to have data on Bangladeshis living illegally throughout the nation. This is one of their main arguments. Even yet, the Indian government has occasionally released data on the estimated number of illegal immigrants living there.

Specifically, in March 1992, the Ministry of Home Affairs (MHA) disclosed that more than 700,000 Bangladeshis were staying illegally in different border states of India. The numbers were broken down by state and time. Later, in May 1997, the Home Minister of India, Mr. Inderjit Gupta, stated in Parliament that there were 10 million illegal migrants from Bangladesh in India, according to MHA/Intelligence Bureau sources. The India Today magazine in August 1998 gave a detailed breakdown of the numbers by state. The Task Force on Border Management in 2001 estimated the number of illegal migrants to be 15 million. In 2004, the Minister of State for Home Affairs, Shri Sriprakash Jaiswal, cited an estimated 12 million illegal Bangladeshi migrants staying in India as of December 2001, including 5 million in Assam and 5.7 million in West Bengal. However, this statement was later retracted.

Undocumented Bangladeshi nationals settling in India is not limited to illegal border crossings, as many arrive with valid documents but choose to stay beyond their permitted time. According to government records, from 1972 to 1997, a total of 991,031 Bangladeshi nationals entered India with valid documents but failed to return. A recent report from the Border Security Force (BSF) accessed by ANI indicates that since 2019, almost 14,000 Bangladeshi nationals were prevented from entering India at the Indo-Bangladesh border. Of those, 9,233 were caught attempting to flee back after illegally staying in the country, while 4,896 were caught trying to enter India from Bangladesh. Therefore, a total of 14,361 Bangladeshi nationals were intercepted while crossing the border in slightly over three years.

The Indo-Bangladesh Border Fencing Project

The erection of fencing along the India-Bangladesh border was sanctioned by the Government of India in two phases. Phase-I of the Indo-Bangladesh Border Works was initiated in 1989 and involved the erection of fencing in 854.35 kilometers and completion of 2606.35 kilometers of road. Under Phase-II, the government approved an additional 2429.5 kilometers of fencing and 797 kilometers of road at an estimated cost of Rs 287.617 million (Government of India, 2006). In 1998, the project was budgeted at Rs. 10.5 billion and entailed the construction of 900 kilometers of border fence, 2800 kilometers of border roads, and 24 kilometers of bridges along the India-Bangladesh border in the states of West Bengal, Assam, Meghalaya, Tripura, and Mizoram. However, the Assamese government and media expressed dissatisfaction with the fence on the Assamese side. A local newspaper described crossing the fence border as "easy as slicing butter with a knife."[14]

As per the Indian Ministry of Home Affairs' Annual Report 2005-2006, fencing was deemed necessary to discourage illegal infiltration and other anti-national activities from across the border. By 2004-2005, 1502 kilometers of fencing had been completed, and work on 2670 kilometers of the planned 3663 kilometers of roads was also finished (Government of India, 2006). Of the total length of the Indo-Bangladesh border, which is 4096.7 kilometers, Phases I and II have witnessed the completion of 2535.80 kilometers of fencing. Moreover, the construction of 3250.60 kilometers of border roads was accomplished during Phase I and II (Government of India, 2007-08).[15]

In November 16, 2016, former Union Minister of State for Home Kiren Rijiju had stated in Parliament that, according to available information, approximately 20 million illegal Bangladeshi migrants were living in India. According to Union Minister of State for Home Nityanand Rai, on July 26, 2022, 2,399 Bangladeshi nationals were found to be using Indian documents obtained through fraudulent means in the last five years. The Centre has urged state governments to take immediate action to identify illegal Bangladeshi migrants residing in India. Mr. Rai also stated that the states were advised to share the details of these illegal migrants who had illegally acquired Aadhaar cards, so that appropriate legal measures could be taken against them. Recently, the home ministry's yearly report states that the government has initiated the construction of a fence along the India-Bangladesh border to control illegal activities, such as smuggling and infiltration, from across the border. The report mentions that the government has approved the construction of the border fencing in two phases, along with floodlights. The report also mentions that all the ongoing works related to this project are expected to be completed by March 2024.

Socio-Economic Impact on India

In the past, Bangladesh was considered as a poverty-stricken nation and earned the nickname "international basket case" upon gaining independence in 1971. Economic hardships were a significant driver of both legal and illegal migration from Bangladesh, as the lack of economic opportunities created a sense of despair among its people. Economic factors were the main motivation for Bangladeshi migrants to move to India. Presently, Bangladesh has emerged as one of the rapidly growing economies globally, with an annual growth rate of more than 6% since 2005. As per a 2019 report, Bangladesh's Gross National Income per capita stands at 1940 US Dollars, which is comparable to India's 2130 US Dollars. Moreover, Bangladesh has demonstrated superior performance in human development indicators compared to its South Asian counterparts such as India and Pakistan, as per the United Nations Development Programme's Human Development Report 2021-22.[16] The report ranked Bangladesh at 129 out of 191 nations, while India was positioned at 132.

However, the research indicates that the migration issue is in contradiction with the aforementioned statistics. Specifically, the unauthorized migration from Bangladesh has resulted in a significant increase in population in India, leading to adverse effects such as strain on land, depletion of natural resources, and a negative impact on the state's economy. The migration from Bangladesh initially provided significant advantages to the labor-intensive agricultural sector[17]. The migrants brought with them a combination of skills and hard work, and also introduced more advanced cultivation techniques such as double cropping, involving winter and summer crops. As a result, there was a more efficient use of land for farming, and this contributed to Assam becoming a "surplus province" in rice production as early as 1947.[18]

However, the negative impact of this migration is more prevalent. The migrant workers' willingness to work for very low wages and the perception that they are more hardworking has negatively affected the local workers.[19] Additionally, the continuous influx of migrants has exacerbated the unemployment problem in the informal sector of neighboring Indian states. The descendants of these migrants are the primary source of labor for various industries such as construction, road and building development, railway line construction, domestic cleaning, and other unskilled work due to factors such as lack of education, shortage of labor for development activities in the state, and reluctance among local people to undertake such jobs.[20] Migrants also work in semi-skilled jobs like house painting, bricklaying, and carpentry.

While many migrants come to India in search of livelihood opportunities, circumstances often force them to take up illegal activities and they are often involved in activities such as smuggling, robbery, prostitution, begging, and trafficking in women and children. These activities, along with issues such as deforestation, land grabbing, and illegal occupation of public spaces, are putting pressure on India's natural resources. The problem is further exacerbated by the growth of pre-existing slums and the protection offered by different political parties to illegal migrants, who are even enrolled in voter lists and used as vote banks[21]. Political leaders who provide government services and support to migrant or immigrant communities often secure electoral support from these groups. This dynamic creates a reciprocal relationship between the provision of public amenities and voting behavior among immigrant populations. As a result, it has become increasingly difficult to distinguish between them and Indian citizens, leading to a deterioration of law and order in various parts of the country.

The migration of Bangladeshi workers has also created a remittance issue in India, as they primarily send their earnings back to their families in Bangladesh, which negatively impacts the Indian economy. Furthermore, many of these migrants do not use official channels such as bank transfers or money orders, but instead rely on informal methods such as personal contacts to transfer money across the border. One common and popular informal method is known as "Hawala," which involves transferring money through known personal contacts and often leads to other illegal activities.

Social Tensions between Migrants and the Hosts

The migration of Bangladeshi workers to Assam and Tripura has resulted in social tension due to competition for employment and acquisition of cultivable land. It has also caused communal imbalance in neighboring states, leading to tensions. In addition, the presence of these migrants poses a security threat to India, as they are involved in illegal activities such as smuggling and are aiding extremist groups in northeast India. The illegal migration has also inadvertently provided a fertile ground for the growth of extremist ideologies, particularly Islamic militancy, which has begun to establish a stronger foothold in certain areas. This situation has raised significant security concerns for Indian authorities. Moreover, the sensitive nature of this migration issue has made it susceptible to exploitation by various political factions, who often manipulate it for their agendas.

The influx of undocumented migrants has been a significant catalyst for insurgent activities in India's northeastern region. Notably, Assam, a state previously untouched by violent unrest and considered an integral part of India's national fabric, experienced the emergence of insurgency primarily due to the issue of large-scale unauthorized migration from Bangladesh. The substantial presence of these migrants has been perceived as a profound threat to Assam's cultural integrity, political stability, and economic well-being, fundamentally altering the state's demographic and socio-political landscape. As of now, about 35 percent of Assam's residents are believed to be foreigners. All Assam Students Union (AASU) for the first time raised the issue of foreigners and demanded their deportation in 1979 in Assam.[22]

The persistent maintenance of distinct identities by long-term migrants in India creates multifaceted social divisions. This phenomenon generates rifts between the host population and migrant communities, fosters disparities among demographically similar groups such as Indian Muslims and migrants, and exacerbates tensions within broader host communities, particularly along religious lines. Despite India's efforts to address this issue with Bangladesh, the government has denied the presence of Bangladeshi migrants and opposed India's border fencing plans, making repatriation of refugees impossible and straining relations between the two countries.[23]

The Way Ahead

The problem is more serious as while India tries to find a bilateral solution, Bangladesh neither admitted the existence of a sizable number of undocumented Bangladeshis in India nor took any significant measures to control the unauthorized entrance of its residents into India. India has been trying for a long time to stop the tide by building a barrier made of barbed wire around the border and stepping up border patrol, but these efforts have not been successful enough to have any beneficial results. Similarly, India's practice of forcibly pushing illegal Bangladeshi immigrants back across the India-Bangladesh border at times hasn't produced results because the arrivals either deliberately opted for another hollow boundary to re-enter India or were forcibly driven back towards India by the Bangladeshi surveillance and security officers.

However, there may be different ways to deal with the issue. Adopting a nationwide refugee statute to discriminate between refugees and unauthorized immigrants, as well as creating a bilateral accord with Bangladesh to repatriate nationals who have been living there illegally, can be a way to deal with such illegal immigrants. However, finding the Bangladeshi immigrants, classifying them appropriately, resettling or repatriating them, and stopping further entry are the key challenges. Second, preventing migration at the source by concentrating on Bangladesh's economic growth, particularly near its border with India, and working with other donor nations and organisations can be an alternative approach too. India might also tie its financial help for Bangladesh to the assistance and support given in addressing the migration issue. India should further consider seeking expertise from international organizations such as UNHCR, IOM, and ICMPD to address complex migration challenges. These bodies offer valuable experience, insights, and resources that could enhance India's capacity to develop comprehensive and sustainable migration management strategies.

India can step up border patrols and surveillance to stop unauthorised crossings, find, and detain illegal immigrants. This can be accomplished by sending out more border security agents and using cutting-edge tools like drones and other surveillance gear. By broadening the scope of already-existing visa categories, developing new visa categories, and streamlining the visa application procedure, India might examine the prospect of offering legal avenues for migration from Bangladesh. Public awareness campaigns can be organised to inform people about the risks and repercussions of illegal migration through outreach programmes in both India and Bangladesh to create knowledge about those hazards and the legal repercussions of being detected.

India can also provide social and economic support to people in the border regions of Bangladesh to discourage them from migrating illegally. This can include providing economic opportunities, education, and healthcare services to people in these areas to improve their standard of living and reduce their incentive to migrate. Working with international organizations such as the United Nations and the International Organization for Migration to find a sustainable solution to the problem of illegal migration from Bangladesh. This can involve seeking technical and financial assistance from these organizations to address the root causes of the problem and find long-term solutions, which can also be a way.

Conclusion

The international phenomena of migration are going to persist in the coming years. Every nation seeks to control immigration in accordance with its needs. However, not every nation is fortunate. They have been worried about illegal (cross-border) immigration as a result. In India, efforts to stop and regulate illegal immigration are still woefully ineffective, and this is expected to hold in the years to come. Hence, in conclusion, the issue of illegal immigration from Bangladesh into India is a complex problem that has serious implications for both countries. The Indo-Bangladesh border is not only long but also heavily populated, with inhabitants sharing a common history, culture, language, and heritage.

Therefore, any attempt to manage the border must take into consideration the people and their welfare, along with the state's security concerns. Without peaceful borders with its neighbors, India cannot fulfill its legitimate role in global affairs during these times of significant global change. It is therefore imperative that India and Bangladesh work together to address the root causes of illegal immigration, including poverty, unemployment, and political instability, while also ensuring the protection of migrants' rights and providing basic services to them. A peaceful and stable border would not only promote economic and cultural exchanges between the two countries but also enhance regional security and stability.

ENDNOTES

1. Roy, H. (2012), Partitioned Lives: Migrants, Refugees, Citizens in India and Pakistan, 1947-65, Oxford University Press, New Delhi.
2. Jha, M., (2018), "India's refugee saga, from 1947 to 2017", LiveMint, Updated: 09 Jan 2018, https://www.livemint.com/Sundayapp/clQnX60MIR2LhCitpMmMWO/Indias-refugee-saga-from1947-to-2017.html, Visited on 15th Dec 2022.
3. Tripathi, S. (2016), "Illegal Immigration from Bangladesh to India: Towards a Comprehensive Solution". https://carnegieindia.org/2016/06/29/illegal-immigration-from-bangladesh-to-india-towardcomprehensive-solution-pub-63931 6/7, Visited on 15th Dec 2022.
4. Datta, Pranati (2005), "Effects of Undocumented Migration from Bangladesh to West Bengal: A Perception Study", Session 111, Forced migration, IUSSP XXV International Conference, France, [Online: web] Visited on 15th Dec 2022.
5. Ray, Jayanta Kumar (2002), "Migration from (East Bengal/ East Pakistan) Bangladesh to India", Dialogue, 3 (3): p. 33.
6. Barkat, Abul.&Zaman ,Shafique, Uz. (2000). Forced Out migration of Hindu Minority: Human Deprivation Due to Vested Property Act in Chowdhury R. Abrar (Ed.), On the Margin; Refugees, Migrants, and Minorities,113-144, Dhaka: Refugee and Migratory Movements Research Unit.
7. Government of Assam, "Infiltration and Deportation of Pakistanis", Directorate of Information and Public Relations Press Note No. 137, July 27, 1965, Shillong, available at http://online.assam.gov.in/documents/218410/316853/Annexure-2-17A-except-9- and-12.pdf, accessed on January 28, 2015.
8. Hasan, S. Rizwana (2003), "Legal Regime on the IDPs in Bangladesh", in Chowdhury R. Abrar and Mahendra P. Lama (eds.) Displaced within Homelands: The IDPs of Bangladesh and the Region, Dhaka: Refugee and Migratory Movements Research Unit, p. 144.

9. Chowdhury, Afsan (2000) "State and the Minority Identity: The Case of Hindus in Bangladesh", in Chowdhury R. Abrar (Ed); On the Margin: Refugees, Migrants and Minorities, Refugee and Migratory Movements Research Unit, 2000, University of Dhaka, Dhaka, pp. 145-166.
10. Mahmood, Raisul Awal (1998), "Bangladeshi Clandestine Foreign Workers", in Reginald Appleyard (ed.) Emigration Dynamics in Developing Countries, Volume II: South Asia (UNFPA &IOM Project on Emigration Dynamics in Developing Countries), England: Ashgate Publishing Limited, p. 181.
11. Ketkar, Prafulla (2006), "Managing Bangladeshi Migrants: Crisis Resolved, Problem Remains", IPCS, 2006, [Online: web] Visited 15th December 2022.
12. Hossain, S. A. (1997). Bangladesh politics: From secular to Islamic trend. In B. Dey & R. Samaddar (Eds.), State, development, and political culture (pp. 80-83). New Delhi: Har Anand Publication Pvt. Ltd.
13. Chatterjee, P. (1998, November, 19). With the assembly election there have been no more round- ups of Bangladeshis. Rediff on the Net. News, pp. 1-2.
14. Indo-Bangla border in Karimganj only in name, The Assam Tribune (31 August 1999); Bangladeshi cut open border fence to sneak into Assam, The Sentinel (21 May, 2000).
15. As on December 31, 2007. Government of India, 2008. Annual Report 2007-2008. Ministry of Home Affairs (annex IV, page 160).
16. Human Development Report 2021-22: Takeaways for Bangladesh, Stefan Liller, Resident Representative, UNDP Bangladesh, Published on September 27, 2022, visited on December 15, 2022: https://www.undp.org/bangladesh/blog/human-development-report-2021-22-takeaways-bangladesh#:~:text=With%20a%20current%20value%20of,the%20regional%20value%20of%200.632.
17. Datta, Pranati, Swati Sadhu, B. N. Bhattarchaya and P. K. Majumdar (2006), "Undocumented Migration from Bangladesh to West Bengal", Kolkata: Population Studies Unit, Indian Statistical Institute, [Online: web] Accessed December 15, 2022, http://www.ipcs.org/nmt_militaryIndex2.jsp?action=show View&kValue=1411&mili tary=1016&status=article&mod=b.
18. Guha, A., 2006, Nationality Question in Assam, the Economic and Political Weekly 1980- 81 Debate, Akansha Publishing House, New Delhi.
19. Pramanik, B. (2003, January). Impact of undocumented migration on demography, informal sector, and security of the country. Paper presented in the Workshop on Undocumented Migration From Bangladesh to West Bengal organised by Population Studies unit held in Indian Statistical Institute, Kolkata.
20. Bhuyan, J.C., 2002, Illegal Migration from Bangladesh and the Demographic Change in the N.E. Region, Published in Dialogue, Journal of Astha Bharati, New Delhi, Vol. 3 No.3, pp. 71-82.
21. Baruah, Sanjib, India Against Itself: Assam and the Politics of Nationality, Oxford University Press: New Delhi, Second impression 2003, pg. 115.
22. Kotwal, Dinesh. (2001). The contours of Assam insurgency. Strategic Analysis. 24. 2219-2233. 10.1080/09700160108455349.
23. Baruah, S., 2008, Assam: Comforting a Failed Partition, viewed on May 21, 2012 at http://www.india-seminar.com/2008/591/591_Sanjib_baruah.htm.

6

India-Vietnam Partnership and the China Factor: Assessing Human Security in the Indian Ocean Region

– **Navonil Dey**

Introduction

In his seminal work *Orientalism* (1978), Edward Said critiques how Western Europe constructed the "Orient" as culturally and intellectually inferior, branding it as pagan, primitive, and uncivilized. This colonial mindset extended to India, where the British propagated the narrative of Indian backwardness, despite the country's millennia old civilizations, such as those of Harappa and Mohenjo-Daro. Similarly, China and Southeast Asia boast rich histories of political interaction, cultural exchange, and societal evolution, predating the West's civil societies. The colonial powers, however, distorted these narratives through domination and erasure, neutralizing Indigenous memories and histories. In the realm of security, Western paradigms often separate state-centric traditional security from Human Security, which emphasizes individual well-being, dignity, and freedoms. Yet, in underdeveloped regions, the absence of state security often precipitates threats to Human Security. Conversely, conflicts between major powers can disrupt critical aspects of Human Security, such as economic stability, political cohesion, food security, and water access.

The two dimensions of security are deeply intertwined, rendering their separate evaluation inadequate. For India, the concept of

Human Security is not a novel import but is deeply ingrained in its philosophical and cultural traditions. India's civilizational ethos, rooted in concepts like *Vasudhaiva Kutumbakam* (the world as one family), inherently embodies the principles of Human Security. This worldview emphasizes harmony, interconnectedness, and the collective well-being of humanity. Tagore's humanism further illustrates this perspective, advocating for universal dignity and mutual respect. India's traditional systems of understanding life, shaped by spiritual and cultural wisdom, have always prioritized the welfare of individuals and communities. This indigenous approach aligns seamlessly with the modern discourse on Human Security, demonstrating that while the terminology may have evolved, the essence of safeguarding human dignity and ensuring collective well-being has long been part of India's socio-cultural fabric.

India, as a pre-modern agricultural society, shared profound ties with Southeast Asia, forged through economic, cultural, and socio-political bonds. A.L. Basham, in his book *The Wonder That Was India*, aptly noted, "The whole of South-East Asia received most of its culture from India", emphasizing India's profound influence on the region. In the post-colonial era, despite the lingering trauma of colonialism, new opportunities have emerged for rebuilding these ties. As Southeast Asia gains prominence in global geopolitics, India's renewed focus on the region, through initiatives like the *Act East Policy*, reflects an acknowledgment of shared histories and mutual interests. However, challenges persist. India faces strategic deterrence from China, which actively supports Pakistan economically, politically, and militarily, thereby fuelling instability in South Asia. Today, as new states emerge from the remnants of colonial blunders and the global map continues to evolve, India and Southeast Asia are reconnecting. This revival, rooted in historical ties, holds the potential to foster regional stability, enhance Human Security, and promote cooperation in the face of shared challenges.

The Triple-Threat

IOR is a vast water body spreading across the Indian Ocean, from the East coast of Africa to the island countries of Southeast Asia and is responsible for most of the world maritime trade as it is also the main route of the Sea Lines of Communication (SLOC). More importantly, this region also includes the Strait of Malacca, the Straits of Johor, and other important straits that connect the Indian and the Pacific Oceans. The IOR is facing continuous threats from the PLA Navy and the developing countries scattered around the Indian Ocean are economically and politically far less powerful than China. India's growing partnership with Vietnam represents a strategic yet deeply humanistic approach to countering regional instability. Rooted in shared histories and mutual respect, this collaboration seeks not only to address the immediate geopolitical challenge posed by China but also to safeguard the well-being and security of the people in the region. As Ajaya Kumar Das observed,

> "For Vietnam, these hard powers (of India) resources are benign and attractive due to the enmity between China and Vietnam. In the future, if India-Vietnam relations turn into a military alliance, that can enhance India's hard power (Das, 2020)."

The cooperation and interdependence between Vietnam and India are necessary to counter China's aggressive policies. China projects its military power in three different ways. Firstly, China continues to assert its influence in the region through military expansion, debt diplomacy, and territorial encroachments. The People's Liberation Army Navy (PLAN) now operates approximately 730 ships, including 61 submarines, and has two operational aircraft carriers, with a third expected to be fully functional in 2024 (Naval Technology, 2024). Even the US Navy does not operate so many naval ships and boats at a time (Wei, 2021). The PLA Navy often visits many nations in the Indian Ocean and has been conducting naval exercises with Pakistan - 'Sea Guardians' for more than six years. Even amid the India-Pakistan skirmish regarding the Kashmir region, both nations have conducted naval exercises (PTI, 2020). Thus, China not only violates the balance of power in the IOR but also disturbs the security of the common people of the sub-continent by raising the tension of war.

Secondly, China's debt diplomacy and 'Salami Slicing' strategy violates the economic security and territorial integrity of a country. It took Aksai Chin from India in the 1960s, the Paracel Islands in 1974, and Johnson Reef and Scarborough Shoal from the Philippines respectively in 1988 and 2012, Vietnam and Taiwan also have lost some of their territory in these processes. Countries in the South China Sea could not make any serious progress against China as they are highly dependent on the trade and business relations that are controlled by China. The debt diplomacy of China is putting the lives of the common people in danger in many underdeveloped nations of South and Southeast Asia, Africa, and West Asia. The South-South Cooperation that has emerged as a way out for the poor countries of Africa and Asia is also threatened. Foreign Policy magazine writes:

> "...Unable to repay China for a loan used to build a new port in the city of Hambantota, in 2017 Sri Lanka signed over to China a 99-year lease for its use, potentially as a strategic base for China's navy. In Djibouti, public debt has risen to roughly 80 percent of the country's GDP (and China owns the lion's share), placing the country at high risk of debt distress. That China's first and only overseas military base is located in Djibouti is a consequence, not a coincidence. Elsewhere in Africa, Burundi, Chad, Mozambique, and Zambia are all either in debt distress or at high risk of it, a situation China's predatory lending practices are exacerbating (Green, 2019)."

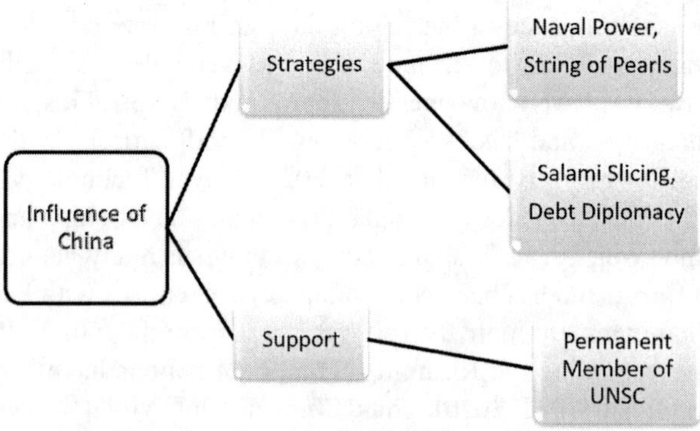

All these countries are located in the IOR and in addition to this, the 'Belt and Road Initiative' (BRI) has also included many states throughout the region. Pakistan too, like many other countries has fallen into this illusion of development that ironically invites and initiates the lack of political and economic security of the masses. China has built roads in Pakistan that stretch from Gwadar port to Tibet via the Pakistan Occupied Kashmir (POK) putting many people's lives from India and Pakistan in the abyss of political uncertainty. Thirdly, all these debt traps and the economic hegemony of China in the IOR led to China's 'String of Pearls' strategy, which has two narratives – Chinese and Global. While China sees it as a safeguard to the energy supply chain from the Arabian countries to the South China Sea, the global narrative is not much different than the previously mentioned tactics of China. It sees the 'string of pearls' as an extension of its salami-slice strategy to the regional level.

India, according to a Chinese website, is afraid of China's increasing regional political influence and a pro-China Myanmar regime and a China-dependent Bangladesh in India's neighborhood. Sri Lanka, despite India's protest, gave the Hambantota Port for lease, it's the country that has recently suffered a great economic crisis, and nonetheless, at this port, Chinese naval ships are making frequent visits (Devonshire, 2009). Moreover, slowly but surely the East African nations are also giving up their territories and ports for lease to China, leading to a great security crisis. African nations like Burundi, Chad, and Mozambique, these countries are already fighting deep poverty, and food and water crises. There is no doubt that the development China offers to these poor countries would come in exchange for a big sacrifice. Why Chinese hegemony matters about human security in the IOR is quite clear. Countries like Afghanistan, Pakistan, Sri Lanka and Myanmar are deeply affected by water, food and environmental

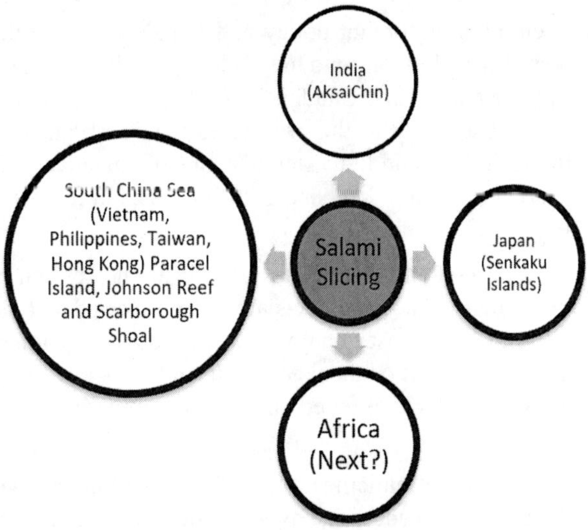

security. The economic condition in all the countries of the Indian Subcontinent is worse. Drought, flood, internal conflict, disease, hunger, and economic crises are a few of the threats, and their numbers are multiplying. These are the kinds of threats that cannot be solved in isolation and so, cooperation is a necessity. Moreover, to create a space for cooperation, these countries need to trust each other and with the presence of a hegemonic power like China, which is consistently disturbing the regional stability, cooperation is not easy. In fostering trust and cooperation with Vietnam, India champions a vision of regional security that is inherently humanistic—addressing not just strategic imperatives but also the dignity, aspirations, and security of the region's people. This partnership embodies the ethos of shared prosperity and mutual respect, creating a robust framework to counter divisive forces while promoting peace and unity.

Human Security aims to bring meaningful improvements to the lives of individuals by fostering a society where people can live free from fear, want, and indignity. This concept, which gained prominence through the 1994 *Human Development Report* by the United Nations Development Programme (UNDP), redefined security to focus on protecting individuals rather than solely safeguarding states. International organisations, including the United Nations, have played a vital role in advancing this idea by promoting policies and initiatives to uplift vulnerable populations globally (UNDP, 1994).

The neutrality as foreign policy and India's stance to the world superpowers did not last long and India's foreign policy saw a paradigm shift during the era of Mrs. Gandhi. It was the 1962 India-China war, and the loss of territory in the process to the PLA that opened the eyes of Indian leaders and India started acting diplomatically. He gave equal importance to both West and Southeast Asia in terms of India's foreign relations:

> "We are of Asia and the peoples of Asia are nearer and closer to us than others…Those contacts are being renewed and the future is bound to see a closer union between India and Southeast Asia on the one side and Afghanistan, Iran, and the Arab world on the west (Nehru, 1947, as cited in Embassy of India, Washington D.C., n.d.)."

Perhaps, the true implementation of Nehru's vision never came true until the recent decades. The overall progress of relations between

India and China has been a mixed outcome of cooperation and competition, ups and downs. Therefore, even if India has developed to a great extent in the last 70 years and has gone through massive modernization of military equipment, the development of China has been even greater. In a nutshell, India is not even close to comparing its economic and military power with China and that is why India needs other countries to counter the hegemonic behaviour of China. To balance the mighty multifaceted prowess of China, India has come up with multidimensional strategies and foreign policies, which would also give a boost to many aspects of threatened securities of the common people of the IOR. Firstly, the formation of Quadrilateral Security Dialogue (QSD) or QUAD has unofficially targeted China's growing military presence in the South China Sea. No matter how bold the leaders are, about QUAD being a non-military group, the very inception of QUAD is related to countering China's hegemony in the 'Indo-Pacific'. The notion of separating Southeast Asia from South Asia has now changed and India has risen from the list of the excludes of NATO members. While the PLA Navy is still dominating the South China Sea, the presence of QUAD countries would only deter China in the region. Vietnam is considered to be one of the QUAD plus members. The whole point of deterring China in the IOR and Indo-Pacific is to ensure any escalation of disputes to a war.

Secondly, debt diplomacy and salami slicing are oftentimes two sides of the same coin of Chinese foreign policy. India on the one hand lost the Aksai Chin province after the 1962 war, but in the 21st century, it protected Bhutan from the initial Chinese salami tactics at Dokalam and resisted Chinese advancements in Ladakh on the other. Very recently Chinese forces have also been countered by the Indian Army in Arunachal Pradesh, which the Chinese Communist Party considers as South Tibet. Even when it comes to China-Pakistan friendship, India has extended its cooperative possibilities in the west as well as in the east. Modi has launched the Look West policy and the Act East policy. While there is no straightforward solution to Chinese aggression, salami slicing, and debt diplomacy, enhancing diplomatic ties with China's and Pakistan's neighbours is a viable approach. India has cultivated strong relations with Iran, Israel, and several Arab nations in the West, alongside Indonesia, Malaysia, Vietnam, Singapore, and Thailand in Southeast Asia. The ASEAN nations, with their robust administrations, seek the cooperation of both India and

China for economic prosperity. Thus, cooperation becomes the key to addressing threats to human security while signalling to China that the modern world will neither tolerate its aggressive policies nor remain wholly dependent on its economy (Ministry of External Affairs, Government of India, 2023; Malik, 2018, p. 212)

Existing Threats to Human Security in IOR

With the rise of the Global South and post-colonial studies, the idea of traditional security has been changed, at least to the developing countries. The IOR has two sets of countries arranged by the Eastern coasts of Africa, and scattered around South-Southeast Asia. Eastern African countries are suffering from serious problems such as food and water crises. Political instability, unstable democracy, corruption and extreme poverty have devastated these countries. East Africa is also suffering from severe health problems, it has the second highest HIV AIDS cases in the world, while the first is Southern Africa. Most of these countries also have lower ranks in the Human Development Index and Gender Equality Index. Therefore, the overall security of the East African countries is worse than any other part of the world. Never to be forgotten that Africa was the continent of slavery and religious conversion, where colonial masters practiced racial discrimination and did not build up schools and colleges like they did in Asia, especially in India. Even in the 21st century, the continent is suffering from civil war, terrorism, insurgency, and forced migration, and eastern African countries are no exception to these miseries.

Kenya, despite being one of the most educated countries in Africa, according to the World Bank about 36.1% of Kenya's total population lives below the international poverty line, students struggle to complete graduation from colleges, and 'Kenya has one of the highest HIV/ AIDS adult prevalence rates in Africa today'. Along with this massive deforestation, poaching, water pollution and land degradation put the country in a grave environmental crisis (AfricaW, 2009). Corruption has become a normal part of everyday life.

Somalia, one of the poorest countries in the world, remains trapped by its over-dependence on international aid, lack of effective leadership, internal conflicts, and a pervasive "crab mentality." According to the World Health Organization (WHO), "Famine in Somalia has put millions of people at risk of severe malnutrition and outbreaks of diseases such as cholera and measles." Furthermore, Somalia's geography and topography render it highly vulnerable to natural disasters, including droughts, famines, floods, and cyclones (WHO, 2022).

Tanzania, even after having a very good rate of literacy (77%), is devastated by health problems. HIV AIDS prevalence rate is 5.1% among adults, while most of its population has been suffering from malaria, diarrhea, typhoid, and many other diseases. Environmental problems are just as big as that of Kenya, while electricity is reachable to only 40% of the total population.

In Ethiopia, children are not going to school due to extreme poverty, and they are associated with child marriage, child prostitution, and child labor. Systematic marginalization and ethnic cleansing are increasing due to the absence of adequate governance. Uganda, while having a well-educated class of people and plenty of water resources, is facing serious environmental and territorial challenges due to its overpopulation. Health Security is another concern that the Ugandans are facing today. The island countries of Seychelles and Madagascar are not exceptions to these crises, and at the same time they are also geopolitically at a crucial strategic location. Seychelles is facing one of the world's worst heroin and drug problems (*United Nations Office on Drugs and Crime, 2021*). In some parts of Madagascar, one in every two children lives under the poverty line and suffers from security challenges.

Since the beginning of this century China has been investing in many African nations. Chinese money goes mostly in the communication sector where it spends capital by building roads, railways, bridges, pipelines etc. China extends its BRI projects to these countries. China also serves humanitarian aids such as medical assistance, and agricultural and educational aid. According to many scholars all these aids and developmental activity ultimately serves China's own national interest. Firstly, these are loans that China is giving these underdeveloped countries in exchange for some control over the country's socio-political life. Secondly, all of these loans need to be repaid to China at either a moderate or high interest rate (Felbab, 2014). China is gradually creating its access to the local natural resource markets of Africa vis. its coal mines, gold mines, oil enriched places. Moreover, these countries would begin to support China's ideology and its goals to become a world leader. No matter what the policies say, the reflection of these policies could be seen on the other side of the IOR. Pakistan and Sri Lanka for example could not repay China's loan and got encumbered with it and had to give control of their two major ports to China.

Nonetheless, China's intention to use them as military bases is quite clear. Sri Lanka, especially, had fallen into a grave economic crisis, triggering an emergency that led to massive migration of population in India, unimaginable inflation, social and political misbalance and its agriculture stepped backward. China has not come as a savior then. China's economic aid to Africa presents a dual narrative: while it has undoubtedly contributed to infrastructure development and economic growth, it has simultaneously raised concerns about sovereignty and long-term stability. The "debt-trap diplomacy" has led to fears that nations receiving Chinese aid may become overly reliant, jeopardizing their autonomy and fostering mistrust toward Beijing's intentions (Brautigam, 2020). While China's involvement has provided vital resources to nations that lack alternatives, its track record of human rights violations, including labor abuses and environmental degradation in host countries, casts doubt on its role as a reliable partner (Human Rights Watch, 2022). These issues highlight the complexity of China's global engagements, which cannot be dismissed as purely malevolent but also cannot escape scrutiny.

Yet, China is not alone in facing such critiques. Russia and the United States have also historically prioritized geopolitical gains over genuine humanitarian aid, eroding trust in their global interventions (Mearsheimer, 2014). Similarly, Japan, despite its democratic and pacifist ethos today, is still shadowed by its imperial past and associated human rights violations, complicating its role as a neutral actor in international relations. Thus, no major power emerges as entirely altruistic, and trust deficits continue to characterize the global political landscape. India, by contrast, emphasizes human-centered development in its foreign policy but cannot play a significant role in war-torn zones due to its domestic challenges and resource limitations. However, India's collaborative approach through partnerships, such as those within the ASEAN framework, provides a foundation for fostering stability. Vietnam, in particular, stands out as a potential partner due to its history of pragmatic diplomacy and minimal involvement in regional conflicts or human rights violations. Vietnam's record positions it as a trustworthy ally in developing multilateral strategies for addressing conflict-prone regions while promoting human security.

Ultimately, while no global power operates without self-interest, multilateral cooperation focusing on human security and inclusive development can provide an alternative to the exploitative tendencies of dominant powers. Nations like India and Vietnam can play pivotal roles in crafting a balanced approach that counters the trust issues associated with unilateral actions by powers such as China, the United States, and Russia. This collective effort is essential for ensuring that economic development aligns with the protection of human dignity and sovereignty.

Human Security and China

The People's Republic of China presents a contradictory image when juxtaposing its humanitarian aid to African nations with its record of human rights violations. Like other historical and emerging superpowers such as the U.S., Britain, and Japan, China is no stranger to human rights abuses. Recently, Chinese state media criticized the U.S. for its handling of prisoners in its "black site" prisons, describing the practices as "brutal and horrifying" (CCR, 2021). However, China's record in regions such as Xinjiang, Hong Kong, and Tibet undermine its credibility. According to Human Rights Watch, Uyghurs in Xinjiang are subjected to arbitrary detention, forced labor, and systemic repression, with many dying in detention camps, including senior citizens (Human Rights Watch, 2022).

China's approach to African nations reflects a strategic focus on economic and geopolitical interests rather than genuine humanitarianism. Countries like Pakistan and Sri Lanka, heavily reliant on Chinese financial and military support, have struggled with instability and underdevelopment. African nations should heed these warnings. For instance, China's loans to Sri Lanka contributed to the country's economic crisis, culminating in the leasing of Hambantota Port to China for 99 years after debt defaults (Reuters, 2023).

China's influence extends beyond Africa to Southeast Asia, where countries like Laos and Cambodia remain heavily dependent on its economic support. Cambodia has facilitated Chinese military base construction, raising concerns about regional security. In Myanmar, China's investments in jade mining under the New Silk Road Initiative have caused widespread environmental degradation. Unregulated mining has led to deforestation, landslides, and pollution, severely affecting the local people's lives and security. In 2020, a landslide at the Wai Khar mine resulted in the deaths of 175 people, underscoring the urgent need for reform (Muller & Strangio, 2020). Furthermore, recent reports highlight that China's Belt and Road Initiative (BRI) has trapped nations such as Kenya in unsustainable debt, forcing cuts to public services (Al Jazeera, 2023).

China's actions emphasize economic gains over social and environmental sustainability, causing trust issues globally. While India lacks the resources to counter China alone, partnerships with nations like Vietnam, which has minimal human rights violations, could foster multilateral approaches to balancing China's influence. Ultimately, African and Southeast Asian countries must diversify partnerships to reduce overdependence on China, prioritizing investments that enhance human security.

India-Vietnam Strategic Partnership

In early June 2022, India and Vietnam signed the *'Joint Vision Statement on India-Vietnam Defence Partnership towards 2030'*. This landmark agreement, formalised by India's Defence Minister Rajnath Singh and his Vietnamese counterpart General Phan Van Giang, reflects a shared vision to strengthen bilateral defence cooperation for strategic and regional interests. Both leaders emphasised the importance of maintaining this partnership to address evolving challenges in the Indo-Pacific and beyond. Over the decades, India and Vietnam have entered into numerous bilateral agreements, reinforcing their collaboration in defence, trade, and strategic domains.

India's increasing presence in Vietnam stems from smaller, incremental developments in soft power and public diplomacy. Vietnam, with its significant strategic position in Southeast Asia, offers a platform for India to enhance its global footprint. Both nations share concerns over safeguarding critical Sea Lines of Communication, energy security, and ensuring an open, rules-based regional order. Additionally, India and Vietnam are aligned in their commitment to counter hegemonic influences in the region.

The defence partnership is a crucial pillar of their cooperation and includes Government-to-Government Dialogues, Defence Line of Credit agreements, Defence Procurement, and multilateral frameworks. The *Defence Protocol 2000* remains a significant milestone in formalising their cooperative measures. In 2023, both nations decided to operationalise a *$500 million Defence Line of Credit* provided by India to Vietnam. This funding will assist in the procurement of defence equipment, including offshore patrol vessels and other maritime security assets, reinforcing Vietnam's capabilities in the South China Sea (*Ministry of External Affairs, 2023*). India has signed a memorandum to increase investment in Vietnam's pharmaceutical sector, aligning with Vietnam's efforts to fulfil over 50% of its domestic pharmaceutical consumption needs (*Business Standard, 2024*). In a forward-looking move, India and Vietnam agreed in 2024 to collaborate on *cybersecurity and defence technology*, with a focus on Artificial Intelligence and secure communication systems. This partnership aims to bolster Vietnam's cyber defence capabilities amid increasing cyber threats (*Economic Times, 2024*). In early 2024, the two countries conducted their largest-ever *joint naval exercise* in the South China Sea. This showcased enhanced interoperability between the Indian Navy and the Vietnam People's Navy, underlining their shared commitment to a free and open Indo-Pacific (*The Diplomat, 2024*).

Therefore, it can be deduced that the gradual development of strategic partnership between India and Vietnam is not just a proof of cooperation between these two countries but also hints at the interstate support at the international level.

Indo-Vietnamese partnership hence has a multi-dimensional reach in Southeast Asia and beyond. The strategic and economic partnership between India and Vietnam reflects a blend of human security objectives and neorealist principles, effectively balancing power dynamics in the Indo-Pacific and South China Sea regions. At its core, this collaboration aims to counter China's economic and strategic monopoly, a hallmark of neorealist's concept of balancing—both internal and external. According to Waltz (1979), internal balancing refers to states improving their capabilities, while external balancing involves alliances. India's increasing investments in Vietnam's industrial and energy sectors, as well as arms trade, exemplify internal balancing, while its partnerships

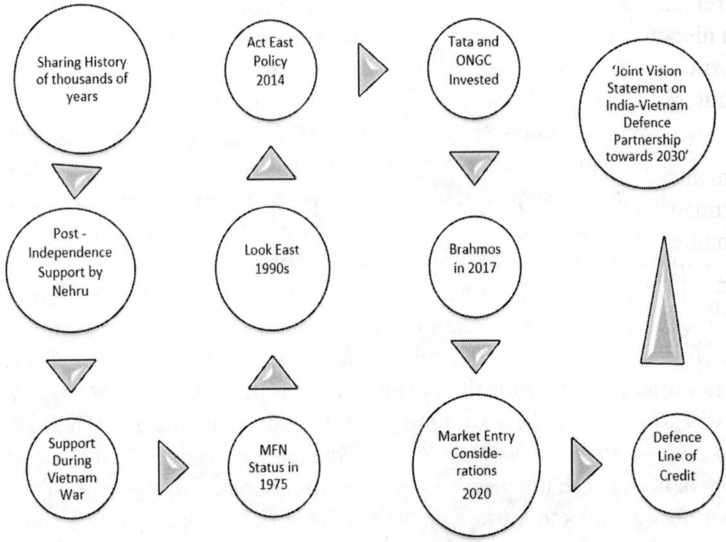

with ASEAN countries and potential naval presence at Cam Ranh Port illustrate external balancing strategies.

> "Human security, while rooted in neoliberals, remains tethered to realist traditions through its dependence on soft and smart power, which focus on influencing states and achieving strategic goals without direct coercion" (Newman, 2010, p. 60).

India's infrastructure projects linking the Indo-China region with its northeastern states, and its emphasis on environmental sustainability in collaboration with Vietnam, highlight this interplay. These initiatives not only address human security, focusing on the welfare of populations through economic and social development but also serve realist goals by consolidating India's influence and limiting China's strategic dominance.

Vietnam's rise as a central figure in ASEAN and its balanced foreign policies with powers like the U.S., Russia, and China exemplify soft balancing. This approach aligns with India's objective of creating a multipolar region, where neither China nor any single power can dominate. The arms trade between India and Vietnam, such as Vietnam's acquisition of BrahMos missiles and patrol boats, strengthens Vietnam's security posture, deterring Chinese aggression in disputed territories like the South China Sea. This reflects a nuanced form of hard balancing, where military preparedness underpins strategic autonomy.

Furthermore, by collaborating on infrastructure projects and enhancing economic interdependence, India and Vietnam extend human security's reach into regions affected by underdevelopment and conflict. Roads connecting India's northeast to Vietnam via Myanmar and Thailand promise to integrate marginalized communities into broader development processes, underscoring human security's role in achieving "freedom from want" and "freedom from fear" (United Nations Development Programme, 1994, p. 22).

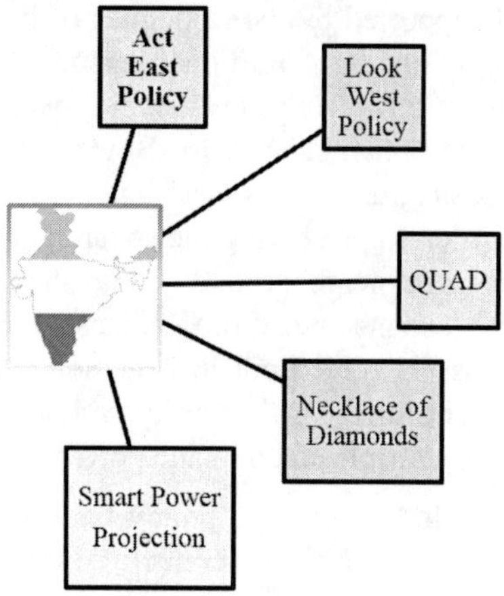

Evaluating India's Role

India's foreign policy, whether directly shaped by anti-China sentiments or not, has consistently emphasized the principles of humanism and collective security, placing the well-being of people at the forefront of its diplomatic strategies. This human-centered approach stands in sharp contrast to China's often regressive and self-serving foreign policies, such as debt diplomacy and salami-slicing tactics, which prioritize Beijing's geostrategic ambitions over the interests of smaller nations. For instance, the Act East policy is not just a geopolitical maneuver but also a framework for fostering economic cooperation, cultural exchange, and sustainable development with Southeast Asian nations.

This policy emphasizes inclusivity and mutual growth, ensuring that all countries benefit, rather than exploiting vulnerabilities. Initiatives like the International Solar Alliance further underline India's commitment to addressing global challenges like climate change, which directly impact human security, particularly in vulnerable regions like the Indian Ocean (International Solar Alliance, 2023) (Ministry of External Affairs, Government of India, 2023). While the QUAD undeniably counters China's growing hegemony in the Indo-Pacific, it does so by promoting a rules-based international order, emphasizing freedom of navigation, and ensuring that the region remains open and inclusive for all stakeholders. This cooperative framework is well supported by the principles of human security by safeguarding the livelihoods of millions dependent on the region's stability, rather than advancing any single nation's dominance. Moreover, India's committed support for Bhutan during the Doklam crisis and its defense of Arunachal Pradesh against Chinese aggression highlights its dedication to preserving the sovereignty and well-being of smaller nations in its neighborhood. India, thus contains China, more importantly, its expansion and pro-China sentiments to a certain extent. These actions are rooted not in hegemonic ambitions but in a genuine commitment to regional security and stability, reinforcing India's image as a responsible and humane power.

In wrapping up, India's foreign policy underscores a profound respect for humanism, prioritising collective security and mutual development. This approach effectively challenges China's regressive, self-centred strategies, offering a model of diplomacy that upholds the ideals of equity, sustainability, and human security. By advocating for a just and inclusive global order, India not only counters the threats posed by Chinese aggression but also reaffirms its role as a leader committed to the welfare of humanity.

India's efforts go beyond merely countering China; they act as a definitive stop signal for the expansionist tendencies, both physical and hegemonic, of the Chinese state. Vietnam emerges as a critical ally in this endeavour, perfectly positioned to complement India's strategic objectives. However, in the intricate dynamics of global politics, it is noteworthy that both India and Vietnam maintain substantial trade relations with China. Despite the complex interdependence created by China's dominance as their leading trading partner, these nations manage to resist succumbing to Beijing's influence. Unlike several countries that have become overly reliant on China's economic benefits and foreign aid, India and Vietnam have demonstrated a unique resilience. They leverage their trade relations while simultaneously confronting Chinese aggression with a calculated and logical approach.

The platform provided by QUAD has further amplified their ability to counterbalance China's assertive strategies. However, it must not be overlooked that India and Vietnam are still developing nations, grappling with numerous internal challenges. These vulnerabilities could have made them more susceptible to China's aggressive and provocative political and socio-economic strategies. Instead, they have turned these challenges into opportunities for collaboration and resistance, showcasing a distinctive approach to balancing immediate economic interests with long-term strategic independence. As Rajesh Rajagopalan aptly observes, India's strategy for balancing against China is not overtly confrontational but instead focused on signaling to China that it is building partnerships, not alliances. These terms are significantly different in both intent and execution. Rajagopalan describes this approach as "hedging," a strategic middle ground between bandwagoning and external balancing. He terms it "evasive balancing," suggesting that while it is pragmatic, it might prove unsustainable in the long run (Rajagopalan, 2020).

However, in the long-term perspective, India seeks to avoid being placed in a false equivalence with China, especially in a negative light. India's approach emphasizes a humane and inclusive path that prioritizes democracy, consent, minority rights, and the upliftment of all, transcending what is merely advantageous for India to focus on what is right for the region and its people. This sentiment is reflected in India's soft power and cultural diplomacy, which underscore values of coexistence, shared growth, and ethical governance. India's current methods of balancing may not yet be robust enough to counter China's expansive influence directly, they undoubtedly reflect a moral and humane strategy. This path positions India as a nation willing to stand for regional stability and equitable development, reinforcing its role as a compassionate and principled actor on the global stage.

Conclusion

The world has gone through bad memories; colonialism, imperialism, and world wars have taught us how to stay impartial and away from war as the consequences of war are destructive. The crises that have risen from the wars and long chapters of colonialism and slavery gave rise to the security threats of the common people around the globe. Human security is only nurtured when the crises are extreme. The United Nations along with other supranational organizations are continuously trying to make the world a better place. Powerful countries must abide by the systematic order of the UN and international law, to respect every country's territorial sovereignty, its border, people and culture. The IOR is pretty much disturbed with security issues; East Africa is troubled with Economic, Political, Environmental, Health, Food, and Water Security. South Asia is struggling with poverty, malnutrition, drug addiction, child mortality, and overpopulation. The Global South is trying to cooperate and India along with its allies is cooperating from the forefront of these countries. The balance of power, sooner or later, is going to get disturbed as China supplies Pakistan with weapons, and is building illegal naval bases alongside the maritime border of South China Sea and countries are falling into debt diplomacy of China, Sri Lanka, Pakistan, Laos, Cambodia are getting fully dependent on China ending up giving away territory and ports.

China has a long history of violation of human rights in its domestic policies and agendas, so nobody can assure that it will not violate human rights and environmental policies abroad, rather, it is quite clear from the memories of Myanmar's Jade Mining that China does not care about the environment. Vietnam comes as a small balancer to the big scenario of the IOR. India-Vietnam ties, if grown stronger, would become a protest voice of the Global South within the Global South. No country would risk going against the policies of China. All the ASEAN countries and their delegates have confirmed that they want both India and China for the prosperity of the region. The IOR is the residence of over one fourth of the world's population. The region is developing fast and people have just about forgotten the distant memories of wars and colonialism. At this crucial point, the balance of power needs to stay undisturbed, India-Vietnam along with the other QUAD members are creating the field to deter the 'Elephant in the Room'- China. The forward moving countries of Africa, South and Southeast Asia are dreaming about a better future by cooperation and making friends, but unequal foreign policies of China are making it harder not to compete with each other. There is a saying that "you cannot bend a full-grown tree", but in the beginning. China's economic policies in Eastern Africa are at the beginning phase and therefore can be countered with better economic policies of India and other potential countries like Vietnam, South Korea, Malaysia, Singapore, etc.

In other parts of the region, the narrative of a separate South and Southeast Asia has already started shifting, and by the commencement of QUAD and QUAD +, the region has been named as Indo-Pacific. Anyways, by the lesson of 'Orientalism' these nations have to avoid any kind of competitive mindset that could lead to regional disputes. Only then would the balance of power and balance of understanding among the IOR countries become stable, while regulating their dependency on China and making stronger bonds with India and Vietnam.

The persistent threats to human security in the IOR underscore the critical need for a phased and collaborative approach to address socio-economic, political, and environmental challenges. A holistic strategy rooted in humanistic values and effective governance is essential for emancipating vulnerable populations and fostering long-term stability.

The first and most fundamental step is the establishment of robust domestic socio-political environments within IOR countries, marked by low corruption, democratic constitutionalism, and inclusive governance. Such systems must evolve organically, free from undue foreign intervention, ensuring local ownership of reforms. Without this foundational framework, subsequent measures will lack sustainability and legitimacy. Building on this, nations such as Afghanistan, Pakistan, Myanmar, Somalia, and Uganda must develop frameworks for stable economic interdependence with their regional neighbors. This entails fostering mutual trade, infrastructure connectivity, and collaborative policy measures that prioritize equitable growth.

However, meaningful economic partnerships can only thrive in environments where political stability and trust are well-established. For countries facing the dire human security crises, international institutions like the United Nations must play a pivotal role. UN-led initiatives should provide immediate relief, while also supporting capacity-building measures that enable these nations to address systemic vulnerabilities. Such interventions must be designed to align with local contexts, empowering communities rather than perpetuating dependency. The increasingly interconnected nature of global politics makes it imperative for nations in the IOR to adopt trust-building measures as a cornerstone of their foreign policies. Trust can be fostered through alliances with nations that demonstrate a strong commitment to human rights, good governance, and regional cooperation. India and Vietnam serve as prime examples of such partnerships, leveraging their shared commitment to stability and development in countering hegemonic influences.

Finally, advancing human security requires sustained investments in environmentally sustainable technologies, modernized agricultural practices, and the preservation of natural resources. Governments must encourage industries to align their operations with environmental priorities and empower farmers through education and access to technology. Collaborative efforts with global economic powers must prioritize the protection of ecosystems, including rivers, lakes, and forests, as integral to sustainable development. The success of the efforts of India and Vietnam depends on a shared commitment to balancing power while prioritizing the welfare of people and the planet – a vision that transcends immediate national interests and paves the way for a sustainable future.

REFERENCES

1. Acharya, A. (2014). *Constructing a Security Community in Southeast Asia: ASEAN and the Problem of Regional Order* (p. 167). Routledge.
2. AfricaW. (2009). *Major problems facing Kenya today - Nairobi*. AFRICAW. Retrieved December 13, 2022, from https://www.africaw.com/major-problems-facing-kenya-today
3. Ahmed, J. M. (2019, April 21). *Top 10 Problems of Somalia*. Modern Ghana. Retrieved December 13, 2022, from https://www.modernghana.com/news/927820/top-10-problems-of-somalia.html
4. Al Jazeera. (2023). *Kenya grapples with debt crisis amid Chinese loans*, Retrieved November 30, 2023, from https://www.aljazeera.com/
5. Brautigam, D. (2020). *The Dragon's Gift: The Real Story of China in Africa*. Oxford University Press.
6. Business Standard. (2024, February 25). *India-Vietnam pharmaceutical cooperation agreement signed*. Retrieved December 6, 2024, from https://www.

business-standard.com/article/economy-policy/india-vietnam-pharmaceutical-cooperation-agreement-signed-124022500123_1.html

7. CCR. (2021, October 29). *New Details of Torture at CIA "Black Sites"*. Center for Constitutional Rights. Retrieved December 15, 2022, from https://ccrjustice.org/home/press-center/press-releases/new-details-torture-cia-black-sites
8. Devonshire, C. (2009, March 18). *China's String of Pearls Strategy*. China Briefing. Retrieved December 10, 2022, from https://www.china-briefing.com/news/china%E2%80%99s-string-of-pearls-strategy/
9. Economic Times. (2024, April 18). *India-Vietnam partner on cybersecurity and AI defence technologies*. Retrieved December 6, 2024, from https://economictimes.indiatimes.com/news/defence/india-vietnam-partner-on-cybersecurity-and-ai-defence-technologies/articleshow/99457658.cms
10. Embassy of India, Washington D.C. (n.d.). *Pandit Jawaharlal Nehru: First Prime Minister of India*. Retrieved from https://www.indianembassyusa.gov.in/ArchivesDetails?id=1690
11. EurAsian Time Desk. (2018, December 8). *Indian Military Base in Vietnam at Cam Ranh Port To Protect Hanoi's Economic and Territorial Interest*. EurAsian Times. Retrieved December 16, 2022, from https://eurasiantimes.com/indian-naval-base-in-vietnam-at-cam-ranh-port-to-protect-hanois-economic-and-territorial-interest/
12. Felbab, V. (2014, February 7). *China's Aid to Africa: Monster or Messiah?* Brookings Institution. Retrieved December 14, 2022, from https://www.brookings.edu/opinions/chinas-aid-to-africa-monster-or-messiah/
13. Green, M. (2019, April 25). *China's Debt Diplomacy – Foreign Policy*. Foreign Policy. Retrieved December 10, 2022, from https://foreignpolicy.com/2019/04/25/chinas-debt-diplomacy/
14. Human Rights Watch. (2022). *World Report 2022: Events of 2021*. Human Rights Watch
15. Human Rights Watch (2022). World Report 2022: China. *Human Rights Watch.* Retrieved December 12, 2022, from https://www.hrw.org/world-report/2022/country-chapters/china
16. Indian Navy. (2022, June 27). *Indian Navy Eastern Fleet Ships Visit Vietnam*. Indian Navy. Retrieved December 16, 2022, from https://www.indiannavy.nic.in/content/indian-navy-eastern-fleet-ships-visit-vietnam
17. International Solar Alliance. (2023). *About ISA: Building a brighter future*. Retrieved December 6, 2024, from https://www.isolaralliance.org/
18. Malik, M. (2018). *China and India: Great Power Rivals.* Boulder, CO: Lynne Rienner Publishers, p. 212.
19. Mearsheimer, J. J. (2014). *The Tragedy of Great Power Politics*. W.W. Norton & Company.
20. Ministry of External Affairs, Government of India. (2023). *India's Foreign Policy - Key Initiatives.* Retrieved from https://mea.gov.in
21. Ministry of External Affairs. (2023, June 15). *India-Vietnam defence relations*.

Retrieved December 6, 2024, from https://www.mea.gov.in/bilateral-documents.htm?dtl/34245/IndiaVietnam_Defence_Relations

22. Ministry of External Affairs, Government of India. (2023). *International Solar Alliance: Powering the future with solar energy*. Retrieved December 3, 2024, from https://www.mea.gov.in/solar-alliance.htm
23. Muller, N., & Strangio, S. (2020, July 13). *A Deadly Gamble: Myanmar's Jade Industry – The Diplomat*. The Diplomat. Retrieved December 15, 2022, from https://thediplomat.com/2020/07/a-deadly-gamble-myanmars-jade-industry/
24. Naval Technology. (2024). *Chinese Naval Modernisation.* Retrieved from https://www.naval-technology.com
25. Newman, E. (2010). *Critical human security studies*. In R. Paris & T. Sisk (Eds.), *Human Security: Concepts and Implications* (p. 60). Cambridge University Press.
26. Nye, J. S. (2004). *Soft Power: The Means to Success in World Politics*. Public Affairs.
27. PTI. (2020, January 15). *China, Pakistan naval exercise concludes*. The Hindu. Retrieved December 10, 2022, from https://www.thehindu.com/news/international/china-pakistan-naval-exercise-concludes/article30572120.ece
28. Rajagopalan, R. (2020). Evasive balancing: India's unviable Indo-Pacific strategy. *International Affairs, 96*(1), 75–93. https://doi.org/10.1093/ia/iiz224
29. Reuters. (2023). *Sri Lanka hands over Hambantota Port to China after debt crisis*, Retrieved November 12, 2023 from https://www.reuters.com/
30. UNDP. (1994, January 1). *Human Development Reports*. United Nations Development Programme. Retrieved 12 11, 2022, from https://hdr.undp.org/content/human-development-report-1994
31. United Nations Development Programme. (1994). *Human Development Report 1994: New Dimensions of Human Security.* Oxford University Press. Retrieved from https://hdr.undp.org/
32. United Nations Office on Drugs and Crime. (2021). *World Drug Report 2021*. Retrieved from https://www.unodc.org
33. The Diplomat. (2024, March 10). *India and Vietnam conduct largest-ever joint naval exercise*. Retrieved December 6, 2024, from https://thediplomat.com/2024/03/india-and-vietnam-conduct-largest-ever-joint-naval-exercise/
34. Waltz, K. N. (1979). *Theory of International Politics*. Addison-Wesley.
35. Wei, L. (2021, September 28). *How big is China's navy compared to the US?* Defence Procurement International. Retrieved December 9, 2022, from https://www.defenceprocurementinternational.com/features/maritime/china-now-boats-the-largest-navy-in-the-world
36. WHO. (2022). *Somalia crisis*. World Health Organization (WHO). Retrieved December 13, 2022, from https://www.who.int/emergencies/situations/somalia-crisis

7

The Future of the Indian Ocean in the New Cold War Era: Certainties and Imponderables

– Shreya Das

Introduction

Along with time, the importance of various regions of the world changes following geopolitical shifts. The Indian Ocean Region is one of those parts of the world that is emerging as the most important theatres of geopolitical conflicts. This chapter assesses the likely future of the Indian Ocean region. The research would be mainly based on qualitative analysis of secondary data. The research questions and objectives are based on geopolitics in the Indian Ocean region. The paper would undertake an analysis of geopolitical and strategic dynamics in the region. The first part of the paper would review existing literature on the subject. The section on research methodology would describe the philosophy, approach, and design of this research. There would be information on data collection and analysis as well. The paper would conclude with a discussion on the findings of the research. It must be acknowledged here that while some factors in the Indian Ocean region's future are certainties, others fall in the category of imponderables.

Research Objectives

1. Analyze geopolitics in the Indian Ocean region

2. Explore the idea of the 'New Cold War or 'Cold War 2.0'
3. Assess the geostrategic future of the Indian Ocean region.

Research Questions

1. How have geopolitical dynamics in the Indian Ocean region evolved since the end of the Second World War?
2. What are the implications of the new cold war?
3. What are the future trends in the Indian Ocean region?

Geopolitical Dynamics between Major Powers in the Indian Ocean Region

After the second cold war ended in 1945, the US emerged as the most powerful sovereign and resident actor in the Indian Ocean Region.[1] The military, economic, and geopolitical strategy of the country in the Indian Ocean region is referred to as the US Indo-Pacific strategy. Since 1945, this strategy has been shaped by the concept of threat perception. The period from 1945 to 1992 is referred to as the 'Cold War Era.'[2] During this period, American foreign policy and military strategy were based on the perceived threat from the socialist bloc. The socialist bloc was led by the USSR, which espoused the ideology of communism. On the other hand, the US was leading the capitalist bloc and wanted to contain the influence of communism in the world. There were a large number of East European countries in the socialist bloc. In the Cold War era, there were serious conflicts of interests between the USA and the USSR on many fronts and issues. However, this era was mainly defined by rival military alliances, the quest for economic dominance and geopolitical competition. There are several instances in conflict between two countries belonging to the two blocs that brought the USA and USSR on the threshold of military confrontation. The Cuban Missile Crisis is one of the most well-known instances in which the two superpowers were on the verge of a nuclear war. The crisis had emerged on the issue of deployment of Soviet missiles in Cuba.[3] Thus it is evident that while the cold war was sustained by a persistent threat perception, it also threatened global peace and human existence.

However, the socialist bloc disintegrated with the withering away of the USSR in the early 1990s.[4] After the disintegration of the socialist bloc, China emerged as a major power among the countries around the

Indian Ocean and replaced the erstwhile USSR as a perceived threat to the US. The US coordinates its activities in the Indian Ocean through its Indo-Pacific Command.[5] Both the Obama and Trump governments have recognized the need to form alliances with cooperative countries in the region to protect mutual interests. The US has formed a strategic grouping with Australia, Japan, and India in response to their increasing assertiveness of China in the region.[6] Australia and Japan are traditional allies of the US. One of the most important similarities between the old and new cold wars is the persistence of a threat perception. In the current era, the US and several other countries feel threatened by the rise of China and its ambitions for territorial expansion.[7]

There is also an element of ideological confrontation in the new cold war as China is also a communist country like the erstwhile Soviet Union. In this way, the perception of threat from China centers around ideological, economic, military, and geopolitical issues. It must be also noted that the US and its allies also consider the rise of China as a threat to the liberal world view represented by the US and other Western countries.[8] After the end of the old Cold War, several strategic alignments and positions have changed in the world order. India was known to be very close to the Soviet Union, although it had declared itself as a non-aligned country with an independent foreign policy. However, in the new millennium the country has significantly improved its relations with the US to the extent that the US now considers India to be its strategic ally.[9] In this way alignments and positions in the global order have been shifting in response to changes in the threat perception over the years.

In the last 10 years, India has been emerging as a significant power in international relations, especially in the region around the Indian Ocean. The country has also moved much closer to the US to the extent that the current US president and other American diplomats do not hesitate to call India one of its most important 'Allies.' India has serious territorial issues with China and has also been involved in military conflicts with it.[10] India is considered to be an emerging rival of China in Asia. Hence the US has been consistently increasing its strategic proximity with India in the last 5 years.[vi] However, the US has been cooperating and working together with Australia and Japan for a long time. The closeness of ties between the US and these two countries is much older in comparison to the proximity between the US and India. The alliance between the US, Australia, and New Zealand has been traditionally based on the notion of reciprocal loyalty. This implies that each country is committed to helping the other in its hour of need. Such a commitment is based on a reciprocity. The three aforementioned countries are formally part of the ANZUS which represents the Australia-New Zealand-United States alliance.[11] It is important to note that this alliance has assumed more importance and additional meaning in the context of Quad which involves the US, Australia, India and Japan. This is mainly due to the increasing importance of the Indian Ocean Region where all the aforementioned four countries have significant stakes. In this research paper, various international alignments would be related to the threat perception from China, which is a significant factor in the Indian Ocean Region.

The New Cold War

The term 'New Cold War' or 'Cold War 2.0' is used to refer to the conflict of interests and strategic competition between the US and China. This strategic competition has ideological, political, economic, and military dimensions.[12] The discussion in the previous section is also consistent with these facts.

In the latter part of the 20th century, China emerged as a significant economic power, which was backed by enhancement in its economic and military might.[13] China wanted to assert its model of socioeconomic development in the international arena and continue to rise as an economic power. However, the US perceives the ascendance of China as a threat. The Chinese model based on communist ideology is one of the main reasons behind this threat perception. Apart from that, China is also posing stiff competition to the US in technological development. Chinese companies such as Huawei, Lenovo, and Haier have become household names in ICT and electronics. China wants to replicate its achievements in other high-tech sectors.[14] Both China and the US are major global powers that want to increase their sphere of influence in the world.[15]

Conflict of Interests and Threat Perception in the US-China Relationship

The US espouses the ideals of liberal democracy, personal freedom, and human rights in the international arena. It has also historically assumed the role of promoting and advancing these values in the world. On the other hand, China views the liberal democratic model to be exploitative and encouraging opportunism. There are frequent protests against government policies and actions in China. On each of these occasions, the government has repressed such protests with a heavy hand. China was heavily criticized by the international community for the Tiananmen Square massacre. On this occasion, the Chinese military had opened fire on peaceful protesters demanding political and economic reforms.[16] Furthermore, China also has a poor track record in human rights. It has been criticized for atrocities against minority communities in Xinjiang province.[17]

In the year 2017, Chinese President Xi Jinping claimed that China is an inspiration for the rest of the developing world. He said that other developing countries should emulate the Chinese model of development which does not compel a country to compromise its territorial integrity or sovereignty. The Chinese leadership thinks that the Western model based on liberal democracy and capitalism increases the dependency of developing countries on Western powers. In this way, there is a direct and perennial conflict between the world views as well as the interests of the US and China.

In the last five years, China has exhibited expansionist tendencies with utter disregard for international law in issues such as free access to seas and open trade.[18] Due to such an approach, China is in a state of conflict with several nations. Such conflicts have increased tension and strategic competition in the areas adjacent to the Indian Ocean. The Chinese leadership has been projecting a sense of historical injustice and victimhood to garner support in Chinese society.[19] It is true to some extent that China has been historically wronged by foreign powers since the 1850s till the inception of the People's Republic of China. However, the claims that the Chinese Communist Party is the only thing standing between the Chinese people and further exploitation are party propaganda. The CCP further claims that it seeks to restore the rightful place of China in the international community. Such a biased interpretation of history is used by the Chinese leadership to justify its territorial ambitions. These factors have further increased the hostilities between the US and China.

Geostrategic Future of the Indian Ocean Region

This is evident from the discussion till now that the new cold war is going to continue in the future as well with little hope for any reconciliation. According to experts on international relations, the Indian Ocean would emerge as a theatre for international rivalry and conflict.[20] In this region, India is fast emerging as the third major power after the US and China. There are some key differences between the first cold war and the new cold war. The first Cold War was mainly characterized by a bipolar world order. On the contrary, the new cold war is witnessing an increase in multipolarity. Lieberherr has opined that the multipolar nature of the current world order would result in more instability in international relations. The competition for economic, geopolitical, and military dominance in the Indian Ocean region can pose a serious threat to international maritime security. Supplies to several industries in Europe depend on the Indian Ocean region. Hence a threat to free navigation in the Indian Ocean would have serious repercussions for supply chains in Europe.

At present three trends are discernible in the dynamics of the Indian Ocean region. First of all, China is involved in massive infrastructure development in the region. India, the nearest competitor of China in the region, is finding it difficult to match China in this respect. Here it should be taken into cognizance that India's activities and projects in the region are mainly focused on maritime security. It is falling far behind China in terms of economic involvement in other countries of the region. The massive involvement of China in infrastructure in Sri Lanka through investments in the Hambantota port is a good example. China has been quite successful in luring Sri Lanka away from India in the region.

The aforementioned developments are directly associated with the issue of China's increasing interference in the matters of the littoral states in the region. After infrastructure development, this is the most observable geopolitical trend in the region. China has been enhancing its strategic presence and economic investments in the region in the past decade. For instance, the objective of the China-Pakistan Economic Corridor (CPEC) is to develop a route to the Indian Ocean region through the territory of Pakistan which is China's closest ally. The CPEC is a part of China's Belt and Road Initiative. China received the Hambantota port on a 100-year lease from Sri Lanka and it is increasing its economic investments in the port.[21] Many littoral countries in the region such as Nepal, Bangladesh, and Maldives are becoming increasingly dependent on technological services provided by Chinese corporations such as Alibaba.

The third prominent trend in the region is its increasing militarization. The Chinese navy has increased its activities in the region by acquiring new bases and naval patrolling. For instance, in 2017 China started a military base in Djibouti, which is the first military base of China in the region. There are reports of Chinese submarines being regularly seen in waters off the Indian coast. At present, Bangladesh, Myanmar, and Pakistan buy most of their military equipment from China. On the other hand, the US, India, Australia, and Japan have increased their military and geostrategic cooperation in the Indian Ocean region through Quad. Quad is an informal alliance between these four countries. Its stated objectives are to increase economic and political cooperation as well as enhance maritime security in the region. Quad is the short form of Quadrilateral Security Dialogue between the US, Australia, India, and Japan. China has always criticized the Quad as an Indo-Pacific counterpart of the North Atlantic Treaty Organization (NATO). It accuses the US of using its relations with the other three countries in this informal alliance to collectively work against Chinese interests in the region. Many researchers believe that the objective of containing China in the Indian Ocean has emerged as the topmost priority in Quad's agenda. The Quad countries have increased their joint military drills in the Indian Ocean in the last five years.[22]

Research Philosophy

This research is based on the philosophy of interpretivism. It is also referred to as post-positivism since it emerged as a critique of positivism.[23] Traditionally, the philosophies of interpretivism, as well as positivism, have been used in social sciences such as international relations.[24] The philosophy of positivism is based on scientific rigor, the primacy of observable facts, and empirical measurements.[25] This is why many social scientists and philosophers also refer to positivism as empiricism.[26] Positivist methods are mainly concerned with findings about the form of an event and its causality. There is no room for any subjective interpretation or factors in research based on the positivist philosophy.[27] This is why the philosophy of positivism is followed mainly in scientific research, which is completely empirical.

On the other hand, research in social sciences requires the interpretation of collected data by the researcher. There is always going to be an element of subjectivity in the findings of such studies because each researcher has their interpretations.[28] Positivist research in international relations would be limited to a description of events, developments, and processes in society. But such findings may not adequately fulfill the objectives of research in international relations. On the contrary, research based on the philosophy of interpretivism would look to find social meanings in the developments and events in international relations. The purpose of interpretations is to find hidden meaning in data.[29] Furthermore, social sciences are based on the dynamics of human society. Hence research in social sciences cannot afford to overlook human factors in international developments and events. This research on international relations involves a subjective interpretation of events for assessing the future of the Indian Ocean region. It involves social dynamics and psychological factors. This implies that the human factors in this research also need to be taken into consideration. Interpretivist research can be effective in studying ideas, norms, identities, and culture in international relations. Each power involved in the political dynamics of the Indian Ocean would have its interpretation of the regional developments. All the factors discussed in this section justify the choice of the interpretivist philosophy for this research.

Research Design

This research can be characterized as exploratory research. Existing literature on research methodology reveals that there are five forms of research designs. These are exploratory, confirmatory, descriptive, explanatory, and causal research.[30] Exploratory research can be defined as a quest for anything new, which has not been studied yet or considered till now.[31] The scope provided by the exploratory research to delve into hitherto unexplored areas of knowledge is one of the main reasons for choosing this design. Exploratory research is mainly used in social science.[32] International relations represent one of the most important forms of applied social science. New developments, events, and processes regularly take place in the arena of geopolitics.

For example, the advent of nuclear weapons or biological weapons introduced the concept of WMD (Weapons of Mass Destruction) into the study of geopolitics. This gave a new dimension and context to the study of international relations. The concept of nuclear proliferation originated after various countries started to develop and acquire nuclear weapons. It is also referred to as the nuclear arms race and is qualitatively different from the conventional arms race. New areas of international relations could be better investigated through exploratory research methods. Hence a completely new field of inquiry requires exploratory research.[33] New developments and events in international relations also lead to the formation of new opinions. Many social scientists and researchers believe that exploratory research is also more suitable to study new opinions.[34] Exploratory research also has the potential to expand the horizon of knowledge related to a discipline in the social sciences.[35]

Research Approach

The inductive approach has been adopted for this research. There are some key differences between inductive and deductive research. Inductive research seeks to develop new theories or hypotheses from specific data. Hence it is considered to be a key process for advancing knowledge.[36] Inductive research acknowledges that reality in essence is a social construction.

It does not involve the testing of existing theories or hypotheses. The inductive approach starts with specific data and then arrives at generalizations based on such data. On the other hand, deductive research tests hypotheses and generalizations based on collected data. In this sense, deductive research moves from general to specific. Experimentation and observation are given primacy in deductive research. Hence it is more suited to the natural sciences. The inductive approach is preferable for social science disciplines such as international relations.

Data Collection

This research has been limited to secondary sources due to the constraints of time and space. Secondary sources used in this research on international relations include reputed books, articles from scholarly journals, news websites, government websites, and publications of international organizations. Such secondary sources have been accessed for collecting data on geopolitics in the Indian Ocean. To seek answers to the research questions, qualitative analysis was applied to secondary data. The rationale for relying solely on qualitative analysis in this research can be explained in terms of key characteristics of qualitative methods. First of all, qualitative analysis of data offers scope for a comprehensive understanding of the meanings hidden in such data.[37] An in-depth understanding of social meanings is more relevant in international relations than statistical analysis of quantitative data. Secondly, qualitative analysis also allows a researcher to incorporate his perspective in the interpretation of data. Hence qualitative analysis is more suited to research that is based on the philosophy of interpretivism. Qualitative methods are also more effective in analyzing opinions. On the other hand, quantitative analysis is more suited to research that seeks a single consistent answer. Opinions vary according to contexts and from person to person. Qualitative analysis is more applicable to findings that depend on the context of a situation or environment. Due to the relevance of opinions and contexts in international relations, qualitative analysis is appropriate for this research.

Results

The results of this study have revealed some key facts about the geopolitics in the Indian Ocean. It is important to comprehend the importance of the Indian Ocean in the larger Indo-Pacific region to evaluate the future of the Indian Ocean region from the right perspective. The Indo-Pacific region includes the tropical waters of the Indian Ocean and the Central and Western Pacific oceans. The seas which link these oceans are recognized as the territorial waters of Indonesia. These seas are also an important part of the entire Indo-Pacific region. This explains the role of ASEAN in the Indo-Pacific Region. The geopolitical shifts in the Indian Ocean region are central to this research. Several reliable secondary sources have been studied to understand the nature, form, context, and implications of such strategic shifts. Nowadays, the term Indo-Pacific finds more mention in international and regional discourses on international relations or geopolitics. In this research paper, it has been mentioned that the objective of research in social sciences is to find out and interpret social meanings in data. The implications of the increasing application of the word Indo-Pacific can be interpreted as a strategic shift in international relations.

Strategic Shifts in Geopolitics

According to secondary data on the Indo-US strategic relationship, the term Indo-Pacific was first used by the Indian Navy.[38] The consequent adoption and use of the term by the US in its strategic discourse reflects that the US and its strategic partners acknowledge the rise and potential role of India in this part of the world. In the opinion of Khurana, the term Indo-Pacific also represents the incorporation of India in the affairs of maritime Asia.[39]

There has been a significant eastward shift in the center of importance in the global economy. Japan and China are already recognized by the international community as two major economic powers. India is also recognized as an emerging economy due to its fast growth and today the influence of the country is extending beyond South Asia. The Indo-Pacific region is quite critical for the global economy, also because several trade routes pass through the Indian Ocean, and it is linked to global supply chains. Furthermore, the geopolitics of the region poses significant security challenges that extend beyond Asia and have global implications. Due to these reasons, the Indo-Pacific has emerged as a singular and integrated geopolitical construct. In such a geopolitical construct, the Indian Ocean region has a central position.

After World War II, there have been significant shifts in the strategic interests of the US in Asia. During the cold war, the primary objective of the US leadership and policymakers was to contain the USSR and its communist ideology.[40] These priorities compelled the US to intervene in Afghanistan through its Central Intelligence Agency with the help of Pakistan. Thereafter, the US was concerned with striking a balance between India and Pakistan. It was also ready to mediate the Kashmir issue between these two countries. After 9/11, the US was primarily concerned with garnering support for its war on terror from Asian countries. At present, the US-China rivalry has acquired a central position in the US strategic discourse on South Asia, which also includes the Indian Ocean region. Many experts in strategic affairs believe that the US has moved closer to India in its bid to contain China. The US considers India to be a key ally from the perspective of American geostrategic interests.

Perspectives of the Southeast Asian Countries

The strategic relevance of the Indian Ocean region has also increased for Indonesia and other Southeast Asian nations. This is the reason why these countries want to increase their engagement with the Indian Ocean region. The various Southeast Asian countries, including Indonesia, are quite concerned with the developments in the Indian Ocean region. They think that China's assertive foreign policy and rivalry with the US is detrimental to peace and stability in the Indian Ocean region. The ASEAN countries want to engage with Quad to increase economic and technological cooperation in the region. Indonesia has framed the Indonesia Ocean Policy (IOP) to pursue its maritime interests. At present, the dynamics in the Indian Ocean region are crucial from the perspective of the IOP agenda. So far Indonesia has supported most of the regional initiatives of the Quad countries. It wants to fulfill its role as a middle power in the Indian Ocean region.

Role of the Quad

Secondary research on the Indian Ocean region also revealed some key facts about the nature and activities of Quad. The navies of the US, India, Japan, and Australia regularly take part in joint maritime exercises coordinated by Quad. According to He & Feng, the regional organizations in the Indo-Pacific region represent the institutionalization of issues and possibilities in the region.[41] However, India's maritime interests are focused primarily on the Indian Ocean region, unlike the other four members of the Quad whose interests extend to the entire Indo-Pacific region.[42] India wants to defend its interests in the Strait of Malacca from the Chinese. The four countries involved in the Quad have several shared economic and geopolitical values. The Chinese leadership has alleged on numerous occasions that the Quad is a military alliance in essence. However, the Quad countries have refuted these allegations by referring to the infrastructure projects in the Quad's agenda.

Continuing Conflict of Interests between the US and China

The competition between the US and China is also reflected in their international projects and investments. Many economists and strategic experts think that both these countries want to use their international projects for economic dominance.[43] It is estimated that in the coming years, China's Belt and Road Initiative (BRI) would witness investments worth \$1.2 to \$1.3 trillion. The initiative would include the development of roads, railways, ports, 5G networks, and power plants. However, the BRI has also received major setbacks due to the pandemic and the failure of several member countries to pay their debts back to China. This is what the G7 countries led by the US want to take advantage of through their Bring Back Better World or B3W initiative. The US claims that the B3W is a better alternative to the BRI, which has resulted in debt traps for countries like Sri Lanka. B3W also includes infrastructure development and aims to invest \$40 trillion by 2035. The competition for economic hegemony has also become a part of the geopolitics in the Indo-Pacific region. The independence and sovereignty of Taiwan is also another contentious issue between the US and China. China does not recognize the independent existence of Taiwan and wants to make it a part of the People's Republic of China.[44]

Such ambitions of China are based on its revisionist interpretation of history, which has led to the formulation of the One China Policy. China wants to incorporate Taiwan into its territory just like Hong Kong. However, the US and Japan have asserted on numerous occasions that they would go to any extent to protect the independence and sovereignty of Taiwan. The ambition to incorporate territories belonging to other countries is also a major reason behind China's conflicts with those countries. For instance, China claims the Indian state of Arunachal Pradesh as South Tibet.[45] The country's territorial and economic ambitions are also responsible for Geopolitical tensions in the Indian Ocean region.

Discussion

An analysis of secondary data for this research has not only revealed current international trends but has also generated insights for the future.

First of all, the Indian Ocean region would continue to represent the current multipolar world order. Economic progress and development in the region would be based on the American models of liberal democracy and a free market economy. Although the Indian Ocean region is going through an economic crisis at present, there would be more investments in infrastructure.[46] This is mainly because of the economic ambitions of the US and China. Both countries want to dominate the Indian Ocean region by establishing their credibility in the region. However, many littoral states in the region may turn to the US and its allies in the region for economic assistance. The experience of several littoral countries with China's debt trap is likely to cause this shift.[47] These countries may also look forward to collectively asserting their interests against China with the support of the US and its allies. China's BRI is already facing challenges due to the impact of the pandemic and geopolitical developments.[48] The B3W initiative may emerge as a better alternative to BRI if more countries join the B3W.

However, the peaceful resolution of the hostilities and conflict of interests in the Indian Ocean region seems to be imponderable. The new cold war may also become more intense due to the rivalry between the US and China. The Quad needs to enhance its image as a common platform for economic, technological, and infrastructural development based on regional cooperation. India has to concentrate on reducing poverty and inequality to contribute more meaningfully as a member of the Quad. Development of infrastructure and technological advancement are also going to be key to the country's progress in the Indian Ocean region. A shift of focus to peace and development can only decrease the militarization of the Indian Ocean region.

Conclusion

All the findings and insights revealed in this research are relevant to the geopolitical dynamics of the Indian Ocean region. Some of these findings may appear to be more relevant for the larger Indo-Pacific region. However, all of them have significant implications for the Indian Ocean region. From this perspective, the role of regional organizations and the United Nations becomes more important. Commitment to international security, cooperation, and dialogue is needed to prevent the hostilities in the Indian Ocean region from escalating into a global conflict.

ENDNOTES

1. Scott, D. (2018). The Indo-Pacific in US strategy: Responding to power shifts. *Rising powers quarterly*, *2*(2), 19-43.https://rpquarterly.kureselcalismalar.com/quarterly/the-indo-pacific-in-us-strategy-responding-to-power-shifts

2. McMahon, R.J. (2021). *The Cold War: a very short introduction.* Oxford University Press.https://pdfcookie.com/documents/cold-wara-very-short-introduction-wylj8xmmddv3
3. Burdekin, R.C., & Siklos, P.L. (2022). Armageddon and the stock market: US, Canadian and Mexican market responses to the 1962 Cuban missile crisis. *The Quarterly Review of Economics and Finance*, *84*, 112-127.https://cama.crawford.anu.edu.au/sites/default/files/publication/cama_crawford_anu_edu_au/2022-04/32_2022_burdekin_siklos_0.pdf
4. Allison, G. (2020). The new spheres of influence: sharing the globe with other great powers. *Foreign Aff.*, *99*, 30.https://www.hks.harvard.edu/sites/default/files/HKSEE/HKSEE%20PDFs/Allison_Spheres%20of%20Influence%2C%20Foreign%20Affairs%2C%20March-April%202020.pdf
5. Anwar, D.F. (2020). Indonesia and the ASEAN outlook on the Indo-Pacific. *International Affairs*, *96*(1), 111-129.https://d1wqtxts1xzle7.cloudfront.net/75450175/Indonesia_ASEAN_Outlook_on_Indo_Pacific_IA_vol_96_issue1_2020-with-cover-page-v2.pdf?Expires=1670154315&Signature=MUC1vNW2t3aHfhjhj8t4PAWQ3iEfUuj-JpJhNJNeQ7rJab6He6Mrl2L1EI84e1~2rJKtK-xcoCjiSAqPJ4Ju4djYbpHqHepXED5z5T5QepD5EwhwrepSNEGw-5N~4XWhARdK3ZzQ6E4z2MjMsKqesfC87xDQIr30tAWPRuSXBanmxAKZHn0EK8kENtWOFkSbCimKn6jVnjbkhxz4AOyLrA~gZjrCq315lQXI-FIXoP5R22zlw0dENRo2rAJV2E1l3xNftKe8eBnrZlxUfcys9UfmUyFT4ikdNsYwi6~Xh0pZHBPtBrafdKh8f4C30sDctJW1vOktWnASiBBRxh7n1Q__&Key-Pair-Id=APKAJLOHF5GGSLRBV4ZA
6. Hosoya, Y. (2019). FOIP 2.0: The evolution of Japan's free and open Indo-Pacific strategy. *Asia-Pacific Review*, *26*(1), 18-28.https://d1wqtxts1xzle7.cloudfront.net/61880019/FOIP_2_0_The_Evolution_of_Japan_s_Free_and_Open_Indo_Pacific_Strategy20200124-45959-ypzujm-with-cover-page-v2.pdf?Expires=1670154700&Signature=asi9wJ79tlpDkpP8H8~x3S0De2xGhat51jDtGHmtrwH~-qW9NKd~Mxb3p5zrnA-BK-zJHrQrRzUKdk0tNTcaClQWfYKnvrrza78TRD387Kj-1eUXlwqHEPjgjmytaMvVp9CzDJtkRk6ZGNSOURIiCKAKA2hCeLTv8H9UY~ayn7ljcFIIAfljsc1YXVKU4gizPaOR4t4PtT4gdRWvnq8O3u-C46YTz2lbNhnZDJ6xtK4-kSf7y--rZKawE1bF2g-3Fgoj7jLc2ahgOYZakrz10yyi90r59raWweW4AI8jjfoRtjJURbVFQyhJ47HmEfgAS59Uwg5WxMmoulpDOnKdQA__&Key-Pair-Id=APKAJLOHF5GGSLRBV4ZA
7. Kuik, C.C. (2016). How do weaker states hedge? Unpacking ASEAN states' alignment behavior towards China. *Journal of Contemporary China*, *25*(100), 500-514.https://www.researchgate.net/profile/Cheng-Chwee-Kuik/publication/296689375_How_Do_Weaker_States_Hedge_Unpacking_ASEAN_states'_alignment_behavior_towards_China/links/5b791757299bf1d5a714aac4/How-Do-Weaker-States-Hedge-Unpacking-ASEAN-states-alignment-behavior-towards-China.pdf
8. De Graaff, N., & Van Apeldoorn, B. (2018). US–China relations and the liberal world order: contending elites, colliding visions? *International affairs*, *94*(1), 113-131.https://www.researchgate.net/profile/Bastiaan-Apeldoorn-2/publication/322268653_US-China_relations_and_the_liberal_world_order_Contending_elites_colliding_visions/links/5f5609e992851c250b99793b/

US-China-relations-and-the-liberal-world-order-Contending-elites-colliding-visions.pdf

9. Blackwill, R.D., &Tellis, A. J. (2015). *Revising US grand strategy toward China*. Council on Foreign Relations.https://books.google.co.in/books?hl=en&lr=&id=xwAICgAAQBAJ&oi=fnd&pg=PR7&dq=India+as+a+strategic+ally+of+the+US&ots=XgIBzixOUc&sig=_xGcE--kaP8aed2cbD33Fd5ltiw&redir_esc=y#v=onepage&q&f=false
10. Baruah, D.M. (2018). India's Answer to the Belt and Road: A Road Map for South Asia.https://carnegieendowment.org/files/WP_Darshana_Baruah_Belt_Road_FINAL.pdf
11. Henry, I.D. (2020). Adapt or atrophy? The Australia-US alliance in an age of power transition. *Contemporary Politics*, *26*(4), 402-419.https://www.tandfonline.com/doi/pdf/10.1080/13569775.2020.1777043?needAccess=true&role=button
12. Karaganov, S. (2018). The new cold war and the emerging greater Eurasia. *Journal of Eurasian studies*, *9*(2), 85-93.https://journals.sagepub.com/doi/pdf/10.1016/j.euras.2018.07.002
13. Westad, O.A. (2019). The sources of Chinese conduct: Are Washington and Beijing fighting a new Cold War. *Foreign Aff.*, *98*, 86.http://viet-studies.net/kinhte/FA_SourcesChineseConduct.pdf
14. Zenglein, M. J., &Holzmann, A. (2019). Evolving made in China 2025. *MERICS papers on China*, *8*, 78.https://kritisches-netzwerk.de/sites/default/files/merics_-_evolving_made_in_china_2025_-_chinas_industrial_policy_in_the_quest_for_global_tech_leadership_-_2._juli_2019_-_80_seiten.pdf
15. Zhao, M. (2019). Is a new Cold War inevitable? Chinese perspectives on US–China strategic competition. *The Chinese Journal of International Politics*, *12*(3), 371-394.https://watermark.silverchair.com/poz010.pdf
16. Nichols, R. (2020). From 4 to 9 June: The Chinese Communist Party's Response to Tiananmen Square '89 and Hong Kong '19. *AKΦ*, 30.https://www.lindsey.edu/academics/majors-and-programs/English/img/AKO-Review20.pdf#page=31
17. Smith Finley, J. (2021). Why scholars and activists increasingly fear a Uyghur genocide in Xinjiang. *Journal of Genocide Research*, *23*(3), 348-370.https://d1wqtxts1xzle7.cloudfront.net/65855747/Smith_Finley_Why_scholars_and_activists_increasingly_fear_a_Uyghur_genocide_in_Xinjiang_pre_publication_version_-with-cover-page-v2.pdf
18. Rehman, I. (2017). India, China and differing conceptions of the maritime order. *wPolicy Review*.https://www.pellcenter.org/wp-content/uploads/2017/06/Rehman-India_China_and_differing_conceptions_of_the_maritime_order.pdf
19. Carrai, M.A. (2021). Chinese Political Nostalgia and Xi Jinping's Dream of Great Rejuvenation. *International Journal of Asian Studies*, *18*(1), 7-25. https://d1wqtxts1xzle7.cloudfront.net/65743114/CARRAI_chinese_political_nostalgia_and_xi_jinpings_dream_of_great_rejuvenation-with-cover-page-v2.pdf
20. Lieberherr, B. (2021). Geostrategic Storm in the Indian Ocean. *CSS Analyses in Security Policy*, *284*.https://www.research-collection.ethz.ch/bitstream/handle/20.500.11850/480516/5/CSSAnalyse284-EN.pdf

21. Ferchen, M., &Perera, A. (2019). Why unsustainable Chinese infrastructure deals are a two-way street. *Carnegie-Tsinghua center for global policy*, *22*.https://carnegieendowment.org/files/7-15-19_Ferchen_Debt_Trap.pdf

22. Kutty, S.N., &Basrur, R. (2021). The Quad: What it is–and what it is not. *The Diplomat*, *24*.https://d1wqtxts1xzle7.cloudfront.net/68191895/The_Quad_What_It_Is_And_What_It_Is_Not_The_Diplomat-with-cover-page-v2.pdf?Expires=1670230926&Signature=QJdruAhs7WY4p5CD-e9ToJgzVBnrlR8ueNiz6uZxafnbgf5wfzo8KHUFNaeWT9EY4ECHLN79reivCZv1iWKdQySb4MYxzrSdQ2s1c9h2gFEetVsRbjWY-4lD0Va8q6agJw-3idsbOwFmLsCxklzLxjz8SyMFN2r~K4n~WBCCPMpNmGbvoagSYYaE5evvkhT4UxlE-MYYi7GDqdLeWb1qnej0Mdbb2~1p3e7npz~TzvNLKmzSbYX~g2m55-xwni-RIbafK2M0vmQ-xAb-WIJz-D2dUTyQaZqe75gNG3OfBO8TAHLajQsWyerlMOCCkfepU3yssR~MyD238AOosCZY8g__&Key-Pair-Id=APKAJLOHF5GGSLRBV4ZA

23. Holliday, A., & Macdonald, M. N. (2020). Researching the intercultural: Intersubjectivity and the problem with postpositivism. *Applied Linguistics*, *41*(5), 621-639.https://watermark.silverchair.com/amz006.pdf?

24. Lamont, C. (2021). *Research methods in international relations*. Sage.https://www.researchgate.net/publication/344403631_Research_Methods_in_International_Relations

25. Kelly, M., Dowling, M., & Millar, M. (2018). The search for understanding: The role of paradigms. *Nurse researcher*, *25*(4), 9-13.https://www.researchgate.net/profile/Marcella-Horrigan-Kelly/publication/322554377_Kelly_M_Dowling_M_Millar_M_2018_The_search_for_understanding_the_role_of_paradigms_Nurse_Researcher_25_4_8-12/links/5c3611d0458515a4c718e283/Kelly-M-Dowling-M-Millar-M-2018-The-search-for-understanding-the-role-of-paradigms-Nurse-Researcher-25-4-8-12.pdf

26. Gamlen, A., & McIntyre, C. (2018). Mixing methods to explain emigration policies: A post-positivist perspective. *Journal of Mixed Methods Research*, *12*(4), 374-393.https://d1wqtxts1xzle7.cloudfront.net/60883739/2018Gamlen_McIntyreMixedMethods20191012-22952-1jvfhnk-with-cover-page-v2.pdf?Expires=1670236775&Signature=Z1~eqitk3N1bX~E4xiwW6I85w2HwziUYh1tIFDCpR2XsoM6e2Tpv4W43gcMWboR0BLi-iNl7ECJuXAkiFSYPVVCG~KKvkiMXaUBuzz7Cd-QmjxopeUhtR97KNLYeU6EGkbkK3FVvGmYoFqr3DqNLy9j1aNvxDWZ9~QYKuMHxWQqzHKgA75t5IJ-wWnP6nxN-EltU7BNmeFxFSb8JXochjjzxCiIpfZiq1Fp-SQt6jHI5IT3NpPGjGQBgxU1~WGNvtj4SPX~rARopzzZFJa0U7H514BW8Mbyei3FluVJCQDTETjVnsxTk5snxd~GmkipZTy2my8VW4vqLne5tTpntI8Q__&Key-Pair-Id=APKAJLOHF5GGSLRBV4ZA

27. Alharahsheh, H.H., & Pius, A. (2020). A review of key paradigms: Positivism VS interpretivism. *Global Academic Journal of Humanities and Social Sciences*, *2*(3), 39-43002 https://gajrc.com/media/articles/GAJHSS_23_39-43_VMGJbOK.pdf

28. Pulla, V., & Carter, E. (2018). Employing interpretivism in social work research. *International Journal of Social Work and Human Services Practice*, *6*(1), 9-14. https://d1wqtxts1xzle7.cloudfront.net/63197938/IJRH2-1929047620200504-61084-3v3zjb-with-cover-page-v2.pdf?Expires=1670237111&Signature=Py0lShS0H-EjT7yBhGXQtfg9GvyY0No3KDIqe4dPId6pHEVUX0l5-4fYxl5r8eULBUY0YYPwGPn9GeKYK4BSKyOG4drr~ruW5ZahqQcEN

oBsAc3ayi70w93Gzwg~v04bkmDlK96VHeamttLnp3Xc2XHCj~DpZXdF7d-Is1Ocz6Qu5jWuZtvnxwDdKsC3b~fZZ3m1W54Js5kP6dXtjmID2cqw1ntEDf38ZEl7mppnoyX7qCxBzws3aq4oZxCIFuHwYNNeavfDWx~Fw-BNkKMjECXVUk2rgB4LLIKGxekkHbJyCP2pzlGmoTgo1n4G4MjR0MlT383E~CptP1KArMzf2w__&Key-Pair-Id=APKAJLOHF5GGSLRBV4ZA

29. Van der Walt, J. L. (2020). Interpretivism-constructivism as a research method in the humanities and social sciences–more to it than meets the eye. *International Journal*, *8*(1), 59-68.http://ijptnet.com/journals/ijpt/Vol_8_No_1_June_2020/5.pdf
30. Rahi, S. (2017). Research design and methods: A systematic review of research paradigms, sampling issues and instruments development. *International Journal of Economics & Management Sciences*, *6*(2), 1-5.https://pdfs.semanticscholar.org/d957/e1a07a961a572ce70f7d5845cb423ac8f0be.pdf
31. Thomas, O.O., &Lawal, O. R. (2020). Exploratory Research Design in Management Sciences: An X-Ray of Literature. *Annals of the University Dunarea de Jos of Galati: Fascicle: I, Economics & Applied Informatics*, *26*(2).https://web.archive.org/web/20210611214026id_/http://www.eia.feaa.ugal.ro/images/eia/2020_2/Thomas_Lawal.pdf
32. Reiter, B. (2017). Theory and methodology of exploratory social science research.vhttps://ttu-ir.tdl.org/bitstream/handle/2346/86610/reiter%20article.pdf?sequence=3
33. Nayak, J. K., & Singh, P. (2021). *Fundamentals of research methodology problems and prospects*. SSDN Publishers & Distributors.http://dspace.vnbrims.org:13000/jspui/bitstream/123456789/4653/1/Fundamentals%20of%20Research%20Methodology_Nayak.pdf
34. Mishra, S.B., &Alok, S. (2022). Handbook of research methodology. http://74.208.36.141:8080/jspui/bitstream/123456789/1319/1/BookResearchMethodology.pdf
35. Bouthillier, X., Laurent, C., & Vincent, P. (2019, May). Unreproducible research is reproducible. In *International Conference on Machine Learning* (pp. 725-734). PMLR.http://proceedings.mlr.press/v97/bouthillier19a/bouthillier19a.pdf
36. Woiceshyn, J., &Daellenbach, U. (2018). Evaluating inductive vs deductive research in management studies: Implications for authors, editors, and reviewers. *Qualitative research in organizations and management: An International Journal*, *13*(2), 183-195. https://www.researchgate.net/profile/Jaana-Woiceshyn-2/publication/324596659_Evaluating_Inductive_versus_Deductive_Research_in_Management_Studies_Implications_for_Authors_Editors_and_Reviewers/links/5b78d9aa92851c1e121f7477/Evaluating-Inductive-versus-Deductive-Research-in-Management-Studies-Implications-for-Authors-Editors-and-Reviewers.pdf
37. Young, B., &Hren, D. (2017). Introduction to qualitative research methods. *Methods in Research on Research*.http://miror-ejd.eu/wp-content/uploads/sites/34/2017/03/Introduction-to-qualitative-research-methods.compressed.pdf

38. Kuo, M.A. (2018). The origin of 'Indo-Pacific'as geopolitical construct. *The Diplomat*, *25*.https://d1wqtxts1xzle7.cloudfront.net/55641133/Origin_of_Indo-Pacific__Diplomat-libre.pdf?1516978718=&response-content-disposition=inline%3B+filename%3DThe_Origin_of_Indo_Pacific_as_Geopolitic.pdf&Expires=1670298218&Signature=S-BjhGVqAD~afyrgyPD23V3jg03jnh43yNSVWCdzgb248ZWKzm4NH7Zz6mZ~KycvTCLrikfvTxkNHPMuQawiAMW39qd5EwelleDwuiHumN2wpKdfZdm2K-oui9whFACSxFCfvjZUInRdtVzvgSj-Ilu0JzeOoAxVRRAflOSiCPWJnSd6LSQHomJ4D~t3KuwerSGLS2T32nLvkKothJqZmYSpG5Ik6VhYTD3dN-ICiSNB7K9Fr5v82FKXTX67fb2xFwV8yENIlRuWoSadTh4Dx5p9YXuWG75UC1Sk6vBBNHXq~FJEDhB3TniugyuDOkPmonU9XCn~lYYm7T35cLqFxA__&Key-Pair-Id=APKAJLOHF5GGSLRBV4ZA

39. Khurana, G.S. (2017). the 'Indo-Pacific 'concept: retrospect and Prospect. *National Maritime Foundation*, *2*.https://www.maritimeindia.org/View%20Profile/636215922419657386.pdf

40. Jia, C. (2017). New trends of US policy toward South Asia: challenges to CPEC. *IPRI Journal*, *1*(1), 95-121.http://www.ipripak.org/wp-content/uploads/2017/04/Article-No.-5w17.pdf

41. He, K., & Feng, H. (2020). The institutionalization of the Indo-Pacific: Problems and prospects. *International Affairs*, *96*(1), 149-168.https://www.researchgate.net/profile/Kai-He-20/publication/338453269_The_institutionalization_of_the_Indo-Pacific_problems_and_prospects/links/5e335f17299bf1cdb9ff3bfc/The-institutionalization-of-the-Indo-Pacific-problems-and-prospects.pdf

42. Roy-Chaudhury, R., & de Estrada, K. S. (2018). India, the Indo-Pacific and the Quad. *Survival*, *60*(3), 181-194.https://ora.ox.ac.uk/objects/uuid:dfcdeb66-5d46-46e6-9936-e727d3a76db4/download_file?file_format=pdf&safe_filename=India%252C%2Bthe%2BIndo-Pacific%2Band%2Bthe%2BQuad.pdf&type_of_work=Journal+article

43. Khan, A., & Khan, S. N. (2022). Bri vs. b3w: A rivalry for economic hegemony: An archival research. *Journal of Social Sciences and Humanities*, *61*(1), 31-44. https://www.jsshuok.com/oj/index.php/jssh/article/view/596/442

44. Bush, R. (2019). *From persuasion to coercion: Beijing's approach to Taiwan and Taiwan's response*. Washington, DC: Brookings Institution.https://www.brookings.edu/wp-content/uploads/2019/11/FP_20191118_beijing_taiwan_bush.pdf

45. Sharma, R. (2021). China's Territorial Claim on Arunachal Pradesh-The North East Frontier State of India.https://rieas.gr/images/asia/raagini101.pdf

46. Voyer, M., Schofield, C., Azmi, K., Warner, R., McIlgorm, A., & Quirk, G. (2018). Maritime security and the Blue Economy: intersections and interdependencies in the Indian Ocean. *Journal of the Indian Ocean Region*, *14*(1), 28-48.https://ro.uow.edu.au/cgi/viewcontent.cgi?article=4373&context=lhapapers

47. Sautman, B., & Hairong, Y. (2019). The "Chinese Debt Trap" and its Sri Lanka Example. *HKUST IEMS Thought Leadership Briefs*, (29), 1-4. https://archives.hkust.edu.hk/dspace/bitstream/9999/47809/1/IEMS-Thought-Leadership-Brief-no29.pdf

48. MwadiMakengo, B., &MimbaleMolanga, J. KamandaLondo, P., Mbutamuntu, J.(2022). Understanding the Strategic Opposition between the Build Back Better World [B3W] and Belt and Road Initiative [BRI]. *Academia Letters*. https://www.researchgate.net/profile/Benjamin-Mwadi-Makengo-2/publication/360282629_Understanding_the_Strategic_opposition_between_the_Build_Back_Better_World_B3W_and_Belt_and_Road_Initiative_BRI/links/626d89a50df856128f8a96dc/Understanding-the-Strategic-opposition-between-the-Build-Back-Better-World-B3W-and-Belt-and-Road-Initiative-BRI.pdf

8

India's Dynamic Foreign Policy: Indo-Pacific Strategy and Balancing Role in Quad

– **Naresh Kumar Behera**

Introduction

India's foreign policy has developed into one that is modern and beneficial to the entire world. In the contemporary world, India has a powerful and independent voice. India's foreign policy is characterized by involvement in various global concerns rather than exclusion. India's participation in the Indo-Pacific region is a new development in its foreign policy strategy. The security of its region is a priority for India. The phrase "Indo-Pacific" refers to an emerging geo-political development. The concept is still evolving. In the 1920s, the German geopolitical expert Karl Haushofer coined the phrase "Indo-Pacific" in his book *"indopazifischen Raum."*[1] In the 1940s, Kalidas Nag, the Indian historian, also used the 'Indo-Pacific' term in his work *"India and the Pacific World"*[2].

Ten years ago, Gurpreet S. Khurana, an Indian Navy officer, also used the term "Indo-Pacific". Following Shinzo Abe's push in 2007, the phrase gained popularity in the current period. Beginning in the early 2000s, countries like the United States, Japan, India, and Australia launched measures to advance the interests of the "Indo-pacific" region. The establishment of Quad or the "Quadrilateral Security Dialogue" contributed to the rise of the "Indo-Pacific" on the global stage. Quad includes Japan, India, Australia and the United States. The "Indo-Pacific" concept is also referred to by the United States, Australia and India on different occasions. Hillary Clinton, US Secretary of State, included the term in U.S.'s *"Pivot to Asia"* policy in 2011. Australia has also used the term in the government paper *"Australia in the Asian Century, 2012"*. India used the phrase in Indian Navy Publication, *"Ensuring Secure Seas: Indian Maritime Security Strategy,2015"*.

Following the revival of Quad, the *"Free and open Indo-Pacific"* concept became the most prominent. Shinzo Abe stated that the foreign policy of Japan is centred on the doctrine, and it is included in the official documents of Japan[3]. In 2017, United States President Donald Trump also included "free and open Indo-Pacific" as the main objective of the U.S.'s Asia policy[4]. By changing the regional strategic balance, this endeavour aims to sustain the current regional order based on US dominance. In 2018, the Indo-Pacific doctrine of France was discussed by French President Emmanuel Macron. France is a major player in the area, according to Macron, not merely as an outsider entering the region but also as a force already residing there[5]. US Department of State published a paper, *"A Free and Open Indo-Pacific, advancing a Shared Vision,2019"*, that dedicated to supporting a "free and open Indo-Pacific region" where all countries, large or small, can pursue economic progress by referring to the international law and fair competition principles and feel secure in their sovereignty. The Indo-Pacific countries' autonomy and freedom of choice will be fiercely contested by all.[6]

The emergence of the Quad grouping again indicates that the "Indo-Pacific" has gained recognition as a geopolitical idea both within and outside of its member nations. The development of the construct is strategically important for the maintenance of geo-political order in the entire Asia-Pacific region. The militarization of the various oceans and seas and China's rapid expansion and influence outside of its own region were the prime reasons for the development. India also maintains a long border with China and is geographically and, historically, economically closely tied to China. In the South Asian region, directly opposing China is a difficult option for India. India supports the international recognition of the Indo-Pacific region for its strategic gain. New Delhi's approach to involvement with the

Quad grouping is motivated by the desire to promote the "inclusive, open, and rule-based order" of the region. After entering the Indo-Pacific arrangements, India established solid bilateral ties with the other countries of the region. Through its role in the Indo-Pacific, India hopes to preserve both regional stability and advancements in maritime security in the Indian Ocean.

From an Informal Dialogue to a Modern Debate: Quad's Evolution

In 2007, a grouping of four big powers called the Quadrilateral Security Dialogue (QUAD) was established. Shinzo Abe, the former prime minister of Japan, initiated the group, and the leaders of India, Australia, and the United States backed it. The founder Quad members originally came together in 2004 as they assisted with the devastating earthquake and tsunami that hit the Indian Ocean. At that time, the four nations came together to help the region with humanitarian aid that was affected by the disaster.[7] Shinzo Abe's interest and other leaders' support signalled the formation. Following that, the informal gathering of Quad members took place in 2007 in Manila during the side-lines of the ASEAN Regional Forum gathering[8]. The groupings could no longer be continued due to Australia's withdrawal from the Quad exercise in response to Chinese diplomatic criticism in 2008. It remained silent for a decade. The idea was revived because, after a decade, the strategic environment grew heated due to the militarization of the oceans by China and the expansion of Chinese hegemony in the international arena.

The great powers were alarmed by China's ascendancy and saw it as a threat to their development. The United States and China are engaged in an economic and military arms race. India and China had a direct border conflict, and Japan had to contend with Chinese influence in the Senkaku Islands. By forming various alliances and groupings, they started their efforts to challenge the hegemony. Again in 2017, with the support of all four members, Quad 2.0 was put into action. The "free and open Indo-Pacific," concept was popularised after the revival of Quad.[9] The concept defines building connectivity and focuses on the security of the Indo-Pacific region. When Quad was first created in 2007, India was viewed as its weak arm. India's goal of retaining mid-level representatives in the Quad is its first and foremost. India preferred to preserve it at the joint/assistant secretary level, whereas other members developed it at the minister/cabinet level.

Second, India was more focused towards its neighbourhood and for the development of its region. Following the resurgence of Quad and recent border disputes between China and India, such as the Doklam incident, the Galwan conflict pushed India to take a more active role in Quad and Indo-Pacific involvement. In 2020, India's invitation to Australia for the Malabar Naval Exercise boosted the progress of Quad 2.0. After a couple of years, the four members conducted the first Quad official meeting in 2021. "The Spirit of Quad" joint statement was released at that summit. In that summit, Quad focused on Global Health, the Covid pandemic, the climate crisis, high standards infrastructure development, clean energy, education and people-to-people relations, cybersecurity, space, critical and emerging technologies.[10] After that, on September 24, 2021, the physical, in-person Quad Leaders' Summit took place at the White House, with President Biden hosting all the leaders of the Quad.[11]

Again, the leaders joined a virtual interaction in March 2022 during the Ukraine war. In that meeting, the Quad leaders discussed the Ukraine conflict and the serious humanitarian challenges due to war. They talked about creating a mechanism for handling future humanitarian crises and disasters in the Indo-Pacific area. In Tokyo, Japan, May 2022, the second Leaders' Summit of the Quad was held. The Quad leaders praised a new Indo-Pacific Maritime Domain Awareness Initiative, in which they strongly supported ASEAN's unity and centrality and unveiled the (Q-CHAMP) Quad Climate Change Action and Mitigation Package.[12] At that summit, Narendra Modi, the Indian Prime Minister, referred to the grouping as a "force for good", which indicates the grouping is committed to all types of developments in the region. The Leaders reaffirmed the value of "democracy, territorial integrity, upholding the principles of sovereignty, and peaceful dispute resolution, as well as their shared commitment to a free, open, and inclusive Indo-Pacific".

However, the development of the term "Indo-Pacific" is connected to strategically countering China's growth and assertiveness in the world, as well as the following 2005 formulation of China's "String of Pearls" policy[13]. There is no mutual-defence agreement in place, like in the European alliance, but China has warned that the organisation is an attempt to establish an "Asian NATO."[14] The Quad leader declined and objected to the Chinese perception. Members of the Quad asserted that the group's goals were to strengthen the four nations' political, economic, and military connections. The Quad's document, "*Spirit of the Quad 2021,*" states that its goal is to create a region that is founded on "democratic ideals, open, inclusive, and accessible to all, and unhindered by force." New Delhi's stand on the Quad is very clear and objectivity-based.

S. Jaishankar, External Affairs Minister of India, stated during the Raisina Dialogue in 2021 that India never had a "NATO mentality" and that the grouping is not anywhere related to "Asian NATO." According to Jaishankar, the Indo-Pacific strategic framework aims to "overcome" rather than "reinforce" the Cold War era[15]. Above all, Quad affirms to support a "free, open, rules-based system that is based on the international rule to achieve security and progress and fend off challenges to the region" and useful for all. After the advent of AUKUS in 2021, new developments by the US raised questions about QUAD's significance. AUKUS is made up of Australia, the United Kingdom, and the United States, and its goal is to give Australia its nuclear submarines. This AUKUS is therefore centred on defence cooperation, and its participants asserted that it would strengthen Indo-Pacific capabilities[16]. Members of the Quad made it clear that AUKUS is for security advances while Quad is a non-military grouping focused on the Indo-Pacific region being "free, open, inclusive, and prosperous" and that AUKUS will not weaken the importance of Quad in this area.

Despite having different goals and organisational structures, both groupings cooperate to achieve influence in the region. It is, therefore, obvious that the two groupings are mutually beneficial. Over time, the grouping became exceptional because of its goal and concern for the peace, stability, and security of the Indo-Pacific region. With all the developments in the Indo-Pacific, QUAD became a forum for promoting "democratic ideals" among nations who shared the same views, developing from a conventional dialogue to a contemporary debate.

India's Indian Ocean Vision and Indo-Pacific Stance

The greater Indian Ocean region, IOR benefits from improved global connectivity. In terms of geography, it is connected Asia to

Africa.[17] In this region, Cold War effects were more pronounced. The first instance of the impending Cold War occurred in the neighbourhood of the region during the Korean war. The United States successfully used this Ocean and its coast to restrict Soviet Communism. The evolving power dynamics in the region have received a lot of attention on the global stage. Due to its advantageous location, the region is a key hub for global trade. It is a hotbed for competitiveness among the IOR countries because of its abundant flora, fauna, and minerals.

Over time, the region became more volatile and sensitive due to the enormous security and governance concerns it faced. One of the key nations in the IOR is India. India has a great historical role in the Indian Ocean region. India has a maritime coastline spanning more than 7,516.6 kilometres[18]. In the region, India's position was regarded as a natural actor. India has significant military and geopolitical interests in the IOR. The geography of India offers it a chance to contribute more significantly to the evolving geopolitical landscape of the region.

India has a long maritime domain and its navy is powerful in the entire region. No other nation in the area has such a strong and spectacular navy. India's involvement in the region is aimed at securing its maritime interests and making them available to other countries through trade, marine cooperation, and naval building. India is historically and culturally linked to the region's neighbouring countries. Indian customs and values have influenced neighbouring countries, and India has also aided them in times of need. Over time, India has become concerned about the security and militarization of the region's seas. India wants to keep the ocean free from becoming militarised. India has many times tried to keep the region's security as top priority. In the past, India also tried to address the security of the ocean in the UN General Assembly. In 1971, India and Sri Lanka passed a resolution regarding establishing a peace zone and making the region free of nuclear weapons.[19]

Over the past twenty years, China's assertiveness and presence over the world have grown. "China is pursuing several infrastructure developments in Southeast Asia. India is worried about a range of Chinese maritime actions in the Bay of Bengal and the Arabian Sea, which is known as a 'string of pearls' strategy or a 'setup of the battlefield' concept."[20] In this strategy, China is building major ports in the Indian Ocean region. At first, China is developing the Gwadar

Port in Pakistan.[21] And other major ports like the Chittagong Port, to promote bilateral commerce and economic growth between China and Bangladesh, China has generously funded the development and building of the Chittagong port.[22] China also took the Hambantota Port of Sri Lanka for a 99-year lease to use it for its benefits.[23] Through various developments, China extended its influence in the region. Along its border with India, China is constructing infrastructure. China's goal of dominating Asia is the first step on its path to becoming a world power. It will have to deal with India at first instance.

In recent times, India's joining of Quad and promotion of the "Indo-Pacific" domain, have divided China and India diplomatically many times. India simultaneously pursues its aim in the Indian Ocean and moves in the Indo-Pacific region to advance its Indian Ocean goal. One of the more recent terms to be included in the global strategic language is "Indo-Pacific" with the revival of Quad 2.0 in 2017.[24] It became more significant for China after the Quad's resurgence. To different powers, the Indo-Pacific inevitably implies different things, but it is a top priority for the Quad nations. For India, it represents its logical progression beyond Act East and a transcendence of South Asia's confines.[25] Firstly, through this engagement, India developed its Act East Policy and foreign policy towards China to be more open and approach-based. India increased its bilateral relations with countries beyond South Asia and Southeast Asia. Second, India's participation increased regional stability, growth, and security, as well as India's priority for the Indian Ocean. Working with people and countries that recognise India's position in a broader context and value its impact and presence is strategically beneficial to India.

Finally, with India's engagement, countries such as the United States, Japan, and Australia recognised India's geopolitical importance. For the development in maritime security of the region's mainland as well as islands, Prime Minister of India, Narendra Modi launched the "Security and Growth for All in the Region," SAGAR initiative."[26] The SAGAR initiative is a part of Modi's larger and pro-active foreign policy. A very strategic action to protect India's interests at home. To achieve marine cooperation and peace as well as for bilateral connections with the IOR littoral states, the SAGAR initiative plays a larger role. The four main components of SAGAR. The first is to defend India's maritime interests, maintain the region's security, growth, and stability, and make its capabilities available for the use of other countries. Secondly, it focuses on enhancing and strengthening its maritime neighbours' capacities for economic and security cooperation. The third calls for cooperation and collaboration to advance safety and security and deal with emergencies. The fourth aims to improve regional sustainability by fostering a more integrated and collaborative future.[27]

Along with SAGAR, the Indo-Pacific Oceans Initiative, IPOI strategy initiated by India also strengthens its maritime boundaries with neighbouring countries. The IORA (The Indian Ocean Rim Association) is another significant development in the region. IORA unifies all 23 oceanic nations through engagement and sustainable development. India is the most significant participant in IORA.[28] Through this organisation, India wants to strengthen its ties with various nations of the Indian Ocean region, with the African nations as well. India's adoption of the "Act East" policy in 2014 is also another step forward for the Indo-Pacific advancement. This larger "Act East Policy," which replaced the previous "Look East Policy," sought to make India's interactions with its neighbours more active and dynamic. India has made a significant effort to promote its "Act East Policy."[29] The "Act East Policy" has evolved into the "Act Indo-Pacific Policy" over time, and India's involvement has extended its neighbourhood vision. India also considered the ASEAN members to be a crucial starting point for promoting regional cooperation. India recognises the significance of ASEAN for upholding the Indo-Pacific regional order, while the ASEAN nations value India's leadership and strategy. With its geopolitical goals, India has long maintained its position as a powerful regional force and a reliable partner in maintaining regional stability.[30] As the centre of global geopolitics shifted to the dynamic continent of Asia in the twenty-first century, India has become a prominent actor in the regional geopolitical scene as a result of all of these events.

Along with developments in the Indian Ocean region, India's Indo-Pacific engagement is primarily based on being a region that is "independent, accessible, and open," with a greater emphasis on the "inclusive" part, seeking progress and prosperity; as a result, it is not to be seen as a region that seeks to rule or to be pushed against other powers. This framework also involves other nations outside the geography of the region.[31] The principle of "international order based on the rules" is demanded by India for the entire region, which signifies everyone will act under the international norms and respect for everyone's territorial sovereignty in the region. "The consent of everyone, not the power of the few" is to serve as the foundation for these laws and customs. "India's free, open, inclusive, Indo-Pacific policy aims to 'balance' its relations with the great powers while maintaining its independence and pursuing a leadership position in the region."[32] India advocates for respect between nations and places a priority on free exchange of ideas, cooperation, regional stability, and economic growth. Based on these, India's inclusive Indo-Pacific growth is described.

India and the United States: A Greater Strategic Partnership

The twenty-first century needs stronger ties between great powers for the advancement of the world. The world benefits from greater cooperation between the U.S. and India. After coming into power, Narendra Modi shifted India's foreign policy towards strategic and national interest-oriented objectives. Modi has accomplished this by reversing New Delhi's previous policy of stringent nonalignment, and opening the door for closer connections with big and intermediate powers. Strategic alliances have received significant weight under Modi. India joined several strategic partnerships with other countries, but several major ones bringing the aforementioned advantages are with the United States, Japan, France, and Russia. India is a key player in Quad, and the United States recognises India's importance and position in the Indo-Pacific region.

After engaging with the US under the Indo-Pacific framework, India and the US's relationship evolved into a worldwide strategic partnership. Relations between India and the US have undergone both good and bad eras throughout history. Platforms such as Quad, IPEF (Indo-Pacific Economic Framework), and I2U2 helped both nations to improve their bilateral and strategic partnerships.[33] The multifaceted interactions or strategic partnerships between New Delhi and Washington are for a few more reasons. First, the US had come to see that India is a trustworthy and peaceful nation that could work with it to advance liberal democratic values and world order. Second, the US became closer to India and developed greater relations because of India's steadily growing acceptance in world politics. Thirdly,

American worries about the expansion of Chinese development in the world and the Asia Pacific were a major factor in the decision to cooperate[34]. Both nations are opposed towards the promotion of democratic values, international norms, cooperation and maintaining stability in the world.[35]

To establish a democratic order in the globe, India and the US have a strategic collaboration in sectors including economics, defence, space, emerging technologies, global health, and politics. Washington also recognizes New Delhi's position on various international conflicts or issues and identified New Delhi as a key partner in the development of the Indo-Pacific framework. India and the US are linked to one another through their participation in or formation of several alliances or groupings. Frameworks like I2U2 and IPEF are most significant. India, Israel, the UAE, and the US are members of the "I2U2," which was established in 2021. The alliance aspires to work together on new projects and cooperative investments in the fields of space, transportation, energy, water, and food security.[36] The "Indo-Pacific Economic Framework" (IPEF), which was founded in 2022, is actively involved in the Indo-Pacific building. This framework is focused on the "geo-economic" aspect of Indo-Pacific construction. The framework's four pillars are 'Trade," "supply chains," "clean energy, decarbonization, infrastructure," and "tax and anti-corruption." Except for the trade pillar, India joined the IPEF's other three pillars. Through the IPEF, member nations from the Quad grouping and Southeast Asian nations are urged to strengthen their economic ties. These forums helped the US and India deepen their bilateral and strategic relationship.

Over the years, India's bilateral relationship with the U.S. has significantly grown into a "global strategic partnership". Under the strategic partnership, economic ties between the US and India significantly improved. In 2022, the trade and economic relations between both countries increased to a higher level, the US will be India's top trading partner, and India will be the US's seventh-largest trading partner.[37] As India-US ties strengthened, the economic and trade relations, it may reach USD 500-600 billion by 2030, said Commerce and Industry Minister of India, Piyush Goyal.[38] India for the first time started the 2+2 Ministerial Dialogue with the U.S. on September 6, 2018, to strengthen the bi-lateral relations and improve in diplomatic and security domains.[39] COMCASA agreement signed by both nations in the inaugural 2+2 dialogue. COMCASA stands for "Communications Compatibility and Security Agreement." Washington delivered secure data and communications technology to New Delhi via COMCASA. It also made it possible for the Indian and American militaries to exchange data in real time across encrypted channels.

In 2018, the United States also gave India "Strategic Trade Authorization-1" (STA-1) status. STA-1 permits the export of cutting-edge US defence and civil space products to India. In 2020, the "Basic Exchange and Cooperation Agreement" (BECA) signed by both countries. "The US National Geospatial-Intelligence Agency and India can communicate unclassified and controlled unclassified geospatial products, topographical, nautical, and aeronautical data, goods, and services due to the BECA."[40] India and the US also cooperate on building critical and emerging technologies. Both countries focused on research and development for next generation telecommunications like 5G and 6G. India expedited critical medical supplies and eased export limits during the COVID year as the US struggled with the COVID. The United States helped India to combat the COVID surge during the pandemic. The US-India partnership is important for finding solutions to global issues and will help establish stability in the entire world through various forms of cooperation. The benefit extends to the entire world, not just the Indo-Pacific region. The "United States Agency for International Development," or USAID, works closely with India's Development Partnership Administration to advance shared global development priorities, particularly in Asia and Africa.

Recently, the two organisations agreed to a five-year cooperation on areas like disaster risk reduction, clean and renewable energy, and climate-smart agriculture. When it comes to a permanent seat on the UN Security Council or in the NSG (Nuclear Suppliers Group), Washington backed the membership of India.[41] Furthermore, the United States openly supported India's position while condemning Beijing's territorial aggressiveness when it came to the border dispute between China and India or in any other instance of aggression. Despite continuing the S-400 agreement with Russia, the United States did not sanction India under the "Countering America's Adversaries Through Sanctions Act." CAATSA is a law that the US uses to sanction nations that interact with Iran, North Korea, and Russia. The greater India-US partnership is also beneficial for both of them. The US needs India's help to maintain the Indo-Pacific order as well as to maintain global order in the face of Chinese aggression, the COVID pandemic, and resource scarcity.[42] India needs a partner like the US to uphold regional stability and combat Chinese expansion in South Asia. China's expansion policy and various strategic movements in the region challenge India's geopolitical stand as well.

Conclusion

India's foreign policy in recent years has been characterised as fearless, independent, and good to others. India interacts in numerous global issues or international crises while maintaining its "strategic autonomy." India also preserves its strategic independence while deciding on its foreign policy with superpowers. The underlying value of "strategic autonomy" or independence serves as the basis of Indian foreign policy. India is a distinctive player on the world scene. India frequently adopts positions that do not serve its interests but are also influenced by its perception of being unique on the international stage, as evidenced by its recent or previous statements on issues of global importance, such as Iraq, Afghanistan, Ukraine, the NATO aerial campaign in Serbia, or the UNSC's handling of climate change. India's reaction to the new American policy is thus characterised by prudence and restraint to avoid getting sucked into the great-power conflict between China and the US.

India is neither pushed toward the West nor more or less affiliated with other blocks. India's approach to establish a regional balance of power in Asia that could be able to restrain China's aggressive objectives in the area. When deciding on its foreign policy toward the Quad or Indo-Pacific framework, India adopts a balancing stance. Furthermore, engagement in the Indo-Pacific framework and joining Quad benefited neighbourhood policies like the "Act East Policy," strengthened strategic ties with the United States, and increased India's geopolitical relevance in the South Asian region. To counter China's rising military power and the threat it poses to India's territorial integrity, border dispute, and influence in the larger Asia-Pacific region, India must externally balance or forge connections with the United States. New Delhi should "develop a varied network of links with multiple important nations, but avoiding relationships that go beyond signalling a particular threat level in Chinese perceptions" in order to make China consider India's position in Asia.

ENDNOTES

1. Weigrt, H.W, *Review: Haushofer and the Pacific,* Council on Foreign Relations, 732-742.
2. Nag Kalidas,1941, *India and the Pacific world.*
3. Kog, K. 2019. *Japan's "Free and Open Indo-Pacific" Strategy: Tokyo's Tactical Hedging and the Implications for ASEAN.* Contemporary Southeast Asia, 286-313.
4. Singh Inder, A.2018, *India and the U.S., Oceans apart*, The Hindu.
5. Scott, D.2018, France's "Indo-Pacific" strategy: regional power projection, Journal of Military and Military Studies,p.p-1-8.
6. *A Free and Open Indo-Pacific: Advancing A Shared Vision.*2019,Department of State, United States of Americ.
7. Pant, H.V.2015, *Indian Foreign Policy: Responds to the U.S.*,Asia Policy, 89-114.
8. Buchan Patrick G., Rimland B. 2020, *Defining the Diamond: The past, present and future of Quadrilateral Security Dialogue*, Centre for Strategic & and International Studies.
9. Australian Strategist Policy Institute.2019, *Quad 2.0: New perspective foe the revived concept.* The Strategist.
10. The White House.2021, *"The spirit of Quad"*, Quad leaders' joint statement, https://www.whitehouse.gov/briefing-room/statements-releases/2021/03/12/quad-leaders-joint-statement-the-spirit-of-the-quad/
11. *Ministry of External Affairs.*2022, Government of India, www.mea.gov.in
12. Ministry of External Affairs.2022, *Prime minister's participation in the Quad leaders' summit,* www.mea.gov.in
13. Kuo, M. A. 2018. *The origin of "Indo-Pacific" as a Geopolitical Construct.* Trans Pacific view, The Diplomat
14. *Quad desires 'Asian NATO', but China has smarter solutions*,2020, Global Times.
15. Jaishankar S. *Quad is not 'ASIAN NATO', India never had NATO mentality*, https://theprint.in/diplomacy/quad-is-not-asian-nato-india-never-had-nato-mentality-jaishankar-says/639924/
16. Shishir, U. 2022. *Do the AUKUS and Quad deter Chinese aggression against India?,* Australian Journal of Maritime and Ocean Affairs, p.p-1-14.
17. Davis E, A. B. 2020. *The Indian Ocean Region in the 21st century: geopolitical,economic and environmental ties.* Australia:Australia India Institute.
18. Ministry of External Affairs, *asean.mgc*. https://mea.gov.in/aseanindia/MGC
19. Ministry Of External Affairs, *Annual Report 1971-72.*

20. Ashraf, J. 2017. *String of Pearls and China's Emerging Strategic Culture.* Institute of Strategic Studies, p.p-166-181.
21. Kanwal, G. 2018. *China's Maritime Silk Road.* Center for Strategic and International Studies(CSIS).
22. Kumar, S. S. 2019. *China's Belt and Road Initiative (BRI): India's Concerns, Responses, and Strategies.* International Journal of China Studies. *10*(1), pp. 27-45.
23. Gangte, L. 2020. *The Debt-Trap Diplomacy Revisited: A Case Study on Sri Lanka's Hambantota.* Artha-Journal of Social Sciences. 19(2), 53-66.
24. Scott D.2018, *The Indo-Pacific in U.S. strategy: Responding to powershifts*, Rising Powers Quarterly Aug.2018. https://rpquarterly.kureselcalismalar.com/quarterly/the-indo-pacific-regional-dynamics-in-the-21st-centurys-new-geopolitical-center-of-gravity/
25. Jaishankar S. 2020, *The India Way*, Haryana, Harpar Collins Publications, India
26. Ministry of Defence,2015. *Mission SAGAR*. www. pib.gov.in
27. Jaishankar S. 2020, *The India Way*. Haryana, Harpar Collins Publications, India
28. Ministry of External Affairs, *Indian Ocean Rim Association and India's Role,*2017. https://mea.gov.in/Portal/ForeignRelation/IORA_new.pdf
29. Ngaibiakching, P. 2020. *India's Act East Policy and ASEAN: Building a Regional Order through partnership in the Indo-Pacific*, Sage Journals, 57(1), pp. 67- 78
30. Horam, M. 2022. *Indian Journal of Asian Affairs, 35*(1), 58-72.
31. Chaudhury, R. 2018, *Modi spells out free, open, inclusive Indo-Pacific policy*, https://www.iiss.org/blogs/analysis/2018/08/modi-free-open-inclusive.
32. Chaudhury, R.2018, *India's 'inclusive' Indo-pacific policy balances relations with US and China.* www.iiss.org
33. Sandhu, A.2022. *Convergence in Indo-Pacific gave new momentum to India-US strategic partnership,* The Print. https://theprint.in/world/convergence-in-indo-pacific-gave-new-momentum-to-india-us-strategic-partnership-amb-sandhu/1187519/
34. Nandy, D. 2019. *India-US bilateral relations in the Post-cold war years: Trends and Directions*, India in the New World Order.
35. US Department of State,2022. *U.S. relations with India, bilateral relations fact sheet*, Bureau of South and Central Asian Affairs.
36. *What is the I2U2.2022*, The New York Times
37. Bhardwaj, N.2022. *US Emerges as India's Largest Trade Partner in FY 2022, Surpasses China,* India Briefing.
38. PTI, P. T. 2022, November. *Outlook*. Retrieved from Outlook. India
39. Press Information Bureau. 2018, Government of India, Ministry of Defence, *Indo-US 2+2 Dialogue*.https://pib.gov.in/Pressreleaseshare.aspx?PRID=1557922#:~:text=Joint%20statement%20on%20the%20inaugural,Secretary%20of%20Defense%20James%20N.

40. *The 3 foundational agreements with US and what they mean for India's military growth. 2020.* The Print. https://theprint.in/defence/the-3-foundational-agreements-with-us-and-what-they-mean-for-indias-military-growth/531795/

41. *US supports India's permanent seat in UN Security Council, entry into NSG: Biden to Modi*, Sept,2021, India Today. https://www.indiatoday.in/world/story/biden-modi-meet-us-supports-india-permanent-seat-security-council-nsg-1857301-2021-09-25

42. Pant, H. V. 2015, *Indian Foreign Policy: Responds to the U.S. Pivot*, Asia Policy. pp-89-114.

9

India's Role in QUAD

– Gopika Pavithran

India and Quad

Since the mid-2000s, India has become a more active player in maritime security to shape the regional and global order. This has resulted in more naval exercises with more countries, actions and statements in support of international law, and separate strategic partnerships with the United States in 2005, Japan in 2006, and Australia in 2009. These bilateral engagements led to the "Quad" experiment in 2007 and a renewed substantive dialogue in 2017.[1] India and some like-minded countries promoted a liberal perspective on the matters of markets and laws in the Indo-Pacific region. China's intervention and their positions in many issues created a strategic turbulence in the world because they are not emerging because of their openness, respect for sovereignty, reciprocity and freedom of navigation.[2] Violent conflicts along the disputed border between India and China have caused a fundamental reorientation of Indian foreign policy.

India's approach to the Indo-Pacific region is captured in Prime Minister Narendra Modi's June 2018 speech at the Shangri La Dialogue in Singapore. He enumerated India's interests in this hyphenated region: an inclusive spirit, special focus on Southeast Asia after its primary focus on the Indian Ocean region, adherence to a rule-based order and the rule of law, open access to the commons including freedom of navigation, support for free trade, promotion of sustainable connectivity without predation, and amid an embrace of increasing competition, a support for cooperation rather than conflict.[3]

The Security and Growth for All in the Region (SAGAR) concept and the Indo-Pacific Oceans Initiative (IPOI) for marine security were both introduced by India in 2015 and 2018. India attempted to connect the SAGAR and IPOI goals with the Quad's goals in 2018. India has three strategic goals. First, it seeks to preserve the republic and its sovereignty by ensuring its territorial integrity and security of the neighborhood from internal and external threats.[4]

Second, it seeks to complete a "20th century nation building project" that ushers in prosperity through robust economic growth and poverty eradication.[5] Finally, India seeks to be a "leading power, rather than just a balancing power"[6] in a multipolar world by being brought into "agenda- setting institutions" with U.S. help, while not sacrificing its strategic autonomy to "restrictive expectations."[7]

These programes aim to restrain Chinese belligerence in the oceans. With India's participation, the Quad has advanced to a venue for international problem cooperation and has had frequent ministerial meetings. For instance, in Delhi, India, a Quad "CT-TTX" (counter-terrorism table-top exercise) was held in November 2019. At India's premier geopolitical forum, the Raisina Dialogue of 2018, 2019, and 2020, senior military officers also spoke on Quad-plus panels. India has also strengthened its bilateral connections with the Quad countries and gone beyond the Quad. India is the only country among the Quad members that directly shares a land border with China – a disputed border, at that, with a troubled history. It is therefore reasonable for India to not want to be seen as being part of an arrangement that is overtly against China. Apart from this, India is conscious of the fact that any grouping with undertones of an alliance will invite apprehensions from Southeast Asian nations that have direct stake and responsibility in the stability of the region.

India and Australia have a mutual logistical support agreement and an agreement on information exchange. Both nations have also held discussions on defence strategy and marine security as well as taken part in bilateral military drills including AUSINDEX (Australia India Exercise) and AUSTRA HIND. JIMEX (the Japan-India Maritime Exercise) and Dharma Guardian are two examples of bilateral military drills in which India and Japan have taken part. Both countries have signed agreements governing the exchange of goods and services as well as the general security of military information (GSOMIA).

Growing Cooperation among Member States

Essentially, it is viewed as a strategic alliance meant to weaken China's hold on the region. To provide freedom of navigation, a liberal economic system, and a rules-based global order is the Quad's main goal. In addition, the coalition wants to provide alternative debt funding to countries in the Indo-Pacific area.

The Quad leaders discuss current international concerns, including key and emerging technologies, connectivity and infrastructure, cyber security, maritime security, humanitarian aid, disaster relief, climate change, pandemics, and education.

India and the United States have strengthened their defence connections through agreements like the Logistics Exchange Memorandum and the General Security of Military Information Agreement (GSOMIA). With the help of accords like the Communications Compatibility and Security Agreement, the Logistics Exchange Memorandum of Agreement, and the General Security of Military Information Agreement, India and the United States have strengthened their defence connections (COMCASA). Joint peacekeeping training exercises and bilateral military drills like VAJRA PRAHAR, YUSH ABHYAS, COPE INDIA, and Tiger TRIUMPH have been conducted by the two nations.

India favors connectivity projects but sees China's infrastructure efforts, led in part by the BRI, as a direct challenge. It perceives China's increasing footprint in the Indian Ocean region to be a mission of either gradualist neo-colonial extraction or predatory lending for dual-use infrastructure that will trigger debt-for-equity swaps, strategic footholds, and outright militarization.[8]

Is the Quad Beneficial to India?

India has both benefits and drawbacks from joining the Quad. As was already indicated, India can counteract China's expanding influence in the Indo-Pacific through the Quad, including the BRI (Belt and Road Initiative), which has seen China build ports in nations bordering India, creating a feeling of encirclement in New Delhi. In contrast to other Quad members, India's Indo-Pacific policy seems to prioritize breadth over depth in its external relationships. India may be pursuing a soft-balancing strategy to restrain China, particularly through "limited alignments and informal ententes,"[9] but this is not the case for other Quad members. For instance, it said that its "Act East Policy is the cornerstone of its participation in the Indo-Pacific region" following the November 2017 Quad summit. With the help of the Quad, India may transcend its position as a middle-power and extend its influence beyond the Indo-Pacific. Additionally, India's engagement in the Indo-Pacific is strengthened by its Act East Policy and Extended Neighbor Policy.[10] India has been more cautious about leading the Quad in the Indo-Pacific and has gone considerably further than any of the other members to include an exit mechanism.[11] Because of its historic nonaligned status and confidence in its own status and material potential, India actively seeks to construct a multipolar order. This runs closer to China's declared preference while the United States, Japan, and Australia prefer a U.S.-led liberal international order that has only thrived under bipolarity or unipolarity.[12] India has historically been the most closed of the Quad economies and is seen by Western countries as a barrier to trade expansion and reforms, despite its verbal commitment to the concepts of free trade and open economies in the Indo-Pacific.

Due in part to its desire to liberalise various sectors more so than other Quad members, it has adopted several positions on free trade agreements in the area that appear to be at odds with one another. It was wary of the TPP and decided not to apply for membership. The Regional Comprehensive Economic Partnership, a free-trade pact between ASEAN, Australia, Japan, South Korea, New Zealand, China, and India, was cautioned about in April 2018 by the government think tank Niti Aayog. This is partly due to its concern that China and other nations will sabotage the accord. This is in part because it fears the agreement being swamped by China and widening India's trade deficit.

The bigger challenge for India is striking a compromise between its goals of safeguarding the commons, defending its industry, and thwarting the BRI with those of fostering trade and investment with China. India, a less developed economy, has less negotiating strength to reject Chinese economic incentives or resilience to endure future

Chinese economic coercion, whereas the economies of Japan and Australia are more dependent on trade with China. Its differences with the United States over whether to allow Chinese companies like Huawei to bid for contracts like 5G infrastructure development reveal a key tension between U.S. national security interests (shared in part by Australia and Japan) and Indian development interests.[13] India's security in the Indo-Pacific region is both internally and externally balancing. To defend its interests in the Indo-Pacific, India has been internally balancing against Chinese military strength by enhancing its military and power projection capabilities. India has prioritised counterbalancing China internationally to protect its strategic interests in the Indo-Pacific by developing or strengthening military alliances with several regional and global powers, most notably the United States.[14]

India's economy is less developed than that of Japan and Australia, which are more reliant on trade with China. As a result, it has less leverage to reject Chinese economic incentives and less resilience to endure potential Chinese economic coercion. In addition, with the Quad as a backdrop, India's bilateral ties with "like-minded" nations can be further expanded through information-sharing agreements, arms exchange agreements, defence partnerships, and more. In terms of the economy, the Quad will also make India a top choice for investment, particularly in light of the COVID-19 epidemic.

India is viewed as a major role in the post-pandemic international order as a result of its efforts to distribute COVID-19 vaccinations to other countries, known as "Vaccine Maitri." The Quad is important for India because it offers the chance to increase its pharmacological expertise and to assert its leadership in the post-pandemic world through economic collaboration, shared democratic principles, and solid defence relations.

Conclusion

To balance China's power projection in the East and South China Seas, the United States and its allies Japan and Australia appear committed to using diplomatic, economic, and especially military means either to contain it within the First or Second Island Chains or at the very least to ensure that it is used responsibly. India demonstrates considerable variance in interests and skills even though it shares the same language and ideas with its Quad partners. Politically, it still views entanglements with suspicion and gains from being sought after as a swing state.

India continues to feel that it will benefit economically more from increasing engagement with a rising China than from containment, despite efforts by other Quad partners to lessen their exposure. The other Quad countries have benefited from and may focus on enhancing the stopping power of water, whereas it is stretched thinner in terms of security by numerous adversaries across multiple domains. India's approach to the Free and Open Indo-Pacific requires a broader range of allies and resources due to its strategic goals.

In the end, this can reduce the Quad's overall utility rather than increase it. The Free and Open Indo-Pacific architecture is one of the main ideals, objectives, and capabilities that the Quad is meant to generate convergence on, but it will be put to the test by centrifugal forces, most notably those from India, which will prevent or at least significantly delay convergence.

Divergent priorities and lower capabilities will continue to constrain India's participation to and integration with the Quad in the medium to long term absent significant adjustments to structural incentives. The strategic divergence exists between the member states' strategies, modalities, and priorities. Second, divergence by definition makes it challenging to present a united front and may encourage adversarial attempts at political dissociation. Thirdly, divergence reveals inconsistent expectations. Unmet inflated expectations can lead to further disagreements and even more protracted confrontations. Within competitive democratic politics, feelings of free-riding, entanglement, or abandonment can fuel nationalist responses. Finally, understanding divergences aids policymakers in understanding the expenses associated with alliance or alignment management. Instead of assuming that the Free and Open Indo-Pacific will be composed of frictionless "natural" alliances, policymakers need to foresee and plan for the costs of negotiation as well as the diplomatic instruments to make sure the construct is long-lasting. The United States, Japan, and Australia may need to consider alternate conceptions if the Quad seems to be turning into more of a three-legged chair with less Indian engagement to achieve interest convergence and a combined capability to balance a rising China.

One such alternative might be to embrace India as one node within a networked security architecture or federated defence concept, alongside several other partnerships, including those with the Philippines, Thailand, Vietnam, Indonesia, and Singapore, and to lower expectations from seeing it as a "major defence partner." Another option might be to make significant diplomatic investments and provide far larger incentives to fundamentally alter India's decision-making process. Third, it can choose to compete with China using a non-zero-sum strategy so that it can, alongside numerous other alliances, including those with the Philippines, Thailand, Vietnam, Indonesia, and Singapore, as one node within a networked security architecture or federated defence concept.

It seems unlikely that the current strategy and pace of harmonising balancing efforts will result in a unified Free and Open Indo-Pacific strategy during the following ten years if one of these improvements is not made. India has always insisted that the Quad becomes an open, constructive forum that ties together the capabilities of member countries to ensure security and stability in the region in a comprehensive way, not limited to security aspects. Making sure the Quad does not overtly identify with "alliance politics" is one reflection of this attitude, which became clear in the way the Quad addressed the Russia-Ukraine conflict. It is clear that China had initially opposed the formation of Quad and since then, China's position has not changed. In 2018, the Chinese Foreign Minister had referred to the Quad, as a "headline-grabbing idea", and accused the group of openly inciting discord among regional powers in Asia. Beijing sees the existence of the Quad, as part of a larger strategy to encircle China, and has pressured countries like Bangladesh to avoid cooperating with the group.

ENDNOTES

1. Sameer Lalwani, Reluctant link? India, the Quad, and the free and open Indo-Pacific C
2. Vinayak Maura, Securing India's economic and security interests in the Indo-Pacific
3. Speech by Narendra Modi, Prime Minister's Keynote Address at Shangri La Dialogue, Ministry of External Affairs of India, June 1, 2018.
4. Dhruva Jaishankar, 'Indian Strategy in a Non-Strategic Age,' in Atul K. Thakur (ed.), India Now and in Transition, Niyogi Books, 2017.

5. Abhijnan Rej, "Reclaiming the Indo-Pacific: A Political-Military Strategy for Quad," Observer Research Foundation, March 2018.
6. Ministry of External Affairs of India, "IISS Fullerton Lecture by Dr. S. Jaishankar, Foreign Secretary in Singapore," July 20, 2015.
7. Alyssa Ayres, "Will India Start Acting Like a Global Power?" Foreign Affairs, November/December 2017, pp. 90-91.
8. Brahma Chellaney, "China's Debt-Trap Diplomacy," Project Syndicate, January 23, 2017
9. T.V. Paul, "Restraining Great Powers: Soft Balancing from Empires to the Global Era," Yale University Press, 2018, p. 26.
10. Ministry of External Affairs of India, "India-Australia-Japan-U.S. Consultations on Indo-Pacific," November 12, 2017.
11. Rajesh Rajagopalan, "India's Strategic Choices: China and the Balance of Power in Asia," Carnegie Endowment, September 14, 2017
12. Sameer Lalwani, Reluctant link? India, the Quad, and the free and open Indo-Pacific
13. Newley Purnell, Rajesh Roy, and Dustin Volz, "U.S. Campaign Against Huawei Runs Aground in an Exploding Tech Market," Wall Street Journal, February 21, 2019
14. Sameer Lalwani, Reluctant link? India, the Quad, and the free and open Indo-Pacific

REFERENCES

1. Alyssa Ayres, "Will India Start Acting Like a Global Power?" Foreign Affairs, November/December 2017.
2. Sameer Lalwani, Reluctant link? India, the Quad, and the free and open Indo-Pacific
3. Vinayak Maura, Securing India's economic and security interests in the Indo-Pacific
4. Speech by Narendra Modi, Prime Minister's Keynote Address at Shangri La Dialogue, Ministry of External Affairs of India, June 1, 2018.
5. Dhruva Jaishankar, 'Indian Strategy in a Non-Strategic Age,' in Atul K. Thakur (ed.), India Now and in Transition, Niyogi Books, 2017.
6. Abhijnan Rej, "Reclaiming the Indo-Pacific: A Political-Military Strategy for Quad 2.0," Observer Research Foundation, March 2018.
7. T.V. Paul, "Restraining Great Powers: Soft Balancing from Empires to the Global Era," Yale University Press, 2018, p. 26.
8. Rajesh Rajagopalan, "India's Strategic Choices: China and the Balance of Power in Asia," Carnegie Endowment, September 14, 2017
9. Newley Purnell, Rajesh Roy, and Dustin Volz, "U.S. Campaign Against Huawei Runs Aground in an Exploding Tech Market," Wall Street Journal, February 21, 2019
10. Brahma Chellaney, "China's Debt-Trap Diplomacy," Project Syndicate, January 23, 2017

10

The QUAD and India-China Relation: An Indian Perspective

– **Kalpesh Bag**

Introduction

India and China are the two major political actors in international politics, Indo-Pacific being a strategic area of concern of late, not only for the mentioned two but also for the western powers and their allied forces. The unwanted tensions in Indo-China relations have been historically triggered by their geopolitical rivalries and border disputes. However, discussions have erupted ever since the Quadrilateral Security Dialogue (QUAD) or "QUAD 2.0" between India, the United States, Australia, and Japan entered into the picture in the Indo-Pacific region about the potential mistrust and suspicion Quad could further cause in the Chinese minds concerning its deteriorating relation with India.

Although, India's approach to the Quadrilateral Consultative Forum is a declaration of New Delhi's diversified foreign policy arc in a developing Indo-Pacific architecture. India's strategic autonomy and pluralism in its foreign policy can be explained by balancing China's expanding outreach to the Indo-Pacific region while still affirming bilateralism with Beijing. This does not imply India is pursuing a China containment strategy, but rather it indicates New Delhi's strategic outreach to strengthen its position within a liberal-order framework. India's vested interest in Quad is more comprehensive and non-traditional security perspective oriented. In the Indo-Pacific framework, China's relationship with India is now more crucial. Similarly, it would be incorrect to interpret India's participation in the Quad as being hostile to China.

Context: The Quad in the Indo-Pacific

The Emergence of the Quad

The genesis of the Quadrilateral Security Dialogue (Quad) dates back to the aftermath of the devastating Boxing Day tsunami in 2004, which prompted an ad hoc coalition known as the "Tsunami Core Group." Comprising the United States, Japan, India, and Australia, this group initially aimed to address new security challenges beyond traditional state sovereignty issues. These challenges, rooted in the non-traditional security perspective, encompassed concerns like disaster management and human security.

In 2006, the concept gained ideological momentum with Japan's then-Prime Minister Shinzo Abe proposing the "Arc of Freedom and Prosperity."[1] This visionary initiative envisioned a network of nations across the Eurasian Continent united by Japan's diplomatic efforts to promote liberty and the rule of law. The first formal meeting of the Quad occurred in May 2007 during the ASEAN Regional Forum (ARF) in Manila, described as an informal grouping focusing on shared interests such as disaster relief.

Initially proposed by the United States in 2006, Quad 1.0 aimed to establish a regional consultative forum rather than a military alliance, despite perceptions by China labeling it as an "Asian NATO".[2] While China and Russia viewed the Quad as potentially shaping security dynamics in the Indian Ocean region, India maintained its autonomous foreign policy stance, although Beijing often perceived New Delhi as pro-American.

The formal advancement of the Quad gained momentum in December 2006 during discussions between India and Japan, coinciding with former Indian Prime Minister Manmohan Singh's visit to Tokyo. This marked the beginning of dialogue processes aimed at developing modalities with like-minded nations in the Asia-Pacific region.

The only military exercise associated with Quad 1.0 was an expanded version of the US-India Malabar series, held in late September 2007 in the Bay of Bengal. This exercise included naval forces from all four Quad nations along with the Singaporean navy, focusing on personnel exchanges, multi-carrier operations, and sea control drills.

However, the Quad faced significant opposition, particularly from China, which formally protested against the initiative. Even non-Quad member nations like the Republic of Korea expressed skepticism about the alliance, emphasizing their reluctance to choose between China's economic influence and the United States' security partnership.

Critics speculated that the Quad might evolve into an Asian NATO or a formal security alliance due to ambiguity surrounding its objectives. In response to mounting Chinese pressure, Australian, Indian, American, and Japanese officials sought to distance the Quad from explicit security agendas, emphasizing its consultative and cooperative nature.

Revival of the Quad (Quad 2.0)

The concept of the Quadrilateral Security Dialogue (Quad) saw a resurgence when Shinzo Abe, upon returning to office in December 2012, described it as "Asia's democratic security diamond." He envisioned a strategic alliance involving Australia, India, Japan, and the United States, extending from the Indian Ocean Region to the western Pacific to safeguard maritime commons.[3]

In October 2017, then-Secretary of State Rex Tillerson and Japanese Foreign Minister Taro Kono proposed the revival of the Quad dialogue. This initiative materialized on November 12, 2017, when assistant secretary-level delegates from the four nations convened in Manila, discussing topics ranging from North Korea's denuclearization to support for a "Free and Open Indo-Pacific" and the promotion of a rules based order in the region.

The first in-person Quad leaders' meeting took place in September 2021, hosted by US President Joe Biden. During this event, Prime Minister Narendra Modi expressed confidence that the quartet would serve as a "force for global good," fostering peace and prosperity in the Indo-Pacific and beyond.[4] Discussions at the meeting focused on managing the COVID-19 pandemic, addressing climate change, and advancing cooperative efforts in various domains.

The most recent Quad meeting occurred on May 24, 2022, where leaders proposed ambitious initiatives aimed at strengthening relationships and addressing 21st-century challenges. These initiatives include enhancing vaccine production and access, promoting high-standard infrastructure, collaborating on climate issues, advancing in emerging technologies, space, and cybersecurity, and nurturing talent development across the member nations.[5]

Since its revival, the Quad's role has evolved to encompass a comprehensive agenda, although each member retains its individual interests. Australia and Japan maintain closer ties with the United States as allies across various domains. In contrast, India's approach within the Quad differs, reflecting its unique strategic perspective.

India's Evolving Approach in the Indo-Pacific: Role and Objectives in the Quad

India's strategic position in the Indo-Pacific region has gained prominence as a counterbalance to China's expanding influence in the Indian Ocean. This strategic imperative is driven by India's concerns over China's encirclement strategy, particularly through port developments like Gwadar and Hambantota in neighbouring countries. Additionally, India seeks to safeguard open sea lanes against potential disruptions posed by China's activities in the South China Sea and its increasing maritime presence in the Indian Ocean, often under the guise of anti-piracy operations.[6]

Prime Minister Narendra Modi articulated India's strategy for the Indo-Pacific during his address at the Shangri-La Dialogue in June 2018. He emphasized India's interests in maintaining an open, rules-based order that ensures freedom of navigation, supports free trade, promotes sustainable connectivity, and fosters cooperation over conflict.[7]

India's recent engagements and high-level dialogues on the Free and Open Indo-Pacific concept align closely with those of other Quad members. However, India's approach stands out due to its unique national interests and strategic priorities. India's strategic objectives in the Indo-Pacific can be categorized into three main areas:

Firstly, India aims to safeguard its territorial integrity and the surrounding region from both internal and external threats, ensuring sovereignty and security. Secondly, India pursues a nation-building agenda for the twenty-first century, aiming at robust economic growth and poverty eradication. Thirdly, India seeks to enhance its global influence by engaging with agenda-setting institutions and positioning itself as a leading power in a multipolar world. This objective is pursued in collaboration with the United States while maintaining India's strategic autonomy and resisting external constraints.

India's Evolving Approach in the Indo-Pacific

India's geographic and geopolitical significance in the Indo-Pacific region plays a crucial role in countering China's expanding influence, particularly in the Indian Ocean. This strategic imperative is driven by India's concerns over China's encirclement strategy, exemplified by its development of port facilities in neighboring countries like Gwadar in Pakistan and Hambantota in Sri Lanka. Additionally, India is vigilant about safeguarding open and free sea lanes of communication amidst China's increasing maritime presence, often justified under the guise of anti-piracy operations.

Prime Minister Narendra Modi articulated India's strategy for the Indo-Pacific at the Shangri-La Dialogue in 2018, highlighting several key interests. These include a commitment to a rules-based international order, freedom of navigation, support for free trade, sustainable connectivity initiatives devoid of predatory practices, and a preference for cooperation over conflict in managing regional dynamics.

Despite aligning with other Quad members on the concept of a Free and Open Indo-Pacific, India distinguishes itself through its unique strategic objectives. First, India prioritizes safeguarding its territorial integrity and sovereignty against both internal and external threats. Second, it pursues a comprehensive nation-building agenda aimed at achieving robust economic growth and eliminating poverty. Third, India seeks to enhance its global stature by participating in and shaping international institutions with the support of partners like the United States, emphasizing its role as a leading power rather than merely a balancing one in a multipolar world.

This approach underscores India's multifaceted strategy in the Indo-Pacific, balancing security imperatives with economic development goals and strategic autonomy. It positions India as a pivotal player in regional affairs, contributing to stability and shaping the evolving geopolitical landscape of the Indo-Pacific. As India navigates these complexities, its engagement within frameworks like the Quad reflects its commitment to advancing shared interests while preserving its distinct national priorities and strategic objectives.

Geopolitical Interests

India's geopolitical interests in the Quad and the broader Indo-Pacific region are multifaceted and strategically nuanced. Here are some key aspects of India's geopolitical interests as outlined:

1. Involvement in ASEAN: India's engagement with ASEAN countries is crucial for its regional diplomacy and economic interests. ASEAN serves as a linchpin for India's "Act East" policy, fostering deeper economic integration, cultural ties, and strategic partnerships in Southeast Asia.
2. Enhancing Connectivity in Asia: India places significant emphasis on enhancing connectivity across Asia, particularly through initiatives like the International North-South Transport Corridor (INSTC) and the Asia-Africa Growth Corridor (AAGC). These efforts aim to bolster trade routes, infrastructure development, and economic linkages across the region.[8]
3. Supporting International Rule of Law: India upholds the rule-based international order and advocates for freedom of navigation in global commons, including the Indo-Pacific region. This stance underscores India's commitment to maintaining maritime security and stability, essential for regional prosperity.
4. Nonalignment Preferences: India's historical stance of nonalignment shapes its geopolitical strategy, emphasizing strategic autonomy and avoiding entanglements in bloc politics. This approach allows India to engage flexibly with various global powers and regional groupings based on its national interests.
5. Strategic Inclusivity (or Promiscuity): India's foreign policy exhibits strategic inclusivity, engaging with a diverse array of countries and groupings beyond traditional alliances. This

approach enables India to pursue multiple partnerships while maintaining independence in decision-making.

6. Preference for Multipolarity: India advocates for a multipolar world order, reflecting its belief in balanced power dynamics and diverse centers of influence. This preference contrasts with the more unilateral or bipolar perspectives often favored by other Quad members.

India's geopolitical interests in the Quad and the Indo-Pacific region reflect its aspirations for regional stability, economic growth, and a rules-based international order. These interests also underscore India's role as a key player in shaping the strategic landscape of Asia, navigating complex dynamics while advancing its national priorities and global aspirations.

Advocating a Multipolar World

India's advocacy for a multipolar world order[9], is deeply rooted in its historical nonalignment, strategic autonomy, and vision for global governance that accommodates diverse centers of power. Here are the key points that illustrate India's stance on advocating a multipolar world:

1. Nonalignment Tradition: India's foreign policy has traditionally been nonaligned, dating back to its post-independence era under leaders like Jawaharlal Nehru. Nonalignment allows India to maintain independence in foreign relations, avoiding alignment with any major power blocs or alliances.

2. Confidence in Own Position: India's growing economic and military capabilities bolster its confidence in shaping global affairs as a major player. India seeks to leverage its position as a significant regional power to influence global norms and governance structures.

3. Preference for Multipolarity: India prefers a multipolar world order, where power is distributed among multiple major actors rather than dominated by a single or a few powers. This aligns with its belief that a multipolar system promotes greater stability, inclusivity, and accommodates diverse geopolitical interests.

4. Divergence from Quad Partners: The Quad, comprising the U.S., Japan, Australia, and India, often emphasizes a liberal international order and strategic coalitions. While India collaborates within the Quad framework on specific issues, its broader vision diverges from the coalition-driven approaches of its Quad partners.
5. Strategic Autonomy: India values its strategic autonomy, which allows it to engage with various global powers and regional groupings based on its national interests and without being constrained by alliance commitments or bloc politics.
6. Critique of Bipolarity or Unipolarity: India is critical of bipolar or unipolar world orders, which it perceives as leading to power imbalances, hegemonic tendencies, and less room for maneuverability for countries with diverse interests like itself.

Overall, India's advocacy for a multipolar world order reflects its strategic aspirations for a balanced global governance structure that accommodates multiple centers of influence. This approach underscores India's role as a key player in shaping the future of international relations while navigating complex geopolitical dynamics in the Indo-Pacific and beyond.

Coping with Human Security Issues Like COVID-19

India's response to the COVID-19 pandemic underscored its proactive engagement in addressing regional and global health emergencies, while also highlighting its strategic alignment within the Quad framework and broader international cooperation. Here are the key aspects of India's role and actions during the pandemic:

1. Regional and Global Medical Assistance: India swiftly provided medical assistance to its neighboring countries and beyond. Countries such as Seychelles, Mauritius, Sri Lanka, Maldives, Iran, and Italy received significant aid from India, including medical supplies and personnel.[6] This proactive assistance demonstrated India's capacity and willingness to contribute to global health efforts.
2. Multilateral Initiatives: India took the lead in organizing multilateral responses to the pandemic. Notably, it initiated the

"Extraordinary Virtual G20 Leaders' Summit" and convened a SAARC web conference to coordinate regional responses. India also established the SAARC Emergency Response Fund for COVID-19, emphasizing regional cooperation in tackling the health crisis.

3. Quad-Plus Engagement: The pandemic catalyzed the expansion of the Quad framework to include additional Indo-Pacific nations and stakeholders, forming what was informally termed as "Quad-Plus."[10] This expansion aimed at leveraging convergent security interests to collectively address the challenges posed by COVID-19 and beyond.
4. Military and Strategic Involvement: India's armed forces played a crucial role in supporting its medical diplomacy efforts. They were instrumental in executing India's missions abroad, facilitating medical evacuations and deploying rapid response teams to assist countries in need.
5. Strategic Alignment and Security Perimeter: The pandemic context also highlighted the Quad's evolving role beyond traditional security concerns. While addressing human security challenges like COVID-19, the Quad members implicitly reinforced their strategic alignment in responding to China's assertive actions and diplomatic maneuvers in the region.[6]

India's response to the pandemic not only showcased its capabilities in crisis management but also reinforced its commitment to regional stability and global health cooperation. By actively participating in multilateral initiatives and expanding collaborative frameworks like the Quad-Plus, India positioned itself as a proactive contributor to shaping the future of Indo-Pacific security and governance. These efforts underscore India's strategic flexibility and its capacity to navigate complex geopolitical dynamics while pursuing its national interests and global responsibilities.

Freedom of Trade and Navigation

India's strategic stance on economic goals in the Indo-Pacific, particularly regarding free trade and navigation,[11] reflects its complex geopolitical position and economic imperatives. Here are the key points regarding India's approach:

1. Support for Economic Goals: India advocates for free trade, ensuring security of common spaces for navigation, and prioritizes non-predatory connectivity projects in the Indo-Pacific. These goals align with India's broader interests in regional stability, economic growth, and integration.
2. Differences with Quad Allies: While India shares these economic goals with Quad allies (United States, Japan, Australia), there are nuanced differences driven by India's unique economic challenges.[12] Unlike its Quad counterparts, India faces significant issues such as poverty, underemployment, and skill shortages, which impact its economic strategy and priorities.
3. Selective Opposition to BRI: India has been cautious about endorsing China's Belt and Road Initiative (BRI), citing concerns over sovereignty, debt sustainability, and the potential for China to dominate regional infrastructure projects. Despite this, India has also sought to engage with China economically, balancing between opposing aspects of the BRI while encouraging Chinese investments in India.
4. Maritime Trade Importance: India's economy heavily relies on maritime trade, with about 90% of its trade being seaborne.[13] This underscores the critical importance of advocating for freedom of navigation in the Indo-Pacific, ensuring open sea lanes and maritime security, which are vital for India's economic growth and stability.
5. Geopolitical Balancing Act: India's approach to economic initiatives in the Indo-Pacific reflects a careful balancing act between promoting its economic interests, engaging with strategic allies like the Quad, and managing relations with China. This dynamic requires India to navigate through asymmetries in capabilities, accommodate varying interests within the Quad, and leverage its economic potential to advance regional stability.

In conclusion, India's advocacy for economic goals in the Indo-Pacific, including free trade and navigation, is shaped by its unique economic challenges and strategic imperatives. Balancing between supporting regional economic integration and safeguarding its national interests, India plays a crucial role in shaping the economic architecture of the region while maintaining strategic autonomy and managing geopolitical complexities.

India's Plural Security Perspective

India's plural security perspective in the Indo-Pacific region reflects a nuanced approach aimed at safeguarding its interests amidst shifting geopolitical dynamics.[14] Here's an elaboration on India's strategic stance:

1. Diversified Strategic Partnerships: India pursues a strategy of hedging by cultivating diverse strategic partnerships across the globe. This approach is rooted in the belief that maintaining multiple partnerships enhances its flexibility and resilience in international relations. However, it also presents challenges such as resource allocation and the potential for sending conflicting messages, particularly among traditional allies like the United States and Japan who may perceive India's partnerships with countries like Iran and Russia as undermining the liberal international order.
2. Maritime Security and Power Projection: India prioritizes the protection of its maritime interests in the Indo-Pacific, given its heavy reliance on seaborne trade. To bolster its capabilities in this domain, India has significantly invested in enhancing its naval and military prowess. This includes being one of the largest arms importers globally over the past decade, with a focus on acquiring advanced military technologies and building strategic alliances with nations such as the United States, Japan, France, and Canada.[15] These alliances facilitate joint naval exercises and access to critical port facilities across the region.
3. Internal and External Balancing: Internally, India continues to strengthen its military capabilities to counterbalance China's growing military presence in the region.[16] Externally, India engages in alliances and partnerships to further bolster its strategic position and ensure a robust defense posture against potential threats. This dual approach of internal and

external balancing underscores India's proactive stance in safeguarding its territorial integrity and geopolitical interests.

4. Quad Dynamics and Multipolar Asian Structure: India views the Quad, comprising the United States, Japan, Australia, and itself, as a strategic initiative aimed at promoting a multipolar Asian order. While the Quad is not explicitly aimed at containing China, it serves as a platform to address regional security challenges and promote a rules-based international order in the Indo-Pacific. India's participation in the Quad is driven by its aspiration to balance China's influence and uphold a diverse and inclusive regional architecture.
5. Impact of China's Rise: China's assertive policies, such as the Belt and Road Initiative (BRI) and its military maneuvers in the South China Sea, have influenced India's strategic calculus in the Indo-Pacific. India perceives these actions as potentially limiting its economic engagement and strategic maneuverability, prompting closer alignment with Quad partners to mitigate perceived threats and enhance regional stability.[17]
6. Power Equilibrium, Not Containment: India's involvement in the Quad is not aimed at containing China but rather at establishing a power equilibrium in the Indo-Pacific. This nuanced approach acknowledges China's growing influence while seeking to maintain a balance that ensures regional stability and safeguards India's interests. The Quad serves as a forum to address common challenges and promote a rules-based international order, rather than targeting any specific country.[18]
7. Security Considerations: Despite its participation in the Quad, India recognizes that the group does not provide a direct security guarantee against China or any other potential adversary. The Quad's primary focus is on non-traditional security issues such as disaster relief, maritime security, and economic cooperation. India's security concerns, particularly in border disputes like the Doklam standoff, remain separate from the Quad's operational scope, which emphasizes broader strategic cooperation rather than mutual defense.

8. Evolution of Quad's Objectives: Over time, the objectives of the Quad have evolved to address emerging challenges and opportunities in the Indo-Pacific region. While initially focusing on maritime security and disaster response, the Quad has expanded its agenda to include economic resilience, technology cooperation, and public health, as evidenced by its response during the COVID-19 pandemic. This evolution reflects the Quad's adaptive approach to regional dynamics and its commitment to enhancing collective capabilities.[19]
9. Strategic Alignment with Liberal Order: India's approach to the Indo-Pacific aligns strategically with the liberal international order promoted by countries like the United States. India emphasizes inclusiveness, consultation, and cooperation in regional development initiatives such as the Asia-Africa Growth Corridor (AAGC), which contrasts with China's unilateral Belt and Road Initiative (BRI). The AAGC underscores India's commitment to fostering connectivity, infrastructure development, and economic growth based on mutual benefits and respect for sovereignty.[20]

In summary, India's approach to the Indo-Pacific is characterized by strategic autonomy, diversified partnerships, and a proactive stance in safeguarding its maritime and geopolitical interests. By engaging with a range of global and regional actors, India seeks to maintain flexibility in navigating complex geopolitical challenges while advocating for a multipolar regional order conducive to its long-term security and economic goals. India's engagement in the Quad and its broader Indo-Pacific strategy are shaped by the pursuit of strategic equilibrium, cooperation on non-traditional security issues, and alignment with a liberal international order. These efforts are intended to promote regional stability, economic development, and inclusive growth while addressing shared challenges collaboratively.

The Dynamics Quad and India-China Relations

Recent geopolitical tensions and strategic divergences have strained relations between China and India. Despite occasional improvements, such as cooperation at COP26 in Glasgow on climate issues, their historical conflicts, including the 1962 border war and subsequent skirmishes, continue to influence their bilateral dynamics.[21] A bilateral agreement in 1968 eased tensions until 2017, with intermittent incidents like the Doklam standoff in 2017 and the more recent border confrontation in December 2021 highlighting ongoing vulnerabilities.[22]

While interactions between India and China have fluctuated, their relationships with other nations, including the United States, Japan, and neighboring Pakistan, play significant roles in regional stability.[23] The reactivation of the Quadrilateral Security Dialogue (Quad 2.0) in 2017–2018, comprising Australia, India, Japan, and the United States, has added another layer to regional geopolitics. The Quad's Indo-Pacific focus aims to address regional power dynamics and promote a rule-based international order, potentially impacting India-China relations.

India's strategic calculus involves navigating its relationship with China while engaging with global partners through forums like the Quad. This approach supports India's preference for a multipolar Asia, in contrast to China's aspirations for regional dominance. China, on the other hand, seeks cooperative frameworks with India within a multipolar Asia framework, as evidenced by initiatives like the Belt and Road Forum.

In conclusion, India-China relations are shaped by their evolving internal and foreign policies, influenced by geopolitical dynamics and global power shifts. India's participation in the Quad and its bilateral engagements with China reflect its strategic efforts to balance regional security imperatives while promoting a multipolar world order. This nuanced approach aims to manage China's assertiveness in South Asia and the Indian Ocean region while preserving strategic autonomy and stability.

Limitations in India-China Relations

Despite occasional efforts to improve relations, several factors impede closer ties between China and India. Firstly, their divergent foreign policy initiatives, particularly regarding security and resource interests in regions like the Indian Ocean and ASEAN, often lead to conflicting priorities. China perceives India as a regional power with limited influence, while India views itself as a custodian of the Indian Ocean, leading to mutual suspicions.

Secondly, differences over economic cooperation pose another challenge. India's strong objections to China's Belt and Road Initiative (BRI) illustrate contrasting economic visions, hindering prospects for a substantial development partnership. Additionally, India remains wary of China's increasing assertiveness in maritime affairs, which could exacerbate tensions over control of maritime spaces, despite no active maritime conflicts between the two countries.

The rejection of the BRI by India exemplifies deep-seated perception gaps and mutual mistrust, suggesting that bilateral relations are unlikely to improve significantly unless these fundamental issues are addressed. China's persistence in urging India to reconsider its stance on the BRI while failing to understand India's concerns further complicates the situation. Consequently, India's Indo-Pacific strategy emphasizes hedging through engagement with Quad countries and enhancing connectivity with ASEAN nations.

Moreover, mutual distrust exacerbates the situation, with each side often attributing negative motives to the other's actions while viewing its own actions positively. This mutual suspicion is rooted in a lack of trust and differing perceptions of each other's national identities.[24] China may not perceive India as a threat but fails to acknowledge India's regional and global aspirations, contributing to India's dissatisfaction with the bilateral relationship.

In conclusion, while sporadic cooperation efforts exist, fundamental differences in strategic goals, economic visions, and mutual perceptions continue to hinder significant improvement in India-China relations. Addressing these underlying issues remains crucial for fostering a more stable and cooperative relationship in the future.

Measures to Wane the Suspicion Caused by QUAD

To mitigate the suspicion and tension caused by perceptions of the Quad and other factors between China and India, several measures could be considered:

1. Mutual Dialogue and Cooperation: Both countries should prioritize open and constructive dialogue on all issues, including contentious topics like border disputes. Establishing regular high-level dialogues can help build mutual understanding and trust over time.[25]

2. Compromise and Negotiation: Both sides should demonstrate willingness to compromise and negotiate in good faith to find mutually acceptable solutions to longstanding issues, such as border disputes. This approach can help reduce tensions and pave the way for broader cooperation.
3. Revisiting Agreements and Understandings: India and China must reaffirm and build upon previous agreements, such as those regarding border management and confidence-building measures dating back to 1993. Clarifying the Line of Actual Control (LAC) and adhering to existing protocols can prevent misunderstandings and incidents along the border.
4. Economic Engagement: Strengthening economic ties and trade relations between India and China can provide a stable foundation for bilateral relations. Closing the trade gap and enhancing economic cooperation could foster greater interdependence and mutual benefits.
5. Building Trust through Collaboration: Both countries should explore collaborative efforts on regional and global issues of mutual interest, such as public health, climate change, and technology standards. Working together in these areas can demonstrate the benefits of cooperation and help build trust.
6. Respecting Each Other's Alliances: India's partnership with the United States and China's alliance with Pakistan are sensitive issues that require careful consideration of each other's legitimate interests. Both sides should strive to avoid actions that undermine the security or interests of the other party's allies.[26]
7. Addressing Perceptions and Public Diplomacy: Acknowledging and addressing public perceptions and misperceptions is crucial. China should work to improve its public image in India, possibly through transparent actions and improved communication about its intentions and policies.
8. Long-term Strategic Stability: Both countries should work towards establishing long-term strategic stability in the region. This includes maintaining military balance, avoiding provocative actions, and committing to peaceful resolution of disputes.

By adopting these measures, India and China can potentially mitigate suspicion, reduce tensions, and pave the way for more stable and cooperative relations in the Indo-Pacific region. Each step should prioritize mutual respect, transparency, and the pursuit of shared interests for sustainable peace and development.

Conclusion

In conclusion, the 21st century has underscored the strategic significance of the Indo-Pacific region, which serves as a vital link in global maritime trade between the West and Asia. China's assertive expansion in the South China Sea and Indian Ocean reflects its ambitions to establish itself as a global power. In this context, the Quadrilateral Security Dialogue (Quad) assumes a critical role in shaping regional dynamics.

The Quad, comprising the United States, Japan, Australia, and India, aims not only for collective development but also seeks to promote global public goods. However, each member state maintains its distinct national interests within the Quad framework. Australia and Japan often align closely with U.S. policies, while India pursues an independent stance on various global issues, as evidenced by its decision to continue importing crude oil from Russia despite U.S. sanctions during the Russia-Ukraine conflict.[27]

Nevertheless, the Quad has demonstrated its potential to address non-traditional security challenges, as seen during the COVID-19 pandemic. It provided a platform for cooperation that extended beyond military and strategic concerns to include humanitarian and health emergencies.

For the Quad to contribute effectively to regional stability, China must move beyond its apprehensions of containment and recognize India's role within the group. By fostering stronger bilateral ties and engaging constructively with India, China can help promote peace and stability in the Indo-Pacific region. This approach could mitigate tensions and pave the way for cooperative efforts on shared challenges, benefiting all stakeholders in the region.

In essence, while the Quad navigates its complexities and diverse member interests, its potential to shape regional security and cooperation remains significant, contingent upon constructive engagement and mutual understanding among its members and with external stakeholders like China.

ENDNOTES

1. Buchan, P. G., & Rimland, B. (2020). *Defining the Diamond: The Past, Present, and Future of the Quadrilateral Security Dialogue*. Center for Strategic and International Studies (CSIS). http://www.jstor.org/stable/resrep24258
2. Panda, J. P. (Aug, 2018). India's Call on China in The Quad: A Strategic Arch between Liberal and Alternative Structures. *Rising Power Quarterly*, 83-111.
3. Panda, J. P. (Aug, 2018). Indias Call on China in The Quad: A Strategic Arch between Liberal and Alternative Structures. *Rising Power Quarterly*, 83-111.
4. PTI. (2021, September 25). *President Biden hosts first Quad leaders summit, PM Modi attends meet*. Retrieved from The Indian Express: https://indianexpress.com/article/world/president-biden-first-quad-leaders-summit-pm-narendra-modi-meet-7533017/
5. House, T. W. (2022, May 24). *Fact Sheet: The Quad Leaders Summit*. Retrieved from The White House: https://www.whitehouse.gov/briefing-room/statements-releases/2021/09/24/fact-sheet-quad-leaders-summit
6. Jash, D. A. (8 March, 2021). The Quad Factor in the Indo-Pacifc and The Role of India. *Journal of Indo-Pacific Affairs*, 1-8.
7. Lalwani, S. (2019). Reluctant Link ? India, The Quad, and The Free and Open Indo-Pacific. *Jstor*, 1-9.
8. Parulekar, D. D. (2022). Scoping an India-Japan Cooperative Framework for Africa: The 'AAGC' and Beyond. *Indian Foreign Affairs Journal*, *17*(1/2), 29–46. https://www.jstor.org/stable/48745123
9. Tourangbam, M. (2019). The UN and the Future of Multilateralism in a Multipolar World: Navigating India's Way. *Indian Foreign Affairs Journal*, *14*(4), 301–308. https://www.jstor.org/stable/48636740
10. O'Neil, A. (2020). Australia: The Art of Strategic Balance. In R. Huisken & K. Brett (Eds.), *CSCAP REGIONAL SECURITY OUTLOOK 2021* (pp. 32–35). Council for Security Cooperation in the Asia Pacific. http://www.jstor.org/stable/resrep28672.11
11. Lalwani, S. (2019). Reluctant Link ? India, The Quad, and The Free and Open Indo-Pacific. *Jstor*, 1-9
12. Kaura, V. (2020). QUAD'S MALABAR MOMENT. *Indian Journal of Asian Affairs*, *33*(1/2), 1–23. https://www.jstor.org/stable/27003432
13. Buchan, P. G., & Rimland, B. (2020). *Defining the Diamond: The Past, Present, and Future of the Quadrilateral Security Dialogue*. Center for Strategic and International Studies (CSIS). http://www.jstor.org/stable/resrep24258
14. Saha, R. (2020). Positioning the Indo-Pacific in India's Evolving Maritime Outlook. *Indian Foreign Affairs Journal*, *15*(2), 125–138. https://www.jstor.org/stable/48630170

15. Malik, M. (Ed.). (2014). *Maritime security in the Indo-Pacific: perspectives from China, India, and the United States*. Rowman & Littlefield.
16. Kumar, P. (2022). India Balancing China: Exploring Soft Balancing Through Indo-Pacific. *Millennial Asia*, *13*(2), 339-359.
17. Malik, M. (2020). India and China: as China rises, India stirs. In *Indian Foreign Policy in a Unipolar World* (pp. 163-191). Routledge India.
18. Deb, S., & Wilson, N. (2021). The coming of quad and the balance of power in the Indo-Pacific. *Journal of Indo-Pacific Affairs*, *4*(9), 111-121.
19. Saha, R. (2022). Quad in the Indo-Pacific: Rhetoric versus Reality. In *Multilateralism in the Indo-Pacific* (pp. 89-102). Routledge.
20. Rajagopalan, R. (2020). Evasive balancing: India's unviable Indo-Pacific strategy. *International Affairs*, *96*(1), 75-93.
21. Srivastava, M. (2022, March 26). *The Paradox of China India Relations*. Retrieved from East Asia Forum: https://www.eastasiaforum.org/2022/03/26/the-paradox-of-china-india-relations/
22. Minds, M. F. (2022, Dec 12). *India-China border clashes erupted on Dec 9*. Retrieved from DW.Com: https://www.dw.com/en/india-china-border-clashes-erupted-on-december-9-says-delhi/a-64071941
23. Baruah, J. P. (2019). Foreseeing India-China Relations: "Compromised Context" of Reapproachment. *Jstor*, 1-9.
24. Gokhle, V. (2021). The India-China-U.S. Triangle. *Carnegie Endowment for International Peace*, 1-6.
25. ash, D. A. (8 March, 2021). The Quad Factor in the Indo-Pacific and The Role of India. *Journal of Indo-Pacific Affairs*, 1-8.
26. Gokhle, V. (March, 2020). The Road From Galwan: The Future of India-China Relations. *Carnegie Endowment For International Peace*, 1-36
27. Srivastava, R. K. (2022, march 8). *U.S announces ban on all Russian oil and gas export*. Retrieved from Zee News: https://zeenews.india.com/world/us-announces-ban-on-all-russian-oil-gas-and-energy-imports-over-ukraine-invasion-2443406.html

REFERENCES

1. Baruah, J. P. (2019). Foreseeing India-China Relations: "Compromised Context" of Reapproachment. *Jstor*, 1-9.
2. Estrada, R. R. (1 june, 2018). India, The Indo-Pacific and The Quad. *Taylor and Francis Group*, 1-15.
3. Gokhle, V. (2021). The India-China-U.S. Triangle. *Carnegie Endowment for International Peace*, 1-6.
4. Gokhle, V. (March, 2020). The Road From Galwan: The Future of India-China Relations. *Carnegie Endowment For International Peace*, 1-36.
5. House, T. W. (2022, May 24). *Fact Sheet: The Quad Leaders Summit*. Retrieved from The White House: https://www.whitehouse.gov/briefing-room/statements-releases/2021/09/24/fact-sheet-quad-leaders-summit

6. Jash, D. A. (8 March, 2021). The Quad Factor in the Indo-Pacific and The Role of India. *Journal of Indo-Pacific Affairs*, 1-8.
7. Lalwani, S. (2019). Reluctant Link? India, The Quad, and The Free and Open Indo-Pacific. *Jstor*, 1-9.
8. Manoj CG, A. G. (2017, july 15). *Doklam Border Stand off.* Retrieved from The Indian Express.
9. https://indianexpress.com/article/india/govt-briefs-opp-china-storm-unlikely-in-monsoon-session/
10. Minds, M. F. (2022, Dec 12). *India-China border clashes erupted on Dec 9.* Retrieved from DW.Com: https://www.dw.com/en/india-china-border-clashes-erupted-on-december-9-says-delhi/a-64071941
11. Mishra, R. (2019). Regional Security Outlook. *Jstor*, 1-4.
12. Panda, J. P. (Aug, 2018). India's Call on China in The Quad: A Strategic Arch between Liberal and Alternative Structures. *Rising Power Quarterly*, 83-111.
13. PTI. (2021, September 25). *President Biden hosts first Quad leaders summit, PM Modi attends meet.* Retrieved from The Indian Express: https://indianexpress.com/article/world/president-biden-first-quad-leaders-summit-pm-narendra-modi-meet-7533017/
14. Rimland, P. G. (2020). The Past, Present and Future of the Quardrilateral Security Dialogue. *Jstor*, 1-12.
15. S.Jaishankar. (2021, March 14). Quad Summit had a motive, its never against anyone. (I. T. Conclave, Interviewer)
16. Singh, D. B. (2019). Quad will damage India-China Relations. *Jstor*, 1-4.
17. Srivastava, M. (2022, March 26). *The Paradox of China India Relations.* Retrieved from East Asia Forum: https://www.eastasiaforum.org/2022/03/26/the-paradox-of-china-india-relations/
18. Srivastava, R. K. (2022, march 8). *U.S announces ban on all Russian oil and gas export.* Retrieved from Zee News: https://zeenews.india.com/world/us-announces-ban-on-all-russian-oil-gas-and-energy-imports-over-ukraine-invasion-2443406.html

11

Securing the Tide: The Grand Design of Aspiring India for the Indian Ocean

– Subham Tripathy

Introduction

There has been disquiet in India over the last several years as a result of China's rapidly growing maritime posture in the Indian Ocean. According to many observers, New Delhi's historical zone of influence has been diminished by Beijing's naval advances. Beijing has promoted ties with littoral governments by leveraging the People's Liberation Army Navy's (PLAN) rising involvement in India's proximate seas, furthering the myth of an "altruistic China." High-tech maritime platforms, including modern destroyers, guided-missile frigates, amphibious warships and submarines are all used by the anti-piracy forces of China in the Indian Ocean to carry out insignificant counterpiracy missions[1]. For New Delhi, the Belt and Road Initiative (BRI) of China has convoluted the situation. Beijing has made plans to build ports, motorways, trains, pipelines, and other vital connection infrastructure that South Asian states have found difficult to reject. The activities undertaken by China are a covert demonstration of its economic might intended to raise Beijing's geopolitical prominence in Asia. Chinese funding of the projects under the BRI is not intended to be based on the "win-win" growth, but rather to increase its power in continental-maritime Eurasia.

What makes India much more cautious is the dual use of the infrastructural projects in South Asia capable of promoting China's both military and business interests. Indian scholars, who stress the risks of Chinese dependence network in South Asia, are unconvinced by the presentation of the BRI by China as a massive infrastructure project. Indian observers believe that China's attempt to wrest control of ports from governments that are heavily indebted to it is an attempt to expand the Chinese naval influence in the Indian Ocean[2]. Despite the significant economic advantages of the BRI, the political establishment of India is still cautious in viewing it favourably.[3] Indian policymakers have publicly expressed their objection to the China Pakistan Economic Corridor (which passes through POK, i.e., the Pakistan occupied Kashmir) and have also spoken out against the infrastructure developments by China in Sri Lanka and Maldives, which have the potential to expand PLA activities in South Asia.[4]

The 'Grand Design of Aspiring India' refers to the strategic framework, which India is employing to fulfill its aspirations in the Indian Ocean. These aspirations will primarily be bi-folding. The first, to check any foreign nations to be as powerful as they can curtail Indian supremacy in the Indian Ocean and the second, to elevate Indian position to a level where other countries cannot challenge India's sphere of Influence and its role as the 'Key Security Provider' in the Indian Ocean Waters. Whereas, with the title, 'Securing the Tides', this article evaluates what is India's grand strategic plan for countering expanding influence of China in the Indian Ocean waters, which is India's domestic sphere of influence. The reason why China has been taken into consideration in the article lies with some facts: firstly, China aspires to be the single dominant power in the Asian continent and beyond[5] which is challenged by India's growing stature in the world. Secondly, China wants to dominate the Indian Ocean waters to ensure security to its sea lanes of communication, which is pivotal for its energy import, and exports of Chinese-made goods because, as per the "Military and Security Developments Involving the People's Republic of China 2021" report by the U.S. Department of Defense (DoD), there are top 10 crude oil suppliers to Beijing[6], out of which, nine of its suppliers are accessed via the Indian Ocean. Therefore, Beijing continues to engage in regional affairs in the Indian Ocean and tries to maintain its influence.

Securing the Indian Ocean is the primary objective for India as it is the core of its Indo-Pacific Vision. Because, due to its rapid ascension in the global order as a result of its strong economic growth and growing military might, China has aspirations to become a great power. A country is granted great power status if it can sway events on land or at the water that are taking place outside of its native land in favour of the native land. This is stated in China's 2015 White Paper, where a notable shift from the former "offshore defense" to a pronounced "open ocean protection" in the maritime domain is understood as follows: After securing the defenses in the South China Sea, it is time to protect Chinese interests to the West, specifically the Indian Ocean.[7]

China's Advancements in the Indian Ocean: Implications for India

Under this heading, 'Chinese Encirclement Plan' or 'Strategy of Encirclement', which explains how Beijing is allying with the countries around India, to isolate New Delhi militarily and diplomatically. 'Strategy of Encirclement' means a political and military strategy that is used by a state against its rival nation to circle it through military bases or friendly territories and isolate it militarily in times of war. China is employing this strategy against India in the Indian Ocean. This is supposed to have started in 2005 when the "String of Pearls" theory first came to light when the phrase was first used by Booz Allen in his 2005 report "Energy Futures in Asia" where he projected that China would try to increase its naval presence throughout the IOR by developing infrastructure in neighbouring friendly countries.[8] This projection seems true when it is observed that China has been building a network of Chinese military and commercial facilities in the Indian Ocean Region (IOR), which stretches from the Horn of Africa in the west to the Chinese mainland ports.

In East Africa, Djibouti, where a military support station had been established by China in 2017, is the country's most valuable asset[9]. By leveraging its debt-trap diplomacy, China is also investing a substantial sum of money in infrastructural development in East Africa, taking advantage of the East African governments' economic pressure. China is involved in 46 seaports across Africa, according to a report from the Centre for Strategic and International Studies (CSIS),[10] and Beijing will undoubtedly exploit these investments to dilate its military and political leverage in the future.

The next trade snarl in the Indian Ocean is the Strait of Hormuz, which is situated in the Persian Gulf. According to a 2017 Reuters article, Chinese businesses began investing more than $10 billion in Duqm in 2016.[11] Besides, China inked numerous significant agreements with Yemen, totalling $508 million in 2012 and 2013, including 3 natural gas-fired power stations, 2 container ports at Aden and Mokha, and the China National Corporation for Overseas Economic Cooperation (CCOEC).[12] Iran is a significant force in this area. Iran is looking for new regional economic partners after US sanctions on the country. In the meantime, China has promised to invest $400 billion in Iran over the following 25 years.[13] This agreement is anticipated to provide China with a boost in the Middle East.

Again, due to Pakistan's increasing distance from the USA, its relations with China have undergone a rapid transformation in recent years. The port of Gwadar, whose building rights had been granted to China for 40 years,[14] is Pakistan's most significant and strategic location. As a result, it assumes more significance as a vital link between the ambitious Belt and Road Initiative of China and the Maritime Silk Route. In line with BRI, the China-Pakistan Economic Corridor (CPEC) will give China direct access to the Gwadar port. India already opposes CPEC because it goes across the Pakistan occupied Kashmir (POK).[15]

China has allegedly been involved in the Maldives for years, according to the CSIS's "Asia maritime transparency programme" report. The most significant ones here are China's island development initiatives in Feydhoo Finothu, Kunaavashi, and Hulumalé (which is close to Malé, the capital of the Maldives).[16] When the Maldives experienced a political crisis in 2018 due to the pro-China presidency of Abdulla Yameen, the country came under international scrutiny. However, India later felt relieved when Ibrahim Mohamed Salih won the 2019 Maldives elections and stabilized the country's affairs.

China's debt-trap approach appears to be most obvious in Sri Lanka, where it has leased the Hambantota port for 99 years.[17] The event of the research and survey vessel of China i.e. the Yuan Wang 5 landing at Hambantota caused a lot of heartburn at that moment.

There were very legitimate concerns that the "spy ship" might take advantage of the opportunity to monitor India's maritime and underwater infrastructure along its extensive coastline.[18]

China's businesses have acquired three Bangladeshi natural gas fields following a 2017 agreement. China will additionally assist Bangladesh in building a 220 km pipeline for oil imports to the Chittagong refinery. China was given access to Chittagong and Mongla ports by Bangladesh in 2019. India is also concerned about the Chinese plan to provide financial assistance to Bangladesh to build a vessel for managing the waters of the Teesta River.[19]

Again, China also has a 70% stake in Myanmar's deep water Kyaukpyu port in the Kyaukpyu Islands which is not so far from the Indian coasts, especially near Andaman and Nicobar Islands and is being developed by China under the China-Myanmar Economic Corridor that also includes a railway line connecting Yunnan province of China to Mandalay part of Myanmar.[20] This gives an upper hand to China to keep an eye on Indian naval movements. Similarly, one major concern that has been there for India for the last three decades is that a SIGINT intelligence gathering station has been established by China on the Great Coco Island of Myanmar in 1992[21] to keep an eye on the Indian naval activities in the Andaman and Nicobar Islands. China can easily keep an eye on India's naval bases and missile launch sites from there.

The above developments clearly show that the 'String of Pearls' is one of the very well-planned and cunning foreign policy strategies of China to counter India's growing stature in the region. China, after being one of the major economic powers after the U.S; is trying to be the superpower of the world and therefore, it is seeing itself in the US' line which makes an obvious question among the Chinese authorities if, the U.S. is free to get its presence in any region of the world then why not China too? However, China gets annoyed when it encounters India, known for its outreach in the region and its blue water naval capabilities, as the major rival to fulfill its ambitions, especially in the Indian Ocean. Hence, the strategy of String of Pearls is highly crucial for China to counter the Indian sphere of influence in the region.

India sees all the developments in the last 2 decades as an obvious threat to its security because India knows that as China did in the

South China sea, it may reuse the same strategy for the Indian Ocean by gradually increasing its presence in the Indian Ocean and then getting aggressive in the region and trying to dominate the Oceanic waters. The biggest threat to maritime peace and security comes from unilateralism, which is the general nature of China.

India's Indian Ocean Strategy

Booz Allen's String of Pearls theory, which first appeared in 2004, was premature but far-sighted. However, despite China's rapid advancement in the Indian Ocean. India still has several advantages because, for China, the Indian Ocean symbolizes "outside lines," whereas, for India, it symbolizes "inside lines." India's geographical positioning in the Indian Ocean gives the upper hand over China. India's Indian Ocean Strategy, which stretches from the western African waters to the South China Sea waters, is not only designed to give a strategic response to China's encirclement policy but also to ensure the Indian Ocean remains India's Ocean. This is very important for India's cause as famous American maritime strategist Alfred Mahan was of the view that the Indian Ocean waters would decide the destiny of the world and the country which controlled the Indian Ocean would dominate Asia.[22]

Starting from Oman, which has excellent political, diplomatic, and economic links with India. In 2006, the two nations engaged in combined military drills, which was followed by the signing of a defense pact. While the country's Ras-al-Had is home to an Indian listening station, the Muscat naval base has berthing privileges for the Indian Navy. In the Gulf of Aden, to undertake anti-piracy operations, the Indian Navy has been using the ports of Oman as bases since 2008.[23] Indian Air Force and Indian Navy now have access to the Duqm facilities, according to a declaration made by India in February 2018.[24] Then, Iran is one of India's oldest and traditional partners in the Gulf of Oman. India has invested heavily to develop the Chabahar port of Iran and operating the Shahid Beheshti Terminal[25] since 2018. With India's presence in Chabahar, it can counter Chinese movement through Gwadar in the Arabian sea. Hence, Chabahar port plays a very important role in India's counter-encirclement policy.

Towards the southwest Indian Ocean, the 'Coastal Surveillance Radar' (CSR) station of the Indian Navy's National Command, Control and Communication Intelligence Network is one of India's security infrastructure components in Mauritius. India and Mauritius have also agreed to work together to "upgrade maritime and air transportation facilities" on the Agalega island. As per the recent satellite images, India is building an airfield and port at Agalega that will not only help India to track and address any threat in the region but also act as an intelligence outpost for New Delhi.[26] Apart from the Agalega, India is also pushing its defense relationship with Seychelles for having a military base in Assumption Island, which can allow India to counter any possible Chinese movements in the south-western Indian Ocean. India is also maintaining its first overseas listening post and radar facility in northern Madagascar,[27] which enables India to counter any possible Chinese advancement in the Mozambique Channel.

India is also having strong defense ties with France. France has two military bases in the Indian Ocean, i.e. Djibouti and Reunion Island. The Reciprocal Exchange of Logistics Agreement[28] between India and France allows the military forces of the two nations access to logistics and support facilities at each other's bases and ports. Similarly, India has a Logistics Exchange Memorandum of Agreement (LEMOA)[29] with the U.S. which allows India to use the Diego Garcia Naval base of the U.S. in case of emergency or a security threat from China, India can use France's Djibouti base and Oman's Duqm port to counter china in the gulf of Aden whereas the U.S's Diego Garcia and France's Le port in the Reunion island can be used by India to confront Chinese growing military postures in southern Indian Ocean. Similarly, it is from 2009 that India installed 26 radars linked with the Indian Coastal Command on all the atolls of the Maldives for seamless coverage of the area. India has also been conducting joint patrolling and surveillance with the Maldives National Defense Force.[30] India has also equipped the Maldives with defense items and is helping it financially to get rid of the 'Chinese Debt Trap'. Thus, India is also countering Chinese influence in the Maldives.

Furthermore, Beijing's "string of pearls" list of ports with Chinese support includes the port facility at Chittagong in Bangladesh for a very long time. While through this and other projects Beijing wants Dhaka to be more dependent on itself, it seems difficult to make Dhaka fall into its trap. The recent offer by Dhaka to the New Delhi of the use of the Chinese-backed strategically important Chittagong port[31] is a big opportunity for India to counter China in the Bay of Bengal. Again, India is building Sittwe Port as part of the Kaladan Multimodal Transit Transport Project, which aims to develop a multimodal road, river, and sea transport corridor for the movement of cargo to Myanmar from eastern ports of India. Through Sittwe, India can counter Chinese-backed Kyaukpyu port developed under the China-Myanmar Economic Corridor in Myanmar.

The island chain of Andaman and Nicobar, situated in the Bay of Bengal serves as the unsinkable aircraft carrier of India near the strategically important maritime trade route of 'The Strait of Malacca'. New Delhi is concentrating on leveraging the Andaman and Nicobar Islands as a significant chain to offset the Chinese footprints in the Indian Ocean, particularly in the Bay of Bengal. China is quite aware that in the event of a crisis, India might block the Malacca Strait with a few ships, which could harm China's cost-effective marine channels of communication. India is also expanding its Andaman Nicobar Command into an amphibious warfare center in addition to converting it into Tri-Service Command for the Indian Navy,[32] Indian Air Force, and Indian Army. This gives India a strategic edge over China in the entire Indo-Pacific.

Further, the strategic deep-sea port that India is building in Sabang[33], Indonesia, will provide it extensive access to the South China Sea. In addition, India and Singapore signed a bilateral agreement that will give Indian Navy ships logistical support, including refuelling, at Singapore's Changi naval station[34], which is situated close to the disputed South China Sea, will prove to be a strategic move that is expected to enrage China. With a focus on oil and gas development as well as military collaboration, India is swiftly deepening its ties with Vietnam. India and Vietnam have been working together on offshore oil and gas development for many years, but now they are entering a new stage with more resource exploration.

Apart from all these, India has been attempting to have a naval presence near every strategically important choke point to the Indian Ocean. One such effort includes the historic agreement between India and Australia, the "Mutual Logistics Assistance Agreement (MLSA),"[35] which will grant both sides access to each other's military bases to provide logistics support. This will offer the Indian Navy a significant edge because it allows them access to the Australian Cocos

Islands, which are close to the straits of Sunda and Lombok. Indian Andaman and Nicobar Islands, on the other hand, are very close to the Strait of Malacca. The main crossing sites between the Indian and Pacific Oceans are these straits. India can therefore completely deny China access to the Indian Ocean.

Role of India as the Net Security Provider

To challenge China's growing engagements in the region, the Indian government has several complementary measures at its disposal. SAGAR (Security and Growth for All in the Region) is one of these crucial policy initiatives. India, in 2015, launched this plan of action for the Indian Ocean. There is a growing realisation of the importance of marine cooperation, commons, and security in the region. India aims to buttress its security and economic interconnections with its maritime neighbours under SAGAR by helping them develop their maritime security capacities. For this, India is collaborating on coastline surveillance, information sharing, capability enhancement and infrastructure creation. To protect its national interests, India is also ensuring that the Indian Ocean region not only upholds international law but also becomes inclusive and cooperative. India was recently accepted as an observer member of the Indian Ocean Commission (IOC). This initiative represents a milestone in India's strategic goal for the Indian Ocean.

Similar to this, India can concentrate on the Indian Ocean Rim Association (IORA) to promote inclusive growth and shared security in the member nations, which will not only strengthen India's position as a net security provider but also ensure Indian soft power's potential to influence these nations. Additionally, India can draw attention to the Indian Ocean Naval Symposium, often known as IONS, which was created by the Indian Navy in 2008. By offering an inclusive and open forum for discussion of maritime problems that are pertinent to the region, this forum would help to create a shared understanding of the future, and India may work to improve maritime cooperation among the navies of the littoral states in the Indian Ocean region. Along with the SAGAR program and through this forum, India can offer humanitarian assistance and disaster relief (HADR), information security and interoperability (IS&I), maritime security, or anti-piracy missions in the region to take these littoral governments in confidence and in a means to maintain and grow its influence in the Indian Ocean.

Developing Own Capability

Developing relations with the maritime neighbours is a very important step in enhancing India's stronghold in the Indian Ocean, but defense modernization is imperative to maintain these military relations and to ensure India's dominance in the region vis-à-vis any foreign power such as China. Therefore, as a part of the country's modernization and development of its marine capabilities, the Indian Navy is concentrating on creating indigenous platforms, sensors, weaponry, and systems. The Indian Navy, which aspires to develop a powerful navy of 500 aircraft and 200 ships by 2050, and 24 attack submarines, has various types of 45 vessels under construction as of November 2022,[36] including corvettes, frigates, destroyers, conventional as well as nuclear powered submarines, and various other ships. According to a declaration in December 2020, made by the Chief of Naval Staff[37], India's fleet has changed from one that was purchased to one that was built.[38] The Indian Navy has increased its investments in various anti-submarine ships like corvettes of the Kamorta-class, aircraft like the Boeing P-8 Poseidon capable of long-range maritime reconnaissance, unmanned aerial vehicles like the IAI Heron-1[39] and ships like the Saryu-class patrol vessels[40] due to the growing interest of the Chinese PLAN in the Indian Ocean region.

To have a web of island airbases both in the Bay of Bengal and the Arabian Sea that would provide an infrastructure which will ensure the freedom to navigate and overflight to all Indian territories. Following the 2020 Chinese incursions into Ladakh, it has been stated that the Indian Navy aims to improve the military installations in the Lakshadweep on the western seaboard as well as the Andaman and Nicobar Islands on the eastern shore.[41] The Indian Government is having 2 plans in the pipeline, i.e., the Indian Navy's Maritime Capability Plan (MCPP) and the Indian Naval Indigenisation Plan (INIP) 2015-2030. Apart from these 2, the Indian Navy has already completed some projects or targets like- Indian Aircraft Carrier (IAC) Project-71 IAC-1, Project 17 Shivalik Class, Project 17A Nilgiri Class, Project 15A Kolkata Class Destroyers, The Project 15B class of Guided Missile Destroyers, Project 1135.6 Frigates, Project 28 ASW Corvettes, Mines Counter Measures Vessels, Shallow Water ASW Crafts, Amphibious Capability, Fleet Support Ships, Subsurface Vessels.[42] The ongoing projects of Indian Naval Modernisation are:

Project 75, Project 75 India, and Project 75 Alpha. In addition, there are speculations of having a second indigenously developed Air Craft Carrier IAC-2 i.e. INS Vishal.[43]

Conclusion

China has a significant strategic vulnerability when it comes to the Indian Ocean, and it has limited options for mitigating that weakness. China's potential to project power into the Indian Ocean is likely to be severely limited shortly. The weak overland transportation links and the growth of China's so-called "Pearls" would not significantly lessen these disadvantages. It is hard to imagine how China would ultimately be unable to defend all of its SLOCs in the Indian Ocean from India in the case of a dispute between the two countries. The geographical centrality of the Indian subcontinent, which is situated alongside the important maritime routes that span the northern Indian Ocean, gives it substantial natural advantages even though its overall military capabilities are significantly lower than those of China.

The geopolitical ties with the Indian Ocean states, which primarily trend towards the United States and/or India, only serve to exacerbate China's disadvantages in this region. India is currently developing regional alignments in which it assumes a position of leadership after decades of shunning them, partially due to ideological reasons, across the Indian Ocean region.

Undoubtedly, China is exerting more economic influence on the area. Although this carries some political clout, it would be incorrect to think that this inevitably translates into the security sphere. No Indian Ocean state (apart from Pakistan) would presently have the right to seriously consider China as a significant security provider, even though China, India, and the United States are actively competing to expand their influence in the region. The majority of states are mostly modelling their economic relations with China after those of other Asian nations while hedging their security bets. In the Indian Ocean, China will undoubtedly continue playing a strategic role, but it is still challenging to see China eliminating its geostrategic weaknesses there. The underlying vulnerability China faces must be taken into consideration by anyone worried about the security dynamics of the Indian Ocean region.

ENDNOTES

1. Brewster, D. (2018). A contest of status and legitimacy in the Indian Ocean. India and China at Sea: Competition for Naval Dominance in the Indian Ocean, 11-44.
2. Mohan Malik. (2018, April 11). Dimensions, Detours, Fissures, and Fault Lines. *The American Interest*. Retrieved December 5, 2022, from https://www.the-american-interest.com/2018/02/19/dimensions-detours-fissures-fault-lines/
3. Ollapally, D. M. (2016). Understanding Indian policy dilemmas in the Indo-Pacific through an India–US–China maritime triangle lens. *Maritime Affairs: Journal of the National Maritime Foundation of India*, *12*(1), 1–12. https://doi.org/10.1080/09733159.2016.1181392
4. Saran. (2015, July 7). The Beijing paradox. Business Standard. Retrieved December 5, 2022, from https://www.business-standard.com/article/opinion/shyam-saran-the-beijing-paradox-115070701418_1.html
5. The Economist. (2022, October 13). China is exerting greater power across Asia—and beyond. *The Economist*. https://www.economist.com/special-report/2022/10/10/china-is-exerting-greater-power-across-asia-and-beyond
6. Military and Security Developments Involving the People's Republic of China 2021. (n.d.). In *Department of Defense, USA*. Office of Secretary of Defence. Retrieved December 6, 2022, from https://media.defense.gov/2021/Nov/03/2002885874/-1/-1/0/2021-CMPR-FINAL.PDF
7. Doraibabu, M. (2019). India and China at Sea: Competition for Naval Dominance in the Indian Ocean, edited by David Brewster | Manohar Parrikar Institute for Defence Studies and Analyses. JOURNAL OF DEFENCE STUDIES. Retrieved December 6, 2022, from https://idsa.in/system/files/jds/india-and-china-at-sea-doraibabu.pdf
8. Baker, B. D. (2015, October 5). Where Is the 'String of Pearls' in 2015? The Diplomat. https://thediplomat.com/2015/10/where-is-the-string-of-pearls-in-2015/
9. Staff, R. (2017, August 1). *China formally opens first overseas military base in Djibouti*. U.S. https://www.reuters.com/article/us-china-djibouti-idUSKBN1AH3E3
10. Assessing the Risks of Chinese Investments in Sub-Saharan African Ports. (2019). In Centre for Strategic and International Studies. Centre for Strategic and International Studies. Retrieved December 7, 2022, from https://www.csis.org/analysis/assessing-risks-chinese-investments-sub-saharan-african-ports
11. Jabarkhyl, N. (2017, September 6). Oman counts on Chinese billions to build desert boomtown. *U.S.* https://www.reuters.com/article/us-oman-china-investment-idUSKCN1BG1WJ
12. TEKINGUNDUZ. (2019, December 13). What is China doing in Yemen? *TRTWorld.* Retrieved December 7, 2022, from https://www.trtworld.com/middle-east/what-is-china-doing-in-yemen-32183
13. Fassihi, F., & Myers, S. L. (2021, March 29). China, with $400 Billion Iran Deal, Could Deepen Influence in Mideast. *The New York Times*. https://www.nytimes.com/2021/03/27/world/middleeast/china-iran-deal.html

14. Indo Asian News Service. (2017, April 20). Operations at Pakistan's Gwadar port leased to Chinese firm for 40 years. *Hindustan Times*. https://www.hindustantimes.com/world-news/operations-at-pakistan-s-gwadar-port-leased-to-chinese-firm-for-40-years/story-00axpKWxj5Q6dhTx3jEYgK.html
15. The Hindu. (2019, September 10). India asks China, Pakistan to end activities related to CPEC in PoK. *The Hindu*. https://www.thehindu.com/news/national/china-pakistan-economic-corridor-is-on-our-territory-india/article29382571.ece
16. Center for Strategic and International Studies. (2020). Chinese Investment in The Maldives: Appraising The String of Pearls. In *Asia Maritime Transparency Initiative*. Retrieved December 7, 2022, from https://amti.csis.org/chinese-investment-in-the-maldives-appraising-the-string-of-pearls/
17. Gupta, S. (2022, June 26). Was cash strapped Sri Lanka duped by China in Hambantota Port? *Hindustan Times*. https://www.hindustantimes.com/world-news/was-cash-strapped-sri-lanka-duped-by-china-in-hambantota-port-101656205405799.html
18. Guha, S. (2022, August 23). China's Alleged Spy Vessel In Sri Lanka Raises Alarm Bells In Delhi, Is India Over-reacting? Https://Www.Outlookindia.Com/. https://www.outlookindia.com/national/china-spy-ship-docking-in-sri-lanka-and-ranil-wickremesinghe-balancing-act-between-two-asian-giants-news-218160
19. *China–Bangladesh strategic linkages*. (2021, May 11). ORF. Retrieved December 8, 2022, from https://www.orfonline.org/expert-speak/china-bangladesh-strategic-linkages/
20. Vaghji, S. (2022, August 11). What's Behind the China-Myanmar Economic Corridor 'Plus' Initiative? *The Diplomat*. https://thediplomat.com/2022/08/whats-behind-the-china-myanmar-economic-corridor-plus-initiative/
21. *China's SIGINT facilities in Cocos Islands, a threat to India | Indiablooms - First Portal on Digital News Management*. (2022, June 24). Indiablooms.com. Retrieved December 8, 2022, from https://www.indiablooms.com/news-details/M/82475/china-s-sigint-facilities-in-cocos-islands-a-threat-to-india.html
22. Katoch, P. (2020, November 13). *Sea and Space Power*. Indian Defence Review. Retrieved December 8, 2022, from http://www.indiandefencereview.com/news/sea-and-space-power/
23. The Hindu. (2019a, June 2). Indian Navy steps up anti-piracy patrol. *The Hindu*. https://www.thehindu.com/news/national/indian-navy deploys-p-8i-from-oman-on-anti-piracy-patrols-in-gulf-of-aden/article27406710.ece
24. Chaudhury, D. R. (2018, February 13). PM Modi's Oman visit: Indian Navy can now access Duqm port. *The Economic Times*. https://economictimes.indiatimes.com/news/defence/pm-modis-oman-visit-navy-can-now-access-duqm-port/articleshow/62894357.cms
25. Laskar, R. H. (2022, September 10). India, Iran close to finalising long-term agreement on Chabahar port. *Hindustan Times*. https://www.hindustantimes.com/india-news/india-iran-close-to-finalising-long-term-agreement-on-chabahar-port-101662801370797.html
26. Jain, A. (2021, May 17). *India Rapidly Building Military Base In Mauritius To Counter China In The Indian Ocean Region*. Latest Asian, Middle-East,

EurAsian, Indian News. https://eurasiantimes.com/is-india-building-overseas-military-bases-to-counter-china-in-indian-ocean-region/

27. Pubby, M. (2007, July 18). India activates first listening post on foreign soil: radars in Madagascar - Indian Express. *The Indian Express*. Retrieved December 14, 2022, from http://archive.indianexpress.com/news/india-activates-first-listening-post-on-foreign-soil-radars-in-madagascar/205416
28. Siddiqui, H. (2019, January 25). *India-France operationalise their Logistics Support Agreement*. Financial Express. https://www.financialexpress.com/defence/india-france-operationalise-their-logistics-support-agreement/1455043/
29. The Hindu. (2016, October 18). *What is LEMOA?* https://www.thehindu.com/news/national/What-is-LEMOA/article15604647.ece
30. Mitra, R. (2022, January 27). *The China-India Cold War in Maldives*. The Diplomat. https://thediplomat.com/2022/01/the-china-india-cold-war-in-maldives/
31. TIMESOFINDIA.COM. (2022, April 28). *Bangladesh PM Sheikh Hasina offers Chittagong Port for use by India as S Jaishankar calls on her*. The Times of India. https://timesofindia.indiatimes.com/india/bangladesh-pm-sheikh-hasina-offers-chittagong-port-for-use-by-india-as-s-jaishankar-calls-on-her/articleshow/91157017.cms
32. *Integrated Defence Staff*. (n.d.). https://www.ids.nic.in/ancommand.php
33. TIMESOFINDIA.COM. (2019, March 21). Why India is developing its maiden deep-sea port in Indonesia. *The Times of India*. https://timesofindia.indiatimes.com/india/why-india-is-developing-its-maiden-deep-sea-port-in-indonesia/articleshow/68511228.cms
34. Gurung, S. K. (2018, July 12). Navy gets access to Singapore's Changi naval base. *The Economic Times*. https://economictimes.indiatimes.com/news/defence/navy-gets-access-to-singapores-changi-naval-base/articleshow/61855776.cms?from=mdr
35. Siddiqui, H. (2020, June 4). India – Australia: Indo-Pacific maritime powers ink MLSA for access to military bases. *Financial Express*. https://www.financialexpress.com/defence/india-australia-indo-pacific-maritime-powers-ink-mlsa-for-access-to-military-bases/1981619/
36. The Hindu. (2022, November 30). Integration of aircraft with INS Vikrant likely by May-June next year: Navy chief. *The Hindu*. https://www.thehindu.com/news/national/integration-of-aircraft-with-ins-vikrant-likely-by-may-june-next-year-navy-chief/article66204249.ece
37. Statesman News Service. (2020, December 5). Navy Day, 2020: Year-End wrap-up on our sentinels of the sea. *The Statesman*. https://www.thestatesman.com/features/navy-day-2020-year-end-wrap-up-on-our-sentinels-of-the-sea-1502939147.html
38. *Indian Navy has transformed from buyer to builder: Naval Chief.* (2014, September 4). Zee News. Retrieved December 15, 2022, from https://zeenews.india.com/news/nation/Indian-navy-has-transformed-from-buyer-to-builder-naval-chief_1465102.html

39. *Indian Army Inducts 2 Heron MK-II UAVs.* (n.d.). Indian Defence News. https://www.indiandefensenews.in/2022/09/indian-army-inducts-2-heron-mk-ii-uavs.html

40. *Indian Navy receives fourth Saryu-class OPV - IHS Jane's 360.* (n.d.). https://web.archive.org/web/20141222193824/http://www.janes.com/article/41200/Indian-navy-receives-fourth-saryu-class-opv

41. Gupta, S. (2020, July 20). Navy's forward posture against PLA aggression in Ladakh muscles out Chinese threat on high seas. *Hindustan Times.* https://www.hindustantimes.com/india-news/indian-navy-s-forward-posture-against-pla-aggression-in-ladakh-muscles-out-chinese-threat-on-high-seas/story-mRYUXdkrCmGQznQod5lWFK.html

42. *Navy's Quest for Modernisation.* (n.d.). https://www.spsnavalforces.com/story/?id=652

43. Linganna, G. (2022, June 14). INS Vishal - Indian Navy's need for a third aircraft carrier. *Frontier India.* https://frontierindia.com/ins-vishal-indian-navys-need-for-a-third-aircraft-carrier/

12

Unravelling Ethnic Gulf in Manipur: A Land at Crossroads

– Keshab Chandra Ratha

Introduction

Long-simmering tensions between the Meiteis and the Kukis have resulted in the effective partition of Manipur into separate ethnic zones. Some people have taken the precaution of painting their ethnicity on their doors in case their homes are accidentally set on fire. Long-term insurgency, recent drug war controversy, illegal immigration from troubled Myanmar via porous borders, land pressure, and a dearth of job prospects all contribute to the region's underlying tensions. Manipur, as a state, is experiencing a variety of social unrest, ethnic violence, and social upheavals at the moment. Rebellion for homeland, ethnic strife over scarce resources, and competing land claims are all part of the picture. As many ethnic groups seek to strengthen their sense of identity, violence and conflict frequently break out, disrupting the state's social fabric and sometimes forcing people to flee the country. Distrust between the Meitei and Kuki groups has widened as a result of the ethnic violence in Manipur (Kipgen, 2021). The state administration has completely failed in the innermost part of tribal areas in terms of providing security, guaranteed livelihood, and educational amenities. Many hill people are internally displaced as a result of military war, internal unrest, systematic violation of human rights, and natural or man-made calamities.

Today's Manipur is a portrayal of violence, corruption, terrible governance, and a society that has been fractured along ethnic lines

(Singh,2008). Lack of development and pervasive corruption at all levels also contribute to ethnic politics. The entire state of Manipur shows signs of inadequate development. People have not seen clean roads, water supplies, drainage systems, sanitary facilities, etc., in a generation. The development process is time-consuming and exhausting. The hill folks have a truly miserable standard of existence. All parties participating in the development activities, including the government, have botched the task of prioritization. There appears to have been little progress made by all significant tiers of government and secular groups like student unions, clubs, and associations based on tribe, ethnicity, location, etc., or by religious groups like Church organizations. Manipur has been labelled a "failed state" due to these issues and subsequent media coverage (Kipgen, 2021).

Key Research Questions and Method

1. What are the major drivers of the present crisis in Manipur?
2. What are the contributing factors attributed as stumbling blocks to the peace process in Manipur?
3. Is there any Chinese connection to the current flare-up in Manipur?
4. What are the suitable measures that need to be undertaken for conflict management practices?

The method of study employed for the project is normative, historical analytical and descriptive. The study has made exhaustive collections both from the primary as well as secondary sources. The researcher has used primary materials such as reports, documents, legislative debates, and so on. And for the secondary sources, the researcher has taken views from the books, journals, articles, newspapers and internet sites. In fact, a number of the discussions and remarks made by the eminent figures has facilitated the scholar in gaining a genuine understanding of the crisis.

Cultural Geography

Manipur has 16 districts, but the state is most usually thought of as having valley and hill districts. The present-day districts of Imphal East, Imphal West, Thoubal, Bishnupur, and Kakching were once part of the Ningthouja-ruled kingdom of Kangleipak. Historians and academics agree that the tribal lands outside the valley were once part of the monarchy, although the tribes themselves, especially the Naga tribes, disagree. The Manipur valley is ringed by low hills that extend into the neighbouring states of Nagaland and Mizoram. These hill regions are home to the Chin-Kuki-Mizo-Zomi group, which consists of the Kuki, Thadou, Hmar, Paite, Vaiphei, and Zou peoples, as well as 15 Naga tribes. Naga tribes from the northern hills frequently raided the Kangleipak kingdom, which at the time was a British protectorate. It is thought that the British political agent in Manipur recruited the Kuki-Zomi from the Kuki-Chin hills of Burma to serve as a buffer between the Meiteis and the Nagas to prevent the valley from being plundered. The Maharaja granted the Kukis territory along the ridges so that they could protect the Imphal valley from invading Nagas, another vicious headhunting warrior tribe (Roy, 2023).

Because of the many various ethnic groups and clans that make up Manipuri society, the state of Manipur has been able to forge its own identity. The people of Manipur display a wide range of cultural practices and customs. They place a high value on custom. One of the most distinctive features of Manipuri culture is the widespread respect for both traditional and modern aesthetic norms. Each ethnic group in Manipur has its unique artistic traditions. The various Manipuri handicrafts and handloom textiles showcase the ingenuity of the region's inhabitants.

Major Drivers of Conflict

Riots and ethnically motivated violence in particular rarely take place in the absence of some driving forces. When various people who live near one another have the freedom to pursue their preferences but fail to take into consideration and respect the position of others, conflicts of interests frequently develop as an unavoidable consequence (Kipgen,2013). There has been a history of ethnic conflict in Manipur, mainly between the Meiteis and the Kukis. Conflicts like these frequently emerge as a result of rivalry for resources, land conflicts, and old grudges. Various ethnic groups have been at odds with one another due to mutual suspicion and territorial demands. Communities in Manipur often find themselves at odds with one another over land disputes. Because they are not recognized as a Scheduled Tribe (ST), the Meiteis, who are concentrated in the Imphal valley, have difficulty migrating to the surrounding hills. As a result, tensions have arisen between the Meiteis and the hill people. Conflicts between neighbourhoods have been exacerbated by the problem of political representation. Various Manipuri ethnic groups work to ensure they have a voice in the state's decision-making and administration. Differences in political influence and economic opportunity have stoked resentment and confrontations (Singh, 2023).

Communities in Manipur have their own unique languages, customs, and more. These differences in culture have the potential to enrich a community, but they also raise the risk of friction. Conflicts and misunderstandings may arise between groups due to cultural and linguistic differences. The communal dynamics in Manipur have been permanently altered by old grudges and conflicts. Mistrust and societal fragmentation have persisted as a result of historical struggles, violence, and insurgent movements. Distrust amongst communities persists due to lingering animosity over these incidents. In Manipur, there are significant socio-economic gaps between various groups. Tensions and complaints may be fuelled by economic, social, and educational inequalities. Relationships within a community can be strained by real or imagined economic inequality.

A legal ruling that gave Meiteis access to affirmative action was the immediate precipitating factor in the unrest. Land disputes arise because tribes can purchase valley property but Meitei cannot purchase hill property due to Article 371(C). The Meitei are in positions of political influence, while certain Kukis have powerful institutional positions in bureaucracy and circulate freely in the halls of power. The bureaucracy, which is dominated by Kukis, appears to have an advantage because some members of the Meitei governing political elite have lower educational degrees. As a result, the Kuki tribal bureaucracy and the Meitei political elite are at odds with one another. Kuki and Meitei both established armed groups to safeguard their respective communities. The state government has designated certain tribally held forests as reserved forests, causing concern among the tribal people who rely on these woodlands for subsistence. To this day, disagreements between Manipur's numerous ethnic groups may be traced back to fundamental differences in farming methods and patterns of land ownership. This conflict boils down to a struggle for control of land, the most valuable commodity in the hill kingdoms.

The Meiteis have a disproportionate part of the country's progress in every area of development, including education, sports and games, transportation, and infrastructure (including an international airport and rail connections). As a result, they enjoy much greater material prosperity than the indigenous peoples. Most state ministers and officials are Meiteis, giving them significant influence in politics and administration. They are perpetually in charge of everything. The Imphal plain has historically reaped the benefits of development in the state, while the hill areas have lagged far behind.

The current political dispensation appears to be hospitable to the Kangleipak sanamahi racist rebirth program. The Kuki-Zo scholars and researchers claim that the entire Manipuri political establishment, including the Meitei member of parliament, is in some way affiliated with the Meitei groups Arambai Tengol and Meitei Leepun. It is said that these two groups are the reborn storm troopers of the former Kangleipak realm (Tombing, 2023a). A combination of political opportunism and the government's insensitivity has set Manipur ablaze.

Chinese Angle

China is linked to Manipur. China has been aggressively taking over land near the border in the north. So, the Indian Army had to be moved to stop China from taking over even more land. The Indian Army's absence has led to a lack of security in Manipur. It cannot be ignored that China is always a threat in the area, but the fact that the Meitei and Kuki are fighting among themselves makes the situation much worse. Part of India's border with Myanmar, which is about 1,700 km long, goes through the state of Manipur. Since the early 1960s, there has been insurgency in Manipur, and terrorists from Manipur can cross into Myanmar at will and hide there. Militants from Myanmar can come to Manipur whenever they want. Manipur is called the "Gateway to the East" for a reason. Insurgents in the North-East get a lot of help from China, which is an unyielding and angry neighbour to the north. Kunming, China, is physically, financially, militarily, and in other ways deeply connected to a lot of tough North-East groups. China always seeks to take advantage of the huge strategic and security gaps in the North and the North-East (Sudarshan, 2023).

What is Missing?

It appears that the Indian government is partially liable for the current situation due to its lopsided policy towards the north east. Moreover, from the very beginning, none of India's governments had a distinct policy regarding the ethnic conflict in the north east, particularly in Manipur (Haokip, 2013). The lack of political will and apathy of consecutive central and state administrations since independence, along with their flawed policies, have greatly fuelled the cycle of violence in the region (Brahmachari, 2019). Peace in Manipur is hard to achieve because of ethnic divisions and poor governance. The political elite has not done anything to make things better or protect the freedom of the press. First, there is a lack of trust. Everyday life is tainted by a pervasive social climate of mistrust between Nagas and Kukis, Nagas and Meiteis, and Meiteis and Kukis (Goswami, 2015).

The Kuki people just do not trust Chief Minister N Biren Singh, and they are especially angry at the Manipur Police, who they say are biased. Leaders of the community from both parties have accused the government of being involved in the attacks on the Kuki and of doing nothing while Meitei vigilante groups went on the spree. The second is a policy problem. People in the community are angry about what they call the "unilateral" decision of the state government to set aside as reserve forests some hilly areas of Manipur where most Kuki live. The civil society groups of the three communities have been working to promote interethnic communication for a long time. But in recent years, they have been neglected. They have been replaced by violent organizations, who appear to play a significant role in escalating ethnic tensions. There is a connection between the court case, the evictions, the disagreement, and the breakdown of communication.

The infiltration of Kukis from neighbouring countries is another threat to national security, yet the government has proven unable to safeguard the country's borders. If the state is truly concerned about the arrival of the Kukis, then the international borders must have been sealed for a very long time. The state shows its inability to identify illegal border crossers and remove them from the country. This quickly sets off a violent reaction. The gap in development and infrastructure between the hills and the valley has fuelled growing animosity toward the indigenous community.

There is an armed group backing the demands of every community. They only practice a very limited brand of identity politics, but it is also true that they are the only ones capable of defending their citizens. The identity politics being practiced in Manipur today could make this violence worse (Newsclick Report, 2023). Manipur's valley and hills served as the dividing line between revenue and non-revenue areas, leaving the state with a somewhat more adamant hill-valley division today (Phanjoubam, 2023). An old kingdom has been torn apart by an outbreak of ethnic hate, turning neighbours into adversaries.

For the situation in Manipur to be resolved for good, a long-term strategy must be implemented that gives residents confidence in their safety on all fronts. Unfortunately, local efforts have often prioritized ineffective, short-term strategies for dealing with conflicts. These methods aim to reduce violence in the short term, but they might backfire if not paired with broader efforts to end the dispute.

The Kuki-Zo tribes have also been called a variety of disparaging names, including "drug traffickers," "poppy cultivators," and "protected forest encroachers." The likelihood of peaceful cohabitation between these two communities is seriously questioned by the ongoing spread of incorrect information and the smear campaign organized by the Meitei majority population. These behaviours can be interpreted as deliberate attempts to denigrate, dehumanize, and deny the Kuki-Zo tribes their basic human rights. It becomes harder to imagine a future in which both cultures live in harmony because of the ingrained hostility that prevails (Kipgen, 2023). It is encouraging that the Central Bureau of Investigation would be looking into specific violent instances.

A Healing Touch

Manipur is home to a wide variety of peoples. Although physically compact, its ethnic variety is comparable to that of India. Understanding the demographic patterns of these various ethnic groups requires some familiarity with their respective histories. The situation in Manipur requires skilled, careful handling due to its tangled history and complex realities. A return to normalcy once a war is over is essential for addressing the concerns of those whose lives were disrupted by it. To take the first step, leaders from both sides of the conflict need to sit down and talk peace. Representatives from groups with a reputation or track record that transcends their identities are crucial to the success of a peace endeavour. The responsibility of bringing peace and reconciliation must fall on the political representatives of both groups, in particular those members of the legislative assembly (MLAs) who belong to the same party but come from different ethnic backgrounds. The fundamental disagreements that exist between the parties call for an extended period of political discourse and reflective thought because they are not easily resolved. The administration should keep making an effort to persuade important members of civil society and politics to communicate with one another.

The responsibility for reaching out to the victims and providing them with more than just material aid lies on the government. The affected victims lack trust. Thus, the state needs to develop the "trust" aspect to heal them. The first steps in building trust in those who are responsible for governance are attributing responsibility for violent acts to important players and holding those actors accountable for their roles in those acts. A compromise must be reached through negotiations, including all community representatives. The government must reassure the Kukis of their entire security. If the Kukis do not get their demands met, the state may have trouble convincing them to participate in peace negotiations. A triangular arrangement could be able to calm the tribe's people down. The state has a challenging task ahead of it. Coercion cannot bring about peace; instead, understanding and discussion between the parties are the only ways to do it (Niumai, 2023).

Furthermore, the Kuki and Meitei community leaders must meet immediately to resolve their issues. Communities will always exist, even if governments change. The Nagas, Kukis, Meiteis, and Pangals will continue to be Manipur's indigenous peoples. Only by recognizing one another's unique contributions and working together to protect forests, mountains, and ecosystems, hope to live in harmony is possible. The present catastrophe has taught that discrimination of any kind makes lasting peace impossible. It is an opportune moment for the Union government to intervene immediately to bring about peace and harmony by resolving the issue of the unequal distribution of resources between the two groups.

The state needs to reassert its power and play a more central role in mediating conflicts between different communities. To do this, there is the need for political leadership that is trustworthy and is seen as impartial by all groups. Politicians must honour their own identities, but they should not behave like ethnic campaigners or fan the flames of division. There needs to be a genuine effort to resolve the identity (social, economic, aspirational) and resource distribution problems that plague various groups of people.

Reviving the Naga Peace Accord necessitates a concerted effort to dismantle the NSCN (IM) and SoO camps in Manipur and prepare the cadre for reintegration into society. There needs to be an organized effort to better regulate the frontier between India and Myanmar. Refugees and rebels with bases in Myanmar can freely cross this porous border. For decades, it has been complained about the border's subpar infrastructure without doing much to fix it. The ethnic conflict in Manipur is difficult to solve and may take a long time. The current situation should serve as a stark warning against taking a reactive stance when developing strategy (Hooda, 2023). Military action is not the only solution to the Manipur conflict; instead, it must be combined with socio-ethnographic and geopolitical strategizing, as well as inter-community discussion that treats all parties involved fairly (Bose, 2023).

A more accepting mentality toward diversity is necessary for future national and economic growth so that divisions within societies do not become a hindrance to development. There should be equal access to opportunities. To succeed in the years to come, a new culture should be adopted that emphasizes cooperation rather than competition. There is a dire need to work together to control diversity rather than exploit it (Sibal, 2023). Even as security forces work to restore peace and order in Manipur, the only way to bring the state back to normal is to launch a process of inter-ethnic conversation to figure out a road map for long-term ethnic reconciliation (Bhaumik, 2023).

What Manipur Calls For?

The following points need to be taken into consideration because of the historic mayhem in Manipur: i) the creation of district councils in the hills under the direct control and finance of the federal government, similar to the former Mizoram District Council. ii) The founding of Central University in Manipur's Southern Hill District; iii) An immediate reform of legal education and legal responsibility in Manipur's hill regions; and iv) The founding of the Population and Statistics Analysis Institute in Manipur's Southern Hill State. v) To start a process to replace affirmative action for tribes of the North East from the perspective of the indigenous race and its inhabitants to address ethnic problems in the hill states of the North East from an inclusive and diverse discourse of race and linguistic variety (Tombing, 2023 b).

Instead of addressing the problems that are producing such obvious differences, the political class takes advantage of them and uses different caste gaps as a source of support for its political agenda. Multireligious communities with disparate cultural and religious practices can also be a cause of conflict, which a majoritarian culture looks to capitalize on to gain political advantage. The most effective political tool for majoritarian political results is majoritarian domination based on religion. Manipur is but one illustration of what happens when diversity and compromise are absent. What is essential is a setting that values progress while encouraging cohesiveness and harmony. This will provide them the chance to grow and succeed.

It is important to comprehend cultural aspects, especially during times of war. The conflict between Meitei and tribal peoples is a sociological and cultural issue. The Northeastern countryside is dotted with several tribal communities, all of which have different moral codes that must be understood to find a solution. The area is overrun with people from many cultures, who frequently clash. Instead of an antagonistic policy, there should be a conversation. Today, there are enough shared values and goals amongst opposing political parties; what is frequently missing is a strong democratic commitment and the capacity to act for the good of the entire country (Narayanan, 2023). Even though states in the region yearn for more independence, striking a good balance necessitates both sensitivity and "out of the box" thinking for spectacular solutions. Now is the time for more sensible voices to take the initiative. The government should take the lead by providing effective and inclusive governance (Verma, 2023). The Manipur crisis needs to be resolved quickly, otherwise it could spark similar clashes elsewhere in the region.

An urgently necessary pragmatic strategy to put out the flames is required. The peace committee must be reconstituted as soon as possible with non-political members. There is a pressing need for proportionate numbers of representations from the Meiteis and the Kukis, including academics, retired public officers, artists, writers, and social workers. Involving women from both communities will encourage a strong conversation that is desperately needed. People who live in Manipur, including members of the Naga, Meitei Pangal, and other communities, will be essential in bridging the gap between the two communities and in developing a convincing plan for the entire state. To lay the groundwork for a potential peace dialogue, the blame game on both sides must be put to rest. As each group of people struggles for survival, the Meiteis and Kukis must reassure one another that they belong together, that Manipur is home to both as it is to the rest of the other communities in the state (Yumnam, 2023). For a practical reconstruction and potential reconciliation to occur, the Meiteis and Kukis must quickly come to this understanding. Without addressing various complex concerns, a reconciliation process cannot be successful. Representatives of these communities must look above their narrow sectarianism to find constitutional solutions if this is to take place. The resolution of the disagreement calls for a process of give and take on the part of all the contending parties. Only a solution like this can be acceptable for everyone involved. Fair and long-lasting results are only possible with this kind of solution. The reconstruction can start with an objective and open mind. While humanity still exists, it is time to strive for a new generation that is full of love and hope.

REFERENCES

1. Bhaumik, Subir (2023) 'Greater Mizoram' may resurface post-Manipur riots, *The New Indian Express*, June 30, https://www.newindianexpress.com/opinions/2023/jun/30/greater-mizoram-may-resurface-post-manipur-riots-2589849.html.
2. Bose, Rakhi (2023) Manipur, Militancy and The Search For 'Homeland', *The Outlook*, June 27, https://www.outlookindia.com/national/manipur-militancy-and-the-search-for-homeland-news-298250
3. Brahmachari, Deborshi (2019) Ethnicity and Violent Conflicts in Northeast India: Analysing the Trends, *Strategic Analysis*, 43:4, 278-296, DOI: 10.1080/09700161.2019.1623497
4. Goswami, Namrata (2015) Why Violence in Manipur May Recur, *The Hindu Centre for Politics & Public Policy*, September 09, https://www.thehinducentre.com/the-arena/current-issues/why-violence-in-manipur-may-recur/article64931530.ece
5. Haokip, Thongkholal (2013) Essays on the Kuki–Naga Conflict: A Review. *Strategic Analysis*, 37(2),251–259. doi:10.1080/09700161.2012.755785.
6. Hooda, D.S. (2023) The big picture in Manipur, *The Indian Express*, June 26, https://indianexpress.com/article/opinion/columns/manipur-violence-manipur-crisis-big-picture-pm-modi-amit-shah-8685882/
7. Kipgen, Nehginpao (2013) Politics of ethnic Conflict in Manipur, *South Asia Research*, February 2, 33(1): 21-38, DOI:10.1177/0262728013475541

8. Kipgen, Lalmin (2023) Disinformation as a Tool in Manipur Conflict, *The Shillong Times,* June 16, https://theshillongtimes.com/2023/06/16/disinformation-as-a-tool-in-manipur-conflict/.
9. Kipgen, Sheikhohao (2021) Ethnic relation and development-a case study of hill valley relationship in Manipur, *International Journal of Humanities and Social Sciences* (IJHSS), ISSN (P): 2319–393X; ISSN (E): 2319–3948 Vol. 10, Issue 1, Jan-Jun; 113–122.
10. Narayanan, M K (2023) Manipur, a rude reminder of northeast tensions, *The Hindu*, June 12, https://www.thehindu.com/opinion/lead/manipur-a-rude-reminder-of-northeast-tensions/article66958382.ece.
11. Newsclick Report (2023) Manipur Needs Politics That Unites: Nandita Haksar, May 12, https://www.newsclick.in/manipur-needs-politics-unites-nandita-haksar
12. Niumai, Ajailiu (2023) Manipur at the Crossroads after Inter-Ethnic Clashes, *Mainstream Weekly,* May 20.
13. Phanjoubam, Pradip (2023) Challenges around idea of land in Manipur, *The New Indian Express,* May 26, https://www.newindianexpress.com/opinions/2021/may/26/challenges-around-idea-of-land-in-manipur-2307519.html.
14. Roy, Esha (2023) Manipur's ethnic faultlines: Kuki-Meitei divide & recent unrest, *The Indian Express*, May 07, https://indianexpress.com/article/explained/explained-politics/manipurs-ethnic-faultlines-violent-protests-kukis-and-nagas-8594147/.
15. Sibal, Kapil (2023) Managing diversity against backdrop of majoritarianism, *The New Indian Express*, June 26, https://www.newindianexpress.com/opinions/2023/jun/26/managing-diversity-against-backdrop-of-majoritarianism-2588471.html
16. Singh, Amom Malemnganba (2023) Meitei Majoritarian Politics of the BJP in Manipur, *Economic & Political Weekly*, Vol. 58, Issue No. 1, 07 Jan.
17. Singh, Gurinder (2008) In Search of Peace in Manipur: Lessons from Nagaland, *Strategic Analysis,* 32:6, 1115-1129, DOI: 10.1080/09700160802404596
18. Sudarshan, V (2023) Do Manipur clashes have a Chinese angle to it?, *The Deccan Herald*, June 06, https://www.deccanherald.com/opini on/do-manipur-clashes-have-a-chinese-angle-to-it-1225271.html
19. Tombing, Thangzakhup (2023 b) The Epochal Manipur Mayhem, *The Shillong Times*, June 27, https://theshillongtimes.com/2023/06/27/the-epochal-manipur-mayhem/
20. Tombing, Thangzakhup (2023 a) Will HM's visit quench the thirst of Sanamahi spirit in Manipur?, *The Shillong Times*, June 10, https://theshillongtimes.com/2023/06/10/will-hms-visit-quench-the-thirst-of-sanamahi-spirit-in-manipur/.
21. Verma, Abhisek (2023) Report on "The Unfolding Ethnic Conflict in Manipur", *Manohar Parikar Institute for Defence Studies & Analyses*, May 22, https://idsa.in/event/Report-on-The-Unfolding-Ethnic-Conflict-in-Manipur
22. Yumnam, Rosy (2023) Manipur! Let's Give Peace a Chance, *The Shillong Times*, June 22, https://theshillongtimes.com/2023/06/22/manipur-lets-give-peace-a-chance/

13

Human Trafficking: An Overlooked Security Threat to India

— **Priyanka Masant**

Introduction

Human trafficking is an illegal trading of human beings, nowadays a booming industry. It emerged as a growing worldwide problem that victimising men, women and children for exploitation in various forms. However, women and girls disproportionately bear the burden of this heinous crime, often becoming the primary targets of trafficking networks. A significant number of girls are traded, bought, and sold both within and across national borders, making trafficking one of the most profitable illegal industries. This trade thrives on the forced movement of individuals, driven by manipulation, threats, coercion, and violence, to exploit them for labour, sexual purposes, or other inhumane activities. Weak border controls, coupled with systemic corruption, further facilitate the rapid expansion of trafficking operations, enabling these networks to operate with impunity. In the context of globalization, the ease of communication and transportation has inadvertently contributed to the seamless movement of trafficked individuals, allowing traffickers to meet the rising demand for human exploitation. This underscores the urgent need for robust policy interventions and international cooperation to address the socio-economic and institutional factors perpetuating this crime.

In the contemporary era, trafficking is known as modern-day slavery. Like historical forms of slavery, it deprived individuals of their freedom, dignity, and basic rights, forcing them into lives of servitude under inhumane conditions. In India, this crisis is particularly alarming, with an increasing number of girls reported missing every year. Many of these missing girls fall prey to trafficking networks. There is a serious possible link between the missing person and trafficking. According to various reports, it is evident that the girls who have earlier been reported as missing in their local police stations, have been rescued after a long period from brothels in an exploitative condition (Nair & Sen, 2005, p. 164). Their plight reflects a deeper societal failure, as they are deprived of their fundamental rights to safety, education, and livelihood, leaving them caught in cycles of abuses.

Exacerbating this crisis is the issue of weak border security, which allows traffickers to operate with impunity. Porous borders provide an easy pathway for cross-border trafficking, enabling the seamless movement of victims and strengthening transnational criminal networks. This lack of stringent control not only facilitates trafficking but also poses a significant threat to national security. Trafficking networks often intersect with organized crime, terrorism, and corruption, further destabilizing the nation. Addressing human trafficking, therefore, requires a dual focus: protecting vulnerable individuals from exploitation and implementing robust measures to secure borders and dismantle trafficking operations. In this sense, trafficking must be seen as a national security issue due to its consequences that extend beyond individual exploitation, compromising the security, functioning of government, and social cohesion of a society.

Understanding Human Trafficking

Human trafficking is a worldwide crime and deprivation of human rights that include the recruitment, transportation, transfer, or receiving of individuals by force, fraud, and abuse of power for exploitative purposes. This is a multifaceted issue with severe repercussions for victims, who frequently endure forced labour, sexual exploitation, organ trafficking, or other forms of slavery. The predominant concept of human trafficking is articulated in the "United Nations Protocol to Prevent, Suppress and Punish Trafficking in Persons, Especially Women and Children", commonly referred to as the Palermo Protocol. In compliance with the Protocol:

> Trafficking in persons shall mean the recruitment, transportation, transfer, harboring or receipt of persons, by means of the threat or use of force or other forms of coercion, of abduction, of fraud, of deception, of the abuse of power or of a position of vulnerability, or of the giving or receiving of payments or benefits to achieve the consent of a person having control over another person, for the purpose of exploitation (United Nations, 2000).

Exploitation under this definition includes, at a minimum, forced labour, sexual exploitation, slavery or practices like slavery, servitude, and organ removal. This definition highlights three key elements, i.e., the act (what is done), the means (how it is done), and the purpose (why it is done). Similarly, in India this offense of trafficking is being criminalised under the Indian Penal Code, which is currently known as *Bharatiya Naya Sahita*. It defines trafficking in persons as:

> Whoever, for the purpose of exploitation recruits, transports, harbours, transfers, or receives a person or persons, by—(a) using threats; or (b) using force, or any other form of coercion; or (c) by abduction; or (d) by practising fraud, or deception; or (e) by abuse of power; or (f) by inducement, including the giving or receiving of payments or benefits, in order to achieve the consent of any person having control over the person recruited, transported, harboured, transferred or received, commits the offence of trafficking. It further specifies that exploitation must also include slavery, forced labour, and sexual exploitation (India Code, n.d.).

The term "exploitation" here encompasses any act of physical exploitation, any type of sexual exploitation, slavery or related practices, enslavement, begging, or the forceful removal of organs. Notably, victim's consent is irrelevant in the identification of trafficking offenses (India Code, n.d.). Furthermore, the primary objective of the ITPA (Immoral Traffic (Prevention) Act) is to prevent and combat sex trafficking, with a particular emphasis on trafficking for commercial sexual exploitation (Parliament of India, 1956). The Palermo Protocol is closely aligned with India's legal definition, which emphasizes acts, means, and purposes as fundamental components. Although the Protocol offers a comprehensive, global framework, Indian legislation like the IPC and ITPA concentrate more on certain types of trafficking that are common in the nation, like sex trafficking, child labour, and bonded labour. India is both a source and destination country for trafficking, with many incidents involving victims being moved from rural to urban areas or over international borders to and from neighbouring countries such as Nepal, Bangladesh, and Myanmar (UNODC, 2020).

Two major factors contribute to the expansion of this criminal network: the demand factor and the supply factor, often referred to as the push-pull dynamic. The push factors are predominantly linked to regions characterized by poverty, gender inequality, low levels of education, vulnerability to natural disasters, inadequate legal enforcement, corruption, and weak border controls. Additionally, globalisation left a remarkable impact that blew up the hidden crime. These conditions create an environment that facilitates the recruitment and trafficking of victims, making such areas the primary sources of supply in the human trafficking chain.

The pull factor, conversely, is founded in industrialized and more developed cities or regions, where the demand for cheap labour, sexual exploitation, and other forms of human trafficking is considerably greater. Migration for employment has been exacerbated by globalization; however, this movement frequently arises without sufficient safeguards. Many individuals, particularly those from rural areas, migrate to cities in quest of better opportunities, but they are misled or coerced by traffickers. Women are particularly vulnerable to increased risks when they are required to navigate unfamiliar environments without adequate support. These booming regions, which frequently provide economic opportunities and a sense of prosperity, attract traffickers who are attempting to satisfy the demand for exploitation. The unsecured borders with Nepal, Bangladesh, Bhutan, and with other neighbouring countries promote a situation for trafficking of humans, while corruption in law enforcement and border control allows traffickers to operate without consequence (Vidhusy, 2016 & Huda, 2006).

Consequently, victims are frequently coerced, manipulated, or forcibly transported to these regions, often under the guise of false promises of improved lives or employment. This dynamic establishes a systematic cycle in which individuals are attracted to exploitative situations that flourish on these clandestine industries. This issue is one of the most urgent human rights and security challenges on a global scale due to its widespread nature.

Trafficking Routes in India: Domestic and Transnational

Human trafficking in India operates through both domestic and transnational routes, each presenting distinct challenges and reflecting broader socio-economic, political, and infrastructural issues. It poses a serious and increasing threat to national security because of the intricate networks that traffickers use both domestically and internationally. It is essential to comprehend these routes to effectively address the multifaceted nature of the trafficking issue and its broader security implications. Traffickers use these paths to take advantage of the vulnerable population. Because of its strategic geographical location, permeable borders, and socioeconomic vulnerabilities, India serves as both a source and destination country for trafficked humans, as well as a transit point between different regions in certain circumstances.

In trafficking "Patterns and routes are often highly complex, ranging from trafficking within one country and cross-border flows between neighbouring countries to inter-continental and globalised trade" (Nair & Sen, 2005, p. 11). These whole illegal activities are carried on between the inter-state, intra-state as well as transnational. Generally, these routes are similarly categorised as origin, transit, and destination points (p. 11). States like, Andhra Pradesh, Karnataka, Goa, Bihar, Madhya Pradesh, Rajasthan, West Bengal, Uttar Pradesh, and Orissa are observed as a source area. While Rajasthan, Goa, Bangalore, Kerala, Mumbai, Delhi, Kolkata, Hyderabad, and Chennai are believed to be as destination places where victims are recruited (Nair & Sen, 2005; Ghosh, 2009; Joffres et al., 2008, p. 4). The trafficking pathways in India are predominantly influenced by poverty, illiteracy, and gender disparity, causing some regions more vulnerable to trafficking.

The traffickers assume multiple levels of players, including investors, lenders, recruiters, buyers, document forgers, guardians, corrupt government officials, brothel owners, and tour guides, which strengthens organised trafficking. They seamlessly integrate into these roles, through financial investments, recruitment tactics, or forging important documents, they exert their influence and control across different sectors. A broad network exists among police, administrative officials, railway and bus authorities or employees, as well as taxi and auto rickshaw drivers or pullers (Roy & Chaman, 2017).

Some research has shown the hidden link between the criminal network and officials that further strengthens the crime. It is found that:

> In June 2013, 17 police officers, including two superintendents, were suspended in Kerala for their involvement in a sex trafficking network run through two airports. In July 2013, disciplinary action was taken against three Kerala police officers for facilitating the transport of trafficking victims to Dubai. In August 2013, two New Delhi police officers were arrested for running an alleged prostitution and extortion racket…Police also reportedly accepted bribes in the form of money and sexual services in exchange for ignoring or failing to pursue trafficking charges, sexually abused trafficking victims, tipped suspected traffickers off to raids, released suspected traffickers after their arrests, and helped suspected traffickers destroy evidence (Sarkar, 2014, pp. 488-489).

This shows a pitiful situation of the law enforcement. Although rigorous laws and strict adherence are required to combat trafficking, but their involvement in the awful network itself creates a sphere of distrust that further encourages trafficking and exploitation of human beings. About the transnational border, India has shared its border with Bangladesh, Nepal, Bhutan, Myanmar, China and Pakistan. India is not just serving as the destination country but also a transit point. While Pakistan is both a country of destination and a country of passage, Bangladesh and Nepal can be viewed as sending countries or countries of origin. Years of research have shown that trafficking of South Asians happens not only within and between South Asian countries, but also to other continents and areas. There has been a rise in both illegal and undocumented migration in the area and reports of human trafficking as well (Sarkar, 2014).

India and Bangladesh share a 4,222-kilometer border, with 20 official posts monitored by the Border Security Force. They frequently fail to maintain close monitoring since they are few and geographically scattered, and traffickers frequently enter illegally. Between Bangladesh and India, there are numerous enclaves. There are 51 Bangladeshi enclaves in India and 111 Indian enclaves in Bangladesh. These enclaves are frequently used by traffickers as recruitment and recruitment locations (International Labour Organization, 2002, p. 31; Sarkar, 2014, p. 490). Trafficking usually uses a lot of border areas as land routes. Illegal migration to India in pursuit of better work accounts for a significant amount of Bangladesh's cross-border trafficking of women and children. To help with this cross-border movement from Bangladesh to India, several illegal migration businesses have risen (Sarkar, 2014).

In addition, Nepal's long border with India makes migration simple. Due to India's open border policy with Nepal, illicit cross-border movement without documentation is common throughout its 1,740-mile border with 14 legal entry spots. Since Nepalese can enter India freely, trafficking is hard to detect. The 1950 pact between India and Nepal allows Nepalese to travel or migrate to India without immigration controls, making it simpler for traffickers to cross unnoticed. Traffickers sometimes utilize trucks to switch girls between trucks and use unauthorized border posts. From all over Nepal, they finally move largely to Kolkata, Delhi, and Mumbai by train or bus (Sarkar, 2014). Joffres et al. stated that the largest suppliers for Commercial Sexual Exploitation (CSE) into India are Bangladesh and Nepal, which account for 2.17% and 2.6% of the international traffic, respectively (Joffres et al., 2008, p. 4). The porous borders shared between India and its neighbouring countries with undocumented movement create a massive opportunity for the traffickers to strengthen their chains that ultimately result in threat and exploitation of the individuals.

Trafficking and National Security

Human trafficking constitutes not only a violation of human rights and dignity but also a significant criminal and security issue. It may heighten conflict by allowing armed and extreme factions to generate income and enhance their power and military capabilities. It may promote displacement and destabilise communities, ultimately intensifying conflict and hindering development. It is also undertaken by security officers and peacekeepers to undermine the capacity of international institutions to fulfil their mandates of fostering stability and security in the nation (Bigio & Vogelstein, 2019). As security challenges, human trafficking is seen as a "threat multiplier" due to its other security challenges. It not only confined to a sole nature of crime but also supported multiple criminal operations, such as, terrorism and money laundering (Bigio & Vogelstein, 2019, p. 20).

As mentioned by "The Responsible and Ethical Private Sector Coalition against Trafficking (RESPECT)", there is a serious link between terrorism and trafficking to threaten the national security. The extremist and armed groups can use human trafficking to make money, gain more power, and support more armed groups. In particular, the self-proclaimed Islamic State in Iraq and Syria and Boko Haram in Nigeria have forced women and girls to work as sex slaves and made money from sex trafficking. Likewise, corrupt regimes may profit from state-sponsored trafficking, which can boost their military. Human trafficking may additionally lead to displacement and destabilization in communities, increasing tension and hampering the development. All these become a challenge to the security forces and peacekeepers of national as well as international institutions to maintain peace (RESPECT, 2019).

The illicit nature of trafficking carries multiple threats to the security of the nation such as socio-economic, border, and internal strengths. It is a serious violation of human rights and similarly a threat to the structure of governance of the country as well. It has a complex criminal network followed by a highly structured method that is maintained through corruption, violence and exploitation. As an organized crime, human trafficking poses a threat to the national security of India because of its complex network of activities such as the smuggling of drugs and weaponry, money laundering, and the financing of terrorist organizations.

Through intricate networks of trafficking that frequently exist in regions such as West Bengal, Bihar, and the Northeast, it depends on unstable borders, weak administration, and systemic corruption. These networks destabilize borderline regions, finance insurgencies and undermine the rule of law by creating parallel systems that undermine the authority of the institutions. Moreover, trafficking also provides a source of funding to organized crimes, puts pressure on law-enforcement agencies, and destroys social stability through exploitation of vulnerable populations. Thus, this would cause a long-term societal unrest. Hence, it requires a set of actions to strengthen legal systems, enhance law enforcement, deepen international cooperation, fight corruption, and invest in victim rehabilitation. Therefore, identifying trafficking as a national security challenge is important in developing effective and coordinated responses.

Prohibition of Trafficking and State Responses

There are numerous steps taken towards the prevention of trafficking in India. Therefore, to prevent it several sections of Indian Penal Code 1860, the SCs and STs (Prevention of Atrocities) Act 1989, The Juvenile Justice (Care and Protection of Children) Act, 2000, Prevention of Corruption Act, 1988, The Immigration Carriers (Liability) Act, 2000, Immigration Act, 2000 are enacted. All these provisions directly or indirectly address the prevention of trafficking (United Nations Office on Drugs and Crime, 2008, pp. 13-25). There are also other acts such as the ITPA 1956, that mainly focuses on the prevention of trafficking for commercial sexual exploitation. As trafficking is a multifaceted crime, it involves a series of issues under its boundary. For instance, it is linked with human rights violation, sexual exploitation, slavery, terrorism, corruption, cross-border issues, etc. Therefore, it needs to be addressed in multiple approaches without restricting to a particular approach.

Conclusion: A Way Forward

A security-centric approach to trafficking enhances the necessity to understand trafficking as a threat to national security, rather than solely observing it as a social issue. The class, caste, gender, and structural violence are some of the contributing factors that make a person more vulnerable and easily prey to trafficking and facilitate traffickers to recruit them in various regions. Although it is a human rights violation, but at the same time a security concern for both the individual and the state. This happens due to corruption, absence of strict patrolling, and a gap between the enforcement of laws and their implementation, and a low level of conviction rate, further allowing trafficking networks to work fearlessly. Therefore, adopting a robust technology to criminalise every actor involved in trafficking, tracing their activities, identifying the routes are essentially required along with protecting victim.

REFERENCES

1. Bigio, J., & Vogelstein, R. B. (2019). *The Security Implications of Human Trafficking*. Council of foreign Relations.
2. Ghosh, B. (2009). Trafficking in women and children in India: Nature, dimensions and strategies for prevention. *The International Journal of Human Rights, 13*(5), 716-738. doi:10.1080/13642980802533109.

3. Government of India, United Nations Office on Drugs and Crime. (2008). Resources book on the legal framework on anti-human trafficking. https://www.unodc.org/documents/human-trafficking/India_Training_material/Resource_Book_on_Legal_Framework.pdf
4. Huda, S. (2006). Sex trafficking in South Asia. *International journal of gynecology & obstetrics, 94*(3), 374-381.
5. *India Code*. (n.d.). Section 143: Trafficking of person. https://www.indiacode.nic.in/show-data?abv=CEN&statehandle=123456789/1362&actid=AC_CEN_5_23_00048_2023-45_1719292564123&sectionId=90508&sectionno=143&orderno=143&orgactid=AC_CEN_5_23_00048_2023-45_1719292564123
6. International Labour Organisation (2002). *Rapid Assessment on Trafficking in Children for Exploitative Employment in Bangladesh.* International Labour Organisation.
7. Joffres, C., Mills, E., Joffres, M., Khanna, T., Walia, H., & Grund, D. (2008). Sexual slavery without borders: trafficking for commercial sexual exploitation in India. *International Journal for Equity in Health, 7*(1), 1-11. doi.org/10.1186/1475-9276-7-22
8. Nair, P. M., & Sen, S. (2005). *Trafficking in Women and Children in India.* Orient Longman.
9. Parliament of India. (1956). THE IMMORAL TRAFFIC (PREVENTION) ACT, 1956. https://www.indiacode.nic.in/bitstream/123456789/15100/1/immoral_traffic_prevention_act_%28itpa%29_1956.
10. Responsible and Ethical Private Sector Coalition against Trafficking. (2019). *The Security Implications of Human Trafficking*. https://respect.international/the-security-implications-of-human-trafficking/
11. Roy, S., & Chaman, C. (2017). Human rights and trafficking in women and children in India. *Journal of Historical Archaeology & Anthropological Sciences, 1*(5), pp. 162-170.
12. Sarkar, S. (2014). Rethinking Human Trafficking in India: Nature, Extent and Identification of Survivors. *The Round Table, 103*(5), 483–495. doi:10.1080/00358533.2014.966499
13. Shamim, I. (2001) *Mapping of Missing, Kidnapped and Trafficked Children and Women: Bangladesh Perspective.* Bangladesh: International Organization in Migration.
14. United Nations Office on Drugs and Crime (UNODC). (2020). *Global Report on Trafficking in Persons.* Retrieved from https://www.unodc.org/documents/data-and-analysis/tip/2021/GLOTiP_2020_15jan_web.
15. United Nations. (2000). *Protocol to Prevent, Suppress and Punish Trafficking in Persons, Especially Women and Children*. Retrieved from https://www.ohchr.org/en/instruments-mechanisms/instruments/protocol-prevent-suppress-and-punish-trafficking-persons
16. Vidushy, V. (2016). Human trafficking in India: An analysis. *International Journal of Applied Research, 2*(6), 168-171.

14

India and the Road to G20 Presidency: Evolution, Trajectory and The Way Forward

– Mohammed Badrul Alam & Reyaz Ahmad Ganaie

Introduction and Theoretical Framework

The end of the Second World War witnessed the commencement of the era of establishment of international organisations and multilateral fora on a scale never witnessed before. The trend gained even more impetus with the onset of the forces of globalisation and the consequent emergence of a global economy. The process of globalisation led to a mushrooming of "international transactions – flows of money, goods, people and messages across international boundaries."[1] It also led to the deepening of ties, especially economic, among states that resulted in fostering greater interdependence. Further, with the emergence of new and non-traditional threats and concerns (climate crisis, terrorism, global financial crises, cross-border drug trafficking to name just a few), it became inevitable for states, irrespective of their differences in terms of ideology and ethos, to acknowledge the need to collaborate to address these challenges in a collective and concerted manner especially because it was quite evident that such challenges could not be solved by any single state howsoever powerful. This new-found interdependence is what the IR theorists Joseph S. Nye Jr. and Robert Keohane referred to as 'Complex Interdependence' and Hans Morgenthau's realist theory explained on the salience of national interest tinged with power and survival. It is against this backdrop of growing interdependence and pursuit of national interests among the states that the Group of Twenty (or more commonly referred to as G20) came into being.

The Genesis of the G20: Financial Crises as the Stimuli

Established in 1999, the G20 refers to a forum of twenty (nineteen countries plus the European Union) of the world's largest economies. The G20 members include: India, Japan, Australia, the US, the UK, Argentina, Canada, France, China, Germany, South Korea, Italy, Russia, Indonesia, Mexico, Saudi Arabia, South Africa, Brazil, Turkey, and the European Union. The G20 members represent around eighty-five percent of the global GDP, over seventy-five percent of the global trade, and about two-thirds of the world population.[2] The underlying rationale for establishing this forum was to bring together the most industrialized and developing economies to enhance multilateral cooperation and coordination for securing international economic and financial stability. Even though the G20 was preceded by similar groupings with almost identical objectives like the G7 and G77, the fact that the most powerful of these blocs, the G7, was left reeling for cover when the Asian financial crisis of 1997-1999 caused worldwide economic upheaval provided impetus for establishing the G20 to bring together world's most advanced and emerging economies to "harmonize their approaches"[3] to resolve pressing challenges. The effects of the Asian financial crisis led the then Canadian finance minister, Paul Martin, and the US treasury secretary, Larry Summers, to convene a meeting of select finance ministers and central bank governors in December 1999. This initiative paved the way for the establishment of the G20.[4]

For almost a decade, the G20 continued to function at the level of finance ministers and governors of central banks of the member states. Later, in the wake of the US financial crisis of 2008 which caused significant worldwide economic woes, the G20 was elevated to the summit level. The rationale for elevating the forum to summit level has been aptly summed by Stewart M. Patrick as thus: "With the global economy teetering, U.S. President George W. Bush invited the G20 heads of state and government to Washington for an emergency summit, during the waning days of his administration. By elevating the forum to the leaders' level, he conceded that the Western market democracies—working through the smaller G7 grouping—could no longer manage the world economy on their own. They needed the resources and will of emerging economies."[5] The G20 forum proved to be a crucial block whose timely intervention prevented the 2008 US financial crisis from turning into a catastrophe on the scale of the Great Depression. Elaborating on the critical role played by the G20 in the wake of 2008 financial crisis, Stewart M. Patrick argues that "the G20 acted decisively, mobilizing massive liquidity, breathing new life into the Bretton Woods institutions and preventing the Great Recession from becoming another Great Depression."[6]

From 2008 till 2010, G20 leaders met twice a year (in London and Pittsburgh in 2009 and in Toronto and Seoul in 2010). Since 2011, when the G20 summit was chaired and hosted by France, the summits have been held annually.[7] Since then, heads of state or heads of government of member states have held regular summits 'with the single goal of preventing another global financial crisis'.[8] The Summit is held under the leadership of a rotating presidency. To decide as to which member state gets to hold the annual presidency, all the member states of the G20 except the European Union are divided into five different groups.[9] Members of a particular group then have to negotiate among themselves to select the next G20 president when it is that particular group's turn to choose the next president.

Unlike other major international organisations, the G20 functions without a written charter and a permanent secretariat. 'The presidency, aided by the countries holding the presidency before and after it (the *Troika*), is responsible for setting the agenda of each year's summit.'[10] Thus, it is the particular member state holding the annual presidency which sets-up a temporary secretariat to function as the hub for steering that particular country's presidency of the forum.

Expanding Ambit of Objectives of the G20

While the G20 was established (1999) and later raised to the summit level (2008) with a singular focus on managing global financial crises, over the years the objectives of the forum have seen a significant enlargement. Although the primary objective of the G20 continues to be the promotion of global economic stability, the forum now encompasses issues like sustainable development, infrastructure development, combating terrorism, women empowerment, energy cooperation, promotion of tourism, and financial inclusion among others. The G20 as a forum aims to enhance international economic cooperation and coordination among its member states and seeks to promote policies that foster strong, sustainable, and balanced global economic growth. The G20 strives to ensure financial stability worldwide. It focuses on addressing vulnerabilities and risks in the global financial system, enhancing regulation and oversight of financial institutions, and promoting measures to prevent future financial crises. The G20 encourages open and inclusive international trade and investment. It supports efforts to reduce trade barriers, promote a fair and level playing field for businesses, and foster a transparent global trading system.

As a means of promoting open and transparent global trade, the G20 seeks to improve global governance by fostering dialogue and cooperation among member countries. It aims to strengthen international institutions and frameworks to address global challenges effectively, including issues related to finance, trade, development, and climate change. The G20 advocates and seeks to promote free trade and deplores the adoption of protectionism as a trade policy. Besides finance and trade, the G20 also recognizes the importance of sustainable and inclusive development. It focuses on promoting sustainable and inclusive growth, addressing poverty and inequality, and advancing social and environmental sustainability. The G20 also promotes job creation, improving labour market conditions, and enhancing social inclusion. It recognizes the importance of decent work and the need for policies that foster employment opportunities and protect workers' rights. The G20 supports infrastructure development as a driver of economic growth and development. It encourages investment in quality infrastructure projects, including those that are sustainable, resilient, and inclusive. Lastly, another important objective of the G20 is to promote financial inclusion, meaning that individuals and businesses, particularly those in underprivileged populations, have access to affordable education, healthcare, financial services and products.

Apart from the aforementioned objectives, the annual summits of the forum also deal with a specific theme which again provides a clue regarding the overall direction of the forum. For example, in 2021 the G20, under the Presidency of Italy, adopted the theme of 'People,

Planet, and Prosperity'. Similarly, in 2021 the 15th G20 Summit was held by Saudi Arabia under the theme 'Realising Opportunities of the 21st Century for all'.[11] The Indian presidency of the forum has been given the theme of 'Vasudhaiva Kutumbakam' or 'One Earth, One Family, One Future'.

Summits of the G20: A Historical Overview

The G20 summit refers to the annual meeting of the heads of state/ government of member states of the forum. These summits are held under the presidency of a particular member state. These meetings are important in that the leaders of top-ranking economic powerhouses of the world sit together to discuss and deliberate on global issues and concerns and decide on the ways of addressing the same. So far seventeen summit meetings of the G20 have been held while the eighteenth is scheduled to be held in India in September 2023. The member states which have hosted past summits include the United States, the United Kingdom, Canada, South Korea, France, Turkey, Russia, Australia, Germany, Argentina, Saudi Arabia, South Africa, Italy and Indonesia.

Each summit meeting acts as a platform for the member states of the G20 to reaffirm their commitment to the objectives of the forum while at the same time providing them with a space to discuss current and emergent global issues. The first G20 summit, held in Washington D.C. in 2008, was meant to help the member states navigate the financial tumult created by the 2008 financial crisis. The summit was successful in that the member states agreed in principle to work together more concertedly to tackle the effects of the 2008 financial crisis and they also affirmed to remain committed to free market principles.

The second summit, held in London in April 2009, was in essence an extension of the first summit in that the member states were still working on finding ways to correct the financial architectural faults that had caused the financial crisis the previous year. Among other agenda items included in the summit was the idea of building consensus on the need for boosting global trade and reducing protectionism. The agenda also included the reaffirmation of commitment by the member states towards Millennium Development Goals (MDGs). The third summit was held in Pittsburgh, Pennsylvania, in September 2009. The major outcome of this summit meeting was the acceptance of the idea that the G20 would now be the new permanent council for international economic cooperation, an idea which was vigorously pursued and pushed by President Obama. The emergence of consensus on this issue meant that the much larger G20 would supplant the smaller G8. "The G20 will now essentially eclipse the G8, which will continue to meet on major security issues but carry much less influence."[12]

The fourth G20 summit was held in Toronto, Canada in June 2010. The key agenda of this summit included deliberations on the means and methods required to stimulate economic growth and to explore strategies required to recover from the still ongoing global economic recession. While the European Union suggested deficit cuts and austerity measures as the way forward, the United States, India and China, on the other hand, argued in favour of increased stimulus funding as the remedy for fighting recession. The situation in Afghanistan, where the US-led military intervention in late 2001 had resulted in the overthrow of the Taliban regime and the subsequent instituting of democratic processes, was also discussed during the summit dialogue.

The fifth G20 summit was held in Seoul, South Korea in November 2010. This summit, like the preceding ones, was highly skewed in favour of financial and economy-related issues. The major agenda items for the summit included deliberations on and the need for accelerating global economic recovery, sustainable and balanced economic growth, and the need for modernising international financial institutions. The G20 Seoul Summit Leaders' Declaration issued at the end of the summit highlighted the need for concerted action to "break the dramatic fall in the global economy to establish the basis for recovery and renewed growth."[13] The declaration also contained the framework of the so-called Seoul Action Plan. The SAP is in essence a reflection of the consensus reached during the summit on mitigating the effects of global economic recession and the varied modus operandi agreed upon to achieve market stabilisation and sustainable growth.[14]

The sixth G20 summit was held in Cannes, France. The summit took place in the backdrop of the Eurozone crisis[15] and it did not prove successful insofar as the member states couldn't agree on concrete measures and solutions to restore and strengthen the global economy.

However, in other areas like agriculture and food security, the summit proved to be successful in taking novel initiatives to improve agricultural production worldwide. About the objective of guaranteeing food security for all, the Cannes Summit Final Declaration entitled 'Building Our Common Future: Renewed Collective Action for The Benefit of All' reads as thus: "We [meaning the leaders of the member countries of the G20 who collectively issued this declaration at the end of the summit] commit to sustainably increase agricultural production and productivity. To feed a world population expected to reach more than 9 billion people by 2050, it is estimated that agricultural production will have to increase by 70% over the same period. We agree to further invest in agriculture, in particular in the poorest countries, and bearing in mind the importance of smallholders, through responsible public and private investment."[16]

Held in the city of Los Cabos in Mexico in June 2012, the seventh G20 summit was unique in that it reflected a clear trend in the increasing participation and importance of emerging economies in sustaining the global financial institutions, particularly the IMF. Commenting on the importance of this shift, Peter Wolff argued that "One of the few tangible outcomes of the summit was the increase in IMF resources by more than US$ 450 billion, with substantial contributions from China, Brazil and Russia. These resources are intended as the "last line of defence" for the euro's continued existence, even though the summit declaration says that the money is available to all IMF members. The emerging economies have thus bought a larger say in the running of the IMF and a further review of capital shares in 2014, with the prospect of more voting rights in the future."[17]

The eighth summit meeting of the G20 was held in Saint Petersburg, Russia in September 2013. The summit was held at a time when Syria was dealing with a deadly civil war. The United States and Russia were at loggerheads with each other since they harboured antagonistic objectives concerning the Syrian question. While the United States wanted to obtain authorization from the United Nations to launch military strikes against the Bashar-al Assad regime in Syria; Russia, on the other hand, was a staunch supporter of the Assad regime and had therefore blocked US efforts at the UN. Thus, the summit virtually became a contest between the two states with each trying to garner as much support in support of its cause. On the economic front, the summit declaration contained pledges by the member states to work together to promote sustainable and inclusive growth, reduce corruption, improve food security, financial inclusion, infrastructure, and human resource development and domestic resource mobilization.[18]

The ninth summit of the G20 was held in November 2014 in Brisbane, Australia. Raising global growth, creation of quality jobs, poverty eradication, energy cooperation and other related issues found a mention in the communiqué issued at the end of the summit. The tenth summit was held in Antalya, Turkey in November 2015. The official communiqué issued at the end of the summit included pledges related to issues like 'implementation of sound macroeconomic policies in a cooperative manner to achieve strong, sustainable and balanced growth', lifting of collective G20 GDP by two percent, integration of 'youth into labour markets including through the promotion of entrepreneurship', reducing corruption, energy collaboration, 'effective, strong and collective action on climate change and its effects', the 'need for a coordinated and comprehensive response to tackle [refugee] crisis, as well as its long term consequences'.[19]

The eleventh summit of the forum was held in Hangzhou, China in September 2016. The main issues or themes which found a mention in the G20 Leaders' communiqué include fighting tax evasion and tax havens, opposition to protectionism, fighting 'populist attacks' on globalisation, and stepping up aid for the refugees.[20]

Held in the city of Hamburg, Germany in July 2017, the twelfth summit of the G20, apart from deliberating on recurring themes related to global trade and economy, also discussed new issues like fighting corruption, coordination and cooperation on displacement and migration, food security, rural youth employment, and women's empowerment.[21] The thirteenth summit of the forum was held in Buenos Aires, Argentina, on 30 November 2017 and December 1, 2018. The summit marked the completion of a decade of G20 summits. The summit declaration while focussing on the need to foster close economic cooperation also emphasised the need for strengthening a rules-based international order, better jobs and higher standard of living, gender equality, access to education, 'importance of shared actions to address the root causes of displacement and to respond to growing humanitarian needs', and the need to 'tackle climate change, while promoting sustainable development and economic growth'.[22]

The fourteenth G20 summit was held in Osaka, Japan in June 2019. The central focus of this summit continued to be economic growth and trade cooperation, however, other issues also found substantial mention in the summit declaration. These issues include the need for digitalisation and free flow of data, climate change, reducing corruption and promoting transparency in public and private sectors, women's empowerment, promoting tourism, agriculture, global health, and displacement and migration.[23]

By the time the fifteenth summit of the G20 was scheduled to be held in Riyadh, Saudi Arabia in November 2020, the Covid-19 pandemic had wreaked havoc worldwide and therefore the summit was held virtually. The actual summit was preceded by an emergency meeting of G2O members on March 26, 2020, wherein they deliberated on the ways to mitigate the challenge posed by the Covid-19 outbreak. The Riyadh Summit was dominated by concerns related to the pandemic even though other issues were also discussed. The G20 leaders affirmed to work together to 'protect lives, provide support with a special focus on the most vulnerable, and put economies back on a path to restoring growth, and protecting and creating jobs for all.'[24] In the wake of Covid-19 pandemic issues like health, transportation and travel, access to education, and women's empowerment were discussed in great detail and these also found space in the final declaration.

The sixteenth G20 summit was held in Rome, Italy in October 2021. The summit was dominated by calls for equitable distribution of Covid-19 vaccines throughout the world. The summit declaration called upon member states to remain 'determined to use all available tools for as long as required to address the adverse consequences of the pandemic, in particular on those most impacted, such as women, youth, and informal and low-skilled workers, and on inequalities'.[25] Another major theme of the summit was to devise ways to bring back economies of member states to growing trajectories given that almost all states' economies had suffered because of pandemic-induced restrictions. Apart from these issues, the recurring themes of strengthening international economic and trade cooperation, environment, energy cooperation, and gender equality and women's empowerment were also part of the deliberations and summit declaration.

Before India took on the mantle of G20 presidency, the G20 presidency gavel was held by Indonesia, where in the city of Bali, the seventeenth G20 summit was held in November 2022. The summit proved to be a diplomatically and politically charged affair since Russia had begun a full-scale military offensive on Ukraine in February 2022. Therefore, some member states wanted Russia to not be invited to the summit meeting. China, on the other hand, sided with Russia by arguing that no member state or states had the right to remove another state's membership. Eventually what transpired is that President Putin chose not to attend the summit and in his stead, it was Russia's foreign minister Sergey Lavrov who represented Russia. Interestingly, Ukrainian President Volodymyr Zelenskyy was invited to participate by video-conference as a guest.

The summit declaration unequivocally denounced Russia's actions in Ukraine. In this regard the declaration stated: "Most members strongly condemned the war in Ukraine and stressed it is causing immense human suffering and exacerbating existing fragilities in the global economy – constraining growth, increasing inflation, disrupting supply chains, heightening energy and food insecurity, and elevating financial stability risks."[26] The significance of countries such as India, Brazil, South Africa, Mexico, Indonesia, and Turkey was on display during the summit, for it is because of the support these countries extended to the United States that the language of UN Resolutions condemning Russian aggression in Ukraine was incorporated in the summit declaration. It was Indian Prime Minister Narendra Modi's idiom that 'today's era must not be of war' – which he had used earlier in his statement to Putin in a bilateral meeting on the margins of the Shanghai Cooperation Organisation summit in Samarkand in September 2022 – that concluded the summit's declaration on Ukraine.[27] Referring to Modi's blunt message to President Putin, the G20 Bali Declaration noted that "The peaceful resolution of conflicts, efforts to address crises, as well as diplomacy and dialogue, are vital. Today's era must not be of war."[28]

India's G20 Presidency: Opportunities and Challenges

India as an important stakeholder of the G20 group of nations adheres to key objectives of the G20 platform that have been reached on a consensus basis. It includes: establishing and strengthening and reinforcing global architecture, fostering sustainable global economic cooperation, formulating international standards for tackling oppressing and critical problems, providing aid to the most vulnerable nations particularly in the Global South and aiming and striving for recovery on high-quality employment, showing a resolute commitment to a strong, viable as well as a balanced and inclusive growth at a level-playing field across member nations.

In sync with and publicly professed emphasis on the Maha Upanishad concept of 'Vasudhaiva Kutumbakam' , or the 'One Earth, One Family, One Future' and 'World is One Family', the primary focus and road map of the 2023 G20 summit in India are the follows: LiFE (Lifestyles for Environment for promotion of environmentally-conscious practices and is based on India's sustainable initiatives; Boosting Employment; Inclusive, Equitable, Accelerated, Resilient and Sustainable Growth for bringing about appropriate structural transformation including supporting small and medium-sized enterprises in global trade in conformity with labour rights and welfare and agricultural value chains with a particular emphasis on mitigating the adverse impact of the Covid-19 pandemic, increased knowledge-sharing in tourism, agriculture; Skill-mapping, climate financing, global food security, energy security, and green hydrogen; promoting a human-centric approach for developing digital public infrastructure, financial inclusion and tech-enabled development; multilateral institutions for the 21st century and to make it more inclusive, representative and accountable; women-led development geared toward women empowerment and representation in line with goals and objectives of SDGs.

The G20 has two main tracks of engagement: the Finance track for finance ministers and central bank governors and the Sherpa Track. The G20's proceedings are led by the Sherpas, who are appointed as personal emissaries of the leaders of member nations. These sherpas are responsible for overseeing and in leading the negotiations that occur throughout the year, deliberating and debating on the agenda for the summit and coordinating the substantive work of the G20. Both tracks have working groups to address specific themes with representatives from relevant parties and stakeholders.

India has taken a deliberate proactive approach and initiative in G20 agenda commensurate with its core national interests that include: earning respect from around the globe including the Global North and Global South by trying earnestly to bridge its divide; gaining credibility through strength and displaying both hard as well as soft power in an increasingly multipolar and multiplex world; building a diversified and robust defense diplomacy and without any ambition of being a hegemon; creating good neighbourhood policy in the Indian subcontinent by maintain cordiality and flexibility in SAARC, BIMSTEC; reaching out to major powers through multilateral bodies such as QUAD, BRICS, SCO, I2U2; promoting indigenous weapons such as Brahmos, Tejas, Trishul, Vikrant, Arjun, Vajra, etc, for country's defense with the stated goal of 'Atmanirbhar Bharat' adopting both bilateralism and multilateralism along with minilateralism depending upon issues and regions; maintaining 'strategic autonomy' and assertive, forward looking, muscular and yet benign approach in the conduct of foreign policy.

As India takes the center stage in the 2023 Delhi summit of G20 leaders, India reminds the world of the 'scourge of war' as it was reflected in the PM Modi's assertion that 'today's era must not be of war' and which was prominently included in the 2022 Bali Declaration. India's stock has risen from a middle power to an emerging super power and an upper-tier country in the global economy in recent years. India's non-intrusive and non-prescriptive, and a country with no extra territorial ambitions that has been noticed by the international community.[29]

India is probably the only and a rare country in the world today to have strategic and special relationship with both the United States and Russia, and even amongst arch regional rivals, be it Turkey, Iran, Saudi Arabia, and Israel. India has emerged as the home to the world's largest number of Unicorns with startups valued at more than US one billion dollars in the year 2022, surpassing China. India's ambitious drive toward encouraging digital payments through UPI and e-wallets has created records with 48 billion real-time transactions in 2021, almost three times that of China (18 billion) and 6.5 times greater than the US, Canada, UK, France and Germany combined. India's active collaboration with the International Solar Alliance in 2015 has an installed capacity around 61.97 GW as on November 2022. Wind, hydro and nuclear power complement India's drive towards reduced dependence on fossil fuels. India is presently the world's third largest producer of renewable energy. Recent discovery of approximately 5.9 million tons of Lithium in Jammu and Kashmir will make India one of the countries having the seventh largest lithium deposits in the world, and which in turn has the potential of contributing significantly to India's march towards a robust economic growth and ascendancy.[30]

In 2023, apart from holding the G20 Presidency, India is at the helm of SCO and in December 2022, it was also holding the presidency of the UN Security Council. India's humanitarian assistance in recent times to countries such as Turkey, Yemen, Sudan, Nepal, etc, has earned enormous goodwill in the comity of nations. India's emphasis on civilisational ethos and strive for consensus has served it well and that includes on a wide range of issues of immense importance such as disaster management, financial stability, trans-national crime, corruption, terrorism, food and energy security, cybercrime, drug trafficking, etc. in a world which is beset with challenges and uncertainties from the fallout of the Russia-Ukraine crisis, fluid food and energy security situation, North Korea's apparent belligerence, global economic slowdown and the possibility of recession, cataclysmic impact of climate change and global warming, emerging threat to trade and commerce in the Indian Ocean region and in the Indo-Pacific, clouds of warlike situation in Taiwan and South China Sea. India as a leading global power is poised to be a 'brand state' by taking the lead in being an honest facilitator and in converting trust deficit to trust surplus and in swaying window of vulnerabilities to window of opportunities. India as a responsible world power and a key partner and catalyst for real change is committed to overcome ideological, economic and military divisions and cleavages with a determined will, long-term vision with a clear focus and a compassionate approach toward one and all in the global family of nations and thus be a *setu* (bridge) of solidarity and prosperity amidst shifting loyalties, hedging and polarised poly-alignment.[31]

ENDNOTES

1. Kenneth S. Rogerson (2000), "Information Interdependence: Keohane and Nye's complex interdependence in the information age," *Information, Communication & Society*, Vol. 3, No. 3, pp. 415-436.
2. The Group of Twenty, National Portal of India. Available at: https://www.india.gov.in/spotlight/group-twenty-g20#:~:text=The%20Group%20does%20not%20have,%2C%20India%20and%20Brazil%2C%20respectively. (Accessed on 25 May 2023).

3. Manjeet Kripalani and Rajiv Bhatia, "The Group of Twenty Today: India's Opportunity to Lead." Available at: https://www.gatewayhouse.in/the-group-of-twenty-today-indias-opportunity-to-lead/ (Accessed on 4 April 2023). For an overview, please see, Kirton, John J. Governance for a Globalized World, 2015, Routledge: New York. ; Kripalani Manjeet. India in the G20: Rule-taker to Rule-maker, 2021, Routledge India: Delhi; Slaughter Stephen. The Power of the G20: The Politics of Legitimacy in Global Governance, Routledge: New York; Srinivas. G20@2023: The Roadmap for Indian Foreign Policy. 2023, Pentagon Press: Delhi; Special issue on India's G20 Presidency, World Focus, New Delhi, May 2023.
4. *Ibid.*
5. Stewart M. Patrick (October 25, 2021), "The G20 Was Made for Moments Like This," Council on Foreign Relations. Available at: https://www.cfr.org/blog/g20-was-made-moments (Accessed on 23 May 2023).
6. *Ibid.*
7. Ministry of External Affairs, Government of India. Available at: https://mea.gov.in/Portal/ForeignRelation/G20_Brief_for_website_-_27.10__1___1_.pdf (Accessed on 23 May 2023).
8. Manjeet Kripalani and Rajiv Bhatia, "The Group of Twenty Today: India's Opportunity to Lead."
9. There are a total of five groups. Group 1 consists of Australia, Canada, Saudi Arabia and the United Sates. Group 2 consist of India, Russia, South Africa and Turkey. Group 3 has Argentina, Brazil and Russia as its members. Group 4 includes France, Germany, Italy and the United Kingdom while Group 5 consists of China, Indonesia, Japan and South Korea. Except for Group 1 and Group 2, the rest have a predominantly regional character. Every year, the G20 selects a country from another group to be the forum's president.
10. Ministry of External Affairs, Government of India. *Ibid.* For instance in the case of current presidency which is held by India, the *troika* consists of Indonesia (the preceding president), India (the current president), and Brazil (the next scheduled president of the forum).
11. Ministry of External Affairs, Government of India. Available at: https://mea.gov.in/Portal/ForeignRelation/G20_Brief_for_website_-_27.10__1___1_.pdf (Accessed on 20 May 2023).
12. "Officials: G-20 to supplant G-8 as international economic council," *CNN*. Available at: http://edition.cnn.com/2009/US/09/24/us.g.twenty.summit/ (Accessed on 5 June 2023).
13. 'The G20 Seoul Summit Leaders' Declaration November 11 – 12, 2010'. Available at: https://www.oecd.org/g20/summits/seoul/G20-Seoul-Summit-Leaders-Declaration.pdf (Accessed on 3 June 2023).
14. *Ibid.*
15. Eurozone crisis, also known as the European debt crisis, was a balance of payments crisis that lasted from 2009 till mid-2010s and in some states of the European Union it lasted till late 2010s.

16. Cannes Summit Final Declaration "Building Our Common Future: Renewed Collective Action For The Benefit Of All". Available at: https://www.oecd.org/g20/summits/cannes/Cannes%20Declaration%204%20November%202011.pdf (Accessed on 5 June 2023).
17. Peter Wolff, "The G20 summit in Mexico – Nothing but declarations of intent?," German Development Institute. Available at: https://www.idos-research.de/uploads/media/Column_Wolff.25.06.2012.pdf (Accessed on 9 June 2023).
18. The G20 Russia Summit Leaders' Declaration. Available at: https://www.oecd.org/g20/summits/saint-petersburg/Saint-Petersburg-Declaration.pdf (Accessed on 29 May 2023).
19. G20 Leaders' Communiqué, Antalya, Turkey, November 16, 2015. Available at: http://www.g20.utoronto.ca/2015/151116-communique.html (Accessed on 7 June 2023).
20. "G20 agreement to "oppose protectionism" and fight tax evasion" (September 5, 2016), *Le Monde*. Available at: https://www.lemonde.fr/economie-mondiale/article/2016/09/05/accord-du-g20-pour-s-opposer-au-protectionnisme-et-lutter-contre-l-evasion-fiscale_4992783_1656941.html (Accessed on 7 June 2023).
21. 'G20 Leaders' Declaration: Shaping an Interconnected World'. Available at: http://www.g20.utoronto.ca/2017/2017-G20-leaders-declaration.html (Accessed on 3 June 2023).
22. 'G20 Leaders' Declaration: Building consensus for fair and sustainable development'. Available at: https://www.consilium.europa.eu/media/37247/buenos_aires_leaders_declaration.pdf (Accessed on 6 June 2023).
23. 'G20 Osaka Leaders' Declaration'. Available at: https://www.mofa.go.jp/policy/economy/g20_summit/osaka19/en/documents/final_g20_osaka_leaders_declaration.html (Accessed on 4 June 2023).
24. 'G20 Saudi Arabia Riyadh Summit Declaration'. Available at: http://www.g20.utoronto.ca/2020/2020-g20-leaders-declaration-1121.html (Accessed on 5 June 2023).
25. 'G20 Rome Leaders' Declaration'. Available at: https://www.governo.it/sites/governo.it/files/G20ROMELEADERSDECLARATION_0.pdf (Accessed on 5 June 2023).
26. 'G20 Bali Leaders' Declaration'. Available at: https://www.whitehouse.gov/briefing-room/statements-releases/2022/11/16/g20-bali-leaders-declaration/ (Accessed on 7 June 2023).
27. Robin Niblett (22 November 2022), "The G20 Bali summit showcases a more diverse world". Available at: https://www.chathamhouse.org/2022/11/g20-bali-summit-showcases-more-diverse-world (Accessed on 6 June 2023).
28. *Ibid*
29. Col. Rajeev Agarwal, (February 17, 2023), www.firstpost.com, 'One Earth, One Family, One Future': as World Looks at India for Leadership, how New Delhi should set its Course'.
30. *Ibid.*

31. Sujan R. Chenoy. 'India's G20 Presidency: Setting the World Agenda", Observer Research Foundation (ORF), New Delhi, www.orfonline.org, 2 December 2022; also, see, Harsh N. Pant. 'India's Moment: The G20 Presidency and Beyond',; also, see, 'India's G20 Presidency: Challenges and Opportunities', Center for Air Power Studies, www.capsindia.org, 7 December 2022; also, see, 'Opportunities and Challenges of India's G20 Presidency', POLITICO.eu, www.politico.eu, 27 December 2022 ORF, New Delhi, www.orfonline.org, 9 November 2022.

15

India's G20 Presidency: Strengthening Multilateralism for the 21st Century

– **Neeraj Singh Manhas**

Introduction

Even before its independence, India interacted at the world level with international institutes like the League of Nations, World Bank (WB), International Monetary Fund (IMF) and United Nations (UN). Civilisational and historical imperatives have framed India's interaction with the entire world. (Pande, 2020). But not long after its interaction India realised that not enough was being done for the Global South. India made efforts to establish international institutions that are not governed by Western European nations or the United States of America in response to its unjust representation in these institutions. India ought to be a beacon not only for Asia but also for the entire world. (Pande, 2020). When India's G20 presidency began, it vowed not only to represent the Global South but as said by Prime Minister Narendra Modi: *"India's G20 Presidency will work to promote this universal sense of one-ness. Hence our theme – 'One Earth, One Family, One Future"*. (PIB, 2022). The G20 Logo is inspired by the vibrant colours of India's national flag, the Tricolour, but the Earth reflects India's pro-planet approach to life, one in perfect harmony with nature. (PIB, 2022).

At the same time, Prime Minister also emphasized, *"We, the Global South has the largest stakes in the future as three-fourths of humanity lives in our countries. We should also have an equivalent voice. Hence, as the eight-decade-old model of global governance slowly changes, we should try to shape the emerging order."* (BW Online Bureau, 2023). This statement is more than enough to show that India is ready to represent the global South by amplifying its voice in multilateral organisations. It is time that we reform such institutes and focus towards finding solutions to transnational threats.

The Need to Address the Concerns and Priorities

India has identified five priorities of the G20 members which will be discussed at the summits. Growth and prosperity, resilient global value chains, Ministry of Micro, Small & Medium Enterprises (MSMEs), logistics, and WTO reforms are the listed priorities under its G20 presidency from December 1, 2022, to November 30, 2023. (Suneja, 2022). But one agenda was already decided in Bali's G20 Summit, that is, to stop the Russia-Ukraine conflict. This conflict is a major concern and a priority of not only the member states but also every country in the world, and therefore cannot be separated from the G20. (Laskar, 2023). India's passion to ensure that all member countries of G20 voice their concern will be seen throughout its presidency. One such instance is while speaking at the Raisina@ Sydney event in Australia, External Affairs Minister *S Jaishankar* said that as the G20 members are expected to address and resolve global challenges, they bear a great deal of responsibility. *"It is a time when you have a certain convening power, agenda-shaping opportunity but it is also a particular juncture of world politics,"* said Jaishankar. (Standard, 2023).

Several months into the presidency and India already knows that it will succeed in addressing everyone's major concerns and priorities. A statement given in the media by Amitabh Kant claimed that India is confident that disagreements over the Ukraine-Russia conflict will allow it to advance the topics raised during its G20 leadership. *"We have had very constructive and positive discussions. We have already got 99%. The other 1% is not in India's hand, someone else has created that."* Kant also addressed that there is support for reform in the World Bank, climate change resolution, and debt problems of the poorer countries.

India has also garnered the support of other countries who are pessimistic over the way the USA and European countries are approaching the Russia-Ukraine conflict. Another problem is that the central banks of the USA and other developing markets in the developing economies have raised interest rates to combat inflation. This has resulted in a flight of campaign from emerging markets. We must create multinational institutions to address this. *"This will require us to shape multilateral institutes."* (Sidhartha, Gupta, 2023)

The Potential to Create a More Inclusive and Equitable International System

Apart from all agendas of India's G20, one unique agenda picked by India is reform in multilateral institutes to have a higher focus on the equal role, representation, and participation of all countries of the world. Creating such ideals in multilateral platforms has always been an agenda of India. India's top priority at the G20 will be to keep pushing for multilateralism to be changed to build a multipolar international system that is more responsible, inclusive, just, egalitarian, and representative and is capable of confronting the challenges of the twenty-first century. (PIB, 2022)

Unlike the 20th century, which was driven by ideological stands and national interest, where India was part of organisations like NAM to show its political and ideological stand, and G77 to show its economic stand. (Malone, Mohan, Raghavan, 2016) The 21st century is based on the needs of the nation in the globalised world and therefore India is part of many multilateral organisations despite its ideological beliefs like the G20, BRICS organisation consisting of emerging nations like Brazil, Russia, India, China and South Africa, Shanghai Cooperation Organisation (SCO) etc. (Mohan, 2006). By being part of various multilateral and plurilateral organisations India wants to amplify its voice in the global community and ensure that plaguing global issues of energy, climate change, and terrorism reach their solutions. The policies of India are made keeping in mind that the world remains at peace without any enmity.

Multilateral organisations like G20 allow countries to meet regularly and establish global norms, keep a check on the political power of countries and institutions, and ensure greater fairness. (G20, 2022). The global community consists of both the Global North and the Global South and therefore India also seeks to reform global agencies, which it feels are influenced heavily by the world's major powers. Seeing itself as a future major power, India has positioned itself as the voice of equanimity in international bodies, demanding that more powerful nations voluntarily cede some of their influence for the sake of greater fairness in international affairs. (Pande, 2020)

India's G20 presidency has come at a very volatile time, the economies of the world are still recovering from the shocks of the COVID-19 pandemic, and the Ukraine-Russia conflict has not come to a halt. In the midst, the world expects India to take a stand and address the issues which affect the member-states. One way of doing so is also through multilateral organisations, India is part of organisations like BRICS, RIC and SCO comprising of nations like Russia, China, India, Brazil, and South Africa. These organisations were made a long time back based on strong friendship and cooperation. These countries are also believed to be as diverse as India and hence share similar values. At the time of COVID-19, they helped each other through medical and healthcare facilities like vaccines and medicines. They have enough power that if they put enough pressure on Russia, they might convince Russia to end the war, thus addressing one of the biggest issues the world is facing today and is affecting all the G20 members. (Grossman, 2023)

Indian Presidency has set G20 priorities that are not restricted to one region but are transnational. The G20 has a special focus on macroeconomic implications of food and energy insecurity, climate change, strengthening Multilateral Development Banks (MDBs), financing inclusivity, equitable and sustainable growth, digital public infrastructure, and climate financing. India wants that while these issues are addressed by global leaders, their approach should be citizen-centric. (PIB, 2022). Amitabh Kant, a G20 Sherpa, contends that reaching "consensuses on the G20 agenda" is the problem encountered by India's G20 Presidency. Despite geopolitical worries, India will continue to use the G20 forum for its constructive dialogue and diplomacy, which it successfully used in the run-up to the Bali Summit on the crucial topic of opposing Russia's aggression against Ukraine. (Challenges to India's G20 Presidency and Effectiveness of G20 Framework)

India now believes that it is the voice of the Global South. (India Is the Voice of the Global South, 2023). The G20 presidency means fewer presumptions from the side of the West and India will have to show a greater international civic duty. (Sen, 2023) It will have to put pressure on the world to reform its institutions and systems and create an inclusive and equitable international system. Brazil, India, and South Africa are developing economies that awkwardly straddle the North and South's views and interests. India, for instance, has been particularly outspoken on the need for the development of global governance institutions to be centred on minimising and addressing economic disparities in the developing world. (Hampson, Heinbecker, 2011). Similar can also be seen with India and its G20 presidency as Priyanjali Malik writes, the excuse that politics and war are outside the purview of the G-20 cannot be used by Russia and China. The Ukrainian conflict has an impact on the world economy, global warming, nuclear stability, and the UN Charter values that support the rule of law in international interactions. The first two are essential to India's agenda as the G-20 chair this year; the G-20 cannot function without the other two. (Malik, 2023). Indian Prime Minister Modi, in the G20 Bali Summit, claimed *"Now is not the time of war."* (India, "Now Is Not the Time for War, Let Us Strategies for Peace, PM Modi Tells Putin." 2022)

Compared to bigger international institutions like the UN and IMF, membership in the G-20 fosters a sense of shared purpose among the twenty members and reduces members' identification with regional or other organisations. A G-20 agreement on a specific issue might serve as a potent catalyst for action and UN reform. (Hampson, Heinbecker, 2011) In the areas of security, development, global governance, and international institutional innovation, multilateralism, and forums like the G20 allow for new, informal relationships that are likely to arise among nations that are not themselves "great powers" by conventional means. (Hampson, Heinbecker, 2011)

In this paper, we highlight India's stance towards multilateralism under its G20 presidency. We will first look at the current state of multilateral cooperation, its challenges, and the utility crisis. The second part of the paper will talk about the reforms needed in multilateral cooperation to ensure collective and coordinated action, and the last part will focus on India's G20 presidency and how it addresses the biggest transnational issues of the world through multilateralism.

Current State of Multilateral Cooperation

India is a member of many multilateral organisations. In some of these organisations, India is just like another member, but in other organisations, like BRICS, India plays a vital role. But in any case, India has made a point that its position on various economic and political areas in these organisations remains clear. Even for its G20 presidency, India has focused on financing inclusivity, equitable and sustainable growth, digital public infrastructure, and climate financing. It has ensured that these themes gain enough weight that they remain in focus for a longer time. Multilateralism, whether regional or global, has always had a powerful appeal in the Indian foreign-policy discourse. (Green and Gill, 2009)

Immediately after its independence, India started seeking membership in the multilateral organisation to discuss its security and development issues, which impacted India's territory and sovereignty but over the years India's approach has changed. India is not just a member of those few organisations that serve its domestic purpose but also the global purpose. For a long time now, India has been talking about "Asian Unity" in multilateral organisations that involve India and its neighbourhood. China has been doing the same. To advance Pan-Asianism and implement a global Asian security strategy, Asian nations must put aside their distinct cultural, linguistic, economic, and other divisions. This is known as "Asian Unity." (Shome, 2022) But this idea looks deceptive and challenging as regional plurilateral groups of Asia have not been able to gain much success as compared to bigger international organisations. Such regional issues are the biggest challenge of any multilateral organisation.

To illustrate this, we shall take the example of SAARC (South Asian Association for Regional Cooperation) formed in 1985, which failed to fulfil its objective and has not met after 2014. India refuses to attend SAARC summits if cross-border terrorism from Pakistan does not come to an end. (Poudel, 2022) Shome in his article *Asian Unity: No Longer a Pipe Dream* argues that border conflicts come in the way of pan-Asian unity. India and China are at odds over their shared border and security concerns, Japan and China are at odds economically and over past Japanese atrocities committed in China, South Korea and China are at odds over the latter's alleged support for the regime in North Korea, and Vietnam and China are at odds over the South China Sea dispute. So, it is very clear that each nation will prioritise its national interests first instead of promoting the idea of a broader continental identity. (Shome, 2022) He extends his argument to religion, religious extremism in West Asia, the victory of the Taliban regime in Afghanistan, and the sponsorship of Islamist radicalism in Pakistan, making the idea of achieving pan-Asian unity an arduous task. Religion in this context overrides ethnic identity.

Loss of Trust in Multilateralism

Persistent deadlocks and disagreements among member-states arise when an idea or a goal is seen unilaterally. For example, India's new pan-Asian consciousness was built on a foundation of Indian nationalism and not Asian consciousness and knowledge. (Green and Gill, 2009) While Pan-Asianism was based initially on the premises of Asian cultural and spiritual unity, the unique moral mission of the Orient, and the desirability of reviving Greater India, nationalist Indians injected a political character into the concept by advancing the notion of creating some form of Asian political federation under Indian leadership. (Keenlyside, 1982) This has also been established that the smaller countries in Asia and South Asia specifically have feared India and China's dominance in Asia. While both India and China fear each other's dominance this prevents them from taking a unilateral stand in the multilateral organisations. By 2014, China had started pushing for full membership in SAARC but India opposed this. (Roche, 2014)

Chi-Wook Kim has developed the thesis of multilateralism through bilateralism in Asia. The concept is that the framework for de facto multilateralism in regional economic governance is provided by dense networks of bilateral agreements with comparable contents. (Kim, 2015) In his study, Kim contrasts Asia with Europe, where formal multilateral organisations have always been coupled to economic interdependence. The economic governance in Asia, however, is governed by numerous bilateral agreements. Unfortunately, there are no regional trade agreements in Asia that cover the region's main economies. Instead, a centre of international FTA networks has developed as a result of bilateral free trade agreements (FTAs) between

Asia Pacific countries. (Kim, 2015) The socio-political history of Asia has amounted to distrust in the region. Politically speaking, not all countries in Asia follow the liberal democratic order, some bigger nations like Russia and China are authoritarian, this creates ruptures in summit meetings as different countries may not agree on some treatise or inter-governmental cooperation.

Utility Crisis and How It Affects Multilateralism

Since the presidency of Donald Trump in the US, multilateralism is facing a utility crisis. A crisis where powerful member-states think that the organisation is no longer useful for them or it does not serve the national interest of that member-state. (Kumar, 2023) This utility crisis is often associated with de-globalisation. In 2018, the Indian government took steps toward the same. India participated fully in multilateral cooperation, but despite this, the government is taking steps to protect its farmers, shopkeepers, tech companies, and other sectors from foreign competition by boosting tariffs on hundreds of assortments of goods. (Zakaria, 2022) When Mahathir Mohamad, the prime minister of Malaysia, criticised some of Modi's Muslim-related policies. The imports of palm oil from Malaysia were essentially stopped by the Indian government. (Cherian, 2020) Incidents like this not only break the thread of bilateral relations but also rupture the working of multilateral organisations where cooperation and trust are most important. It is important to note here that bilateral relations or regional organisations vary in their contribution to multilateralism. (Ruland, 2011) This utility crisis can also emerge when in a grouping some members hold more power than others. This is usually seen in formal organisations. Brexit is an example of this. Trump decided to leave the Paris Agreement and the UN Human Rights Council.

The hyper-nationalist stance in the foreign policy of various right-wing ruling parties of the world has also caused this utility crisis. As such, governments are away to take stands for transnational issues like climate change, transgender rights, Islamophobia, racism, and anti-migration laws both domestically and at the inter-governmental level. More research is needed on this topic to make a relation between how hyper-nationalist stances taken by right-wing extremist parties are coming in the way of future progress and development.

The Importance of Multilateral Cooperation and Reform

The ability of Asia to create efficient multilateral institutions for the integration process, communication, and collaboration and cooperative problem-solving will form the basis of the new Asian institutional "architecture" and determine whether Asia's future will be marked by cooperation or conflict. (Green and Grill, 2009) In a region mired by poverty, social inequality, and socio-political problems, such institutions become critical.

The 21st-century world has never been more disordered than today. Regional and global governance have produced no output. The rise of right-wing parties in the world has decided to take a hyper-nationalist stand. The poor countries are getting poorer as the rich hoard all the technology and impose sanctions on their own will without thinking about the consequences on the Third World. Instead of picking up normative agendas, institutions established by non-western nations like the countries in Asia, Africa, and Latin America tend to influence regional and global power equations. (Ruland, 2011) And therefore multilateral institutions are critical.

Collective Action and Coordination Required

Globalisation is not only responsible for the integration of economies around the world. But additionally, it is to blame for the growth of non-traditional transnational security concerns such as financial meltdowns, unregulated migration, climate change, food and energy shortages, pandemics, inter-communal conflict, state demise, international terrorism, and transnational organised crime. These challenges can neither be addressed by one nation nor by an inter-governmental body like the United Nations. Therefore, through institutional politics, multilateralism became a desirable tool for the states of the South to exert influence over the allocation of power on a global and regional scale. But reforms in these multilateral institutions are needed. These reforms must be quick and must address the problems faced by the Global South today. In the words of Amitav Acharya, the first-generation leaders of contemporary Asian republics were focused on overthrowing colonial control, objecting to Western domination, reiterating their autonomy and equality, and frequently, requesting concessions and financial support from the West. Consequently, their conception of the world order was infused with what may be referred to as "defensive sovereignty." (Acharya, 2011) But this challenge does not end here as there is currently no coherent Asia thinking about global governance.

The G20, as noted by Chen Dongxiao, is a group of growing powers whose cooperation is "issue-based and interest-oriented," unlike a confederation of like-minded countries. The economies and trade interests of these growing nations are more competitive than complementary, which makes it difficult to build cooperation and coordination between them. (Acharya, 2011) As Chin has lately demonstrated for Brazil, China, India, Indonesia, South Africa, and South Korea, they had been establishing postures and alliances that threatened the hegemony of the established countries for several years. (Chin, 2010)

Multilateral organisations are also accused of undermining domestic democracy because of their elite-driven objectives, lack of explicit democratic delegation and direct people responsibility, and inability to act in concert. (Rabkin, 1998) This has become the central issue of the European Union as well, the former EU commissioner Ralf Dahrendorf had claimed that *internationalization almost invariably means a loss of democracy*. Critics assert that international law and multilateral organisations give elites a pass on the difficult democratic procedures of persuasion and consensus-building. Non-elected NGOs and special interest advocacy networks exist internationally and push for new laws, sometimes without the usual parliamentary process or formal law-making. Without domestic ratification, commitments established under the treaty power may be increased gradually through the operation of international legal procedures. Multilateral institutions give internationalists additional methods to circumvent democratic public opinion. (Kohane, Macedo, Moravesik, 2009)

Over the years, the importance of multilateral grouping has reduced as they are said to be replaced by multiple minilateral groupings (MMG). (Malone, Mohan, Raghavan, 2016). These MMGs whose nature is as informal as a club, and share various significant coincidences of political or economic interests. In recent times, these MMGs have emphasized Indian positions on transnational non-traditional threats like climate change, trade, economic governance, and regional integration and additionally in some niche areas such as South-South and maritime cooperation. To address this and various other problems related to multilateralism, India's G20's T20 Task Force has focused on 'Towards Reformed Multilateralism' (TF7) to construct a roadmap for 'Multilateralism 2.0'. The role of India's G20 in reforming the multilateral institutions will be discussed ahead.

India's G20 Presidency and Promoting Multilateralism

Building international consensus on crucial security and development issues, according to New Delhi, is one of its main goals. This can only be accomplished through multilateral institutions. As a result, multilateral reform was made one of India's top presidential goals. (Kumar, 2023). Apart from all the matters discussed above related to the contemporary challenges to multilateralism. The difficulties have become worse due to the rising great-power tensions in the international arena, deglobalization, populist nationalism, the pandemic, and climatic emergencies. This impasse caused states to look for alternative venues, such as bilateral, plurilateral, and minilateral organisations, which ultimately polarised global politics more. Yet, multilateral reform and cooperation are urgently needed. Today's concerns are global, necessitating global solutions. Moreover, only by working together can pressing global concerns like conflicts, climate change, migration, financial instability, and cybersecurity be resolved. In addition, setbacks like the COVID-19 epidemic have undone the social and economic advancements that the world's society made over the previous two decades.

As discussed above the multilateral platforms have become elite-driven, therefore, the need is to create more informal engagement groups focusing on the longer problems. What seems nowadays is that all the international meetings involving the heads of state narrow down to the Russia-Ukraine crisis, while it is also important to discuss problems that have not ceased despite several efforts, such as climate change. It is also important that such discussions should not be concluded at one meeting or summit. India should also compel the incoming grouping chairs, Brazil, and South Africa, to prioritise multilateral reforms at the top of their presidential agendas. Since both have global high-table ambitions, it would be an easier task for India. (Kumar, 2023). India can keep these agendas active in various plurilateral groups like BRICS and RIC of which it is a part. Moreover, it is high time that the world starts believing in economic cooperation and global governance by keeping aside all its political debates. India has also led an example here. As Pakistan keeps condemning India's decision to host a G20 meet in Jammu and Kashmir, and India overrides. India assures Pakistan that the summit will give India the chance to highlight the potential for tourism in the union territory and to demonstrate how the situation in the Valley has stabilised following the unrest triggered by the revocation of the former state's special status. (Parashar, 2023)

Prioritising Key Areas of Cooperation and Reforming Existing International Institutions

The world knows by now that in recent times, the UN has failed to protect the citizens of the world. The internal politics of the global powers stood in the way of the UN to take proper action. Therefore, reform in existing international institutions has become a priority. The pressure put by nations at the meetings of international institutes does have a role to play. These institutes were built keeping in mind the international order after World War II, but this world order is now fading away and thus new reforms are required as we tackle new problems.

Multiple objectives are involved in the development of reputable global institutions: The institutions must, first and foremost, be inclusive. Second, the institutions must function well. Third, international institutions must function as an efficient global governing framework. Finally, international institutions should provide chances for leaders on the national and international levels to build alliances for reform and action. (Bradford, Linn, 2007) The institutional and summit reforms require strategic direction, vision, and leadership; when combined, these elements can produce a global governance framework that can accomplish the focus, coherence, and coordination needed to address global concerns. To help prevent crises and build a brighter future, it is critically necessary to construct a global governance structure that considers the changing economic and demographic realities and successfully addresses new global concerns of the 21st century. (Bradford, Linn, 2007)

Addressing Problems through Collaboration and Coordination

Bradford and Linn in their essay Reform of Global Governance: Priorities for Action identify that addressing conflicts, climate change, migration, macroeconomic instability, and cybersecurity through collaboration and coordination among countries must become a priority of inter-governmental institutions. The population of the world is projected to rise by almost 2 billion people over the next 30 years, from the present 8 billion to 9.7 billion in 2050, with a potential peak of roughly 10.4 billion in the middle of the 1980s. Thus, a new balance between the economy and the population will develop. (United Nations, n.d.-a)

Second, with commerce and capital movements expanding quickly, as well as in the energy sector, the health, migration, and illicit drug industries, as well as the environmental and security spheres, there has been a tremendous increase in the interdependencies between nations. All of them require international cooperation if significant potential and hazards are to be managed successfully. Thirdly, with the increase in the link between various international issues international organizations with narrowly focused mandates will not be able to handle these interrelationships. Institutions must collaborate successfully across sectoral and thematic boundaries.

Conclusion

From the common man to civil society, all have been waiting for the international system to work in such a manner that the voice of every one is amplified and equitable standards can be maintained for everyone. After the Cold War, the world tried to prioritise the concerns of all the countries but ended up prioritising the concerns of the Global North. After the economic crisis of 2008 and seeing the growth of the Global South economies, the world powers felt more globalisation was needed. But the countries of Asia, Africa and Latin America had been waiting for reform in the international economic order. The formation and existence of multiple multilateral organisations like the G20 showed the promise of cooperation, trust and reform, but soon it all started declining as the multilateral organisation faced a crisis due to mistrust and over-arching political interest of the global powers. With the rise of non-traditional threats like conflicts, climate change, migration, macroeconomic instability, and cybersecurity, global governance also became important. But it too only prioritised the concern of the West.

In 2025, South Africa will get the chance to host the G20 summits. India saw its presidency as an opportunity to amplify the voices of the global south and ask for reforms in the multilateral institutions while standing on its land. The G20s from 2022 to 2025 will show the infrastructure ability of the Global South. It will ensure that the wave of democracy remains alive in multilateral meetings by choosing agendas that solve the prolonged problems of the world. These prolonged problems of climate change, migration, and cross-border terrorism are being discussed in various MMGs, but by getting a chance to host a summit like G20, these countries can put these agendas in the middle and also put focus on the need to reform multilateral organizations. But soon the decline of multilateral organisations will be seen if reforms do not take on time because the emerging transnational issues of climate change, security, migration, and slow development have started to become bigger agendas for the global South and can no longer bear that all the advantages and profits of the globalisation go to the global north.

ENDNOTES

1. "About G20," n.d. About G20.
2. Acharya, Amitav. "Can Asia Lead? Power Ambitions and Global Governance in the Twenty-First Century." Oxford University Press on behalf of the Royal Institute of International Affairs 87, no. 4 (July 2011): 851–69. Can Asia lead? Power Ambitions and global governance in the twenty-first century.
3. BW Online Bureau. (2023, January 12). *With G-20 Presidency, India's Aim Is To Amplify Voice Of Global South: PM.* BW Businessworld. With G-20 Presidency, India's Aim Is To Amplify Voice Of Global South: PM
4. Bradford and Johannes F. Linn, C. I. (n.d.). Reform of Global Governance: Priorities for Action. Brookings. https://www.brookings.edu/research/reform-of-global-governance-priorities-for-action/
5. Cherian, John. "Troubled Relations between India and Malaysia." The Hindu. February 6, 2020. Accessed April 11, 2023. Troubled relations between India and Malaysia - Frontline.
6. Chen, 'China's perspective on global governance and G20'.
7. Dahrendorf, Ralf. 1999. The Third Way and Liberty: An Authoritarian Streak in Europe's New Center. Foreign Affairs 78 (5): 13-17.
8. Elizabeth Roche. 2014, November 27. "Pakistan, 2 others demand greater role for China in SAARC." Mint. DOI: Pakistan, 2 others demand greater role for China in Saarc | Mint
9. G-20 and India's Presidency," n.d. G-20 and India's Presidency G-20 Development Working Group (DWG) meeting to be held in Mumbai from

December 13 – 16, 2022 India will host over 200 meetings in over 50 cities across 32 different work streams G20 delegates and guests to get a glimpse of India's rich cultural heritage and a year-long India experience The theme of India's G20 Presidency "Vasudhaiva Kutumbakam" or "One Earth · One Family · One Future" closely ties with LiFE (Lifestyle for Environment).

10. Grossman, Derek. "India Can Bridge the US-Russia Divide over Ukraine." ORF, March 16, 2023. India can bridge the US-Russia divide over Ukraine | ORF.
11. Green, Michael J., and Bates Gill, eds. Asia's New Multilateralism: Cooperation, Competition, and the Search for Community. Columbia University Press, 2009.
12. G Chin, 'The emerging countries and China in the G20: reshaping global economic governance', Studia Diplomatica, LXIII(2), 2010, pp 105- 123
13. G20 members have agreed on 99% of issues, says India | India News - Times of India. (n.d.). The Times of India. G20 members have agreed on 99% of issues, says India
14. "Hampson, & Heinbecker. (2011). The "New" Multilateralism of the Twenty-First Century. Brill, 17(3), 299–310. The "New" Multilateralism of the Twenty-First Century
15. India, Tribune. "Now Is Not the Time for War, Let Us Strategies for Peace, PM Modi Tells Putin." *Tribuneindia News Service*, September 16, 2022. Now is not the time for war, let us strategise for peace, PM Modi tells Putin.
16. Kumar. (2023, March 6). Multilateral reforms as a priority in the G-20. The Hindu. Retrieved April 11, 2023, from Explained | Multilateral reforms as a priority in the G-20 - The Hindu
17. Kim, Chi Wook. "Building Multilateralism on Bilateralism: Evidence from Networked Governance of FDIs in Asia." Asian Perspective 39, no. 2 (April 2014): 325–55. Building Multilateralism on Bilateralism: Evidence from Networked Governance of FDIs in Asia
18. Kumar, Rajeesh. "Explained | Multilateral Reforms as a Priority in the G-20." The Hindu. March 6, 2023. Accessed April 10, 2023. Explained | Multilateral reforms as a priority in the G-20 - The Hindu.
19. Keohane, Robert O., Stephen Macedo, and Andrew Moravcsik. "Democracy-Enhancing Multilateralism." Cambridge University Press on behalf of the International Organization Foundation 63, no. 1 (2009): 1–31. Democracy-Enhancing Multilateralism.
20. Laskar, R. H. (2023, April 1). Russia-Ukraine conflict cannot be separated from G20, says US head of delegation. Hindustan Times. Russia-Ukraine conflict cannot be separated from G20, says US head of delegation | Latest News India - Hindustan Times
21. Malik, Priyanjali. "G-20: India's Platform for Global Leadership." The Hindu. March 2, 2023.
22. Pande, Aparna. Making India Great : The Promise of a Reluctant Global Power. Happer Collins, 2020.
23. Parashar. (2023, March 18). India overrides objections by Pakistan, to host G20 meet in J&K. The Times of India.

24. http://timesofindia.indiatimes.com/articleshow/98744327.cms?from=mdr&utm_source=contentofinterest&utm_medium=text&utm_campaign=cppst
25. Raja Mohan, C. "India's New Foreign Policy Strategy." *Carnegie Endowment for International Peace*, May 26, 2006.
26. Ruland, Jurgen. "Southeast Asian Regionalism and Global Governance: 'Multilateral Utility' or 'HedgingUtility'?" Contemporary Southeast Asia 33, no. 1 (April 2010): 83–112. https://www.jstor.org/stable/41288816.
27. Rabkin, Jeremy A. 1998. Why Sovereignty Matters. Washington, Press.
28. Sen, By Amiti. "India's G20 Presidency Gives Voice to Global South: Modi." *Businnessline.*, March 3, 2023. Accessed April 5, 2023. India's G20 presidency gives voice to Global South: Modi - The Hindu BusinessLine.
29. Shome, Pranay K. "Asian Unity: No Longer a Pipe Dream." Raksha Anirveda Is a New Age Print Publication (Quarterly) With a Digital Presence. April 30, 2022. Accessed April 10, 2023. Asian Unity: No Longer a Pipe Dream - Raksha Anirveda is a new-age print publication (quarterly) with a digital presence..
30. Suneja, K. (2022, November 23). India identifies five priority issues for its G20 presidency. The Economic Times. India identifies five priority issues for its G20 presidency - The Economic Times
31. Standard, B., & B. (2023, February 18). 180 countries expect G20 countries to address their concerns: Jaishankar. 180 Countries Expect G20 Countries to Address Their Concerns: Jaishankar. 180 countries expect G20 countries to address their concerns: Jaishankar | Business Standard News
32. The Diplomat. "SAARC Is Dead. Long Live Subregional Cooperation." The Diplomat, September 27, 2022. SAARC Is Dead. Long Live Subregional Cooperation – The Diplomat.
33. T. A. Keenlyside, "Nationalist Indian Attitudes Towards Asia: A Troublesome Legacy for Post-independence Indian Foreign Policy," Pacific Affairs 55, no. 2 (1982): 229.
34. United Nations. (n.d.-a). Population | United Nations. https://www.un.org/en/global-issues/population
35. Zakaria, Fareed. "The World Is De-Globalizing. Trump Set the Example." *Washington Post*, January 23, 2020. Opinion | The world is de-globalizing. Trump set the example. - The Washington Post.

16

The Competitive Edge of G-20 in Multilateral Negotiations to Further Inclusive Global Digital Economy

– Nisarg Jani

In a globalized world where economies function in a borderless framework, the 'nation states' have made a comeback. The growing digital economy has led to increasing regulations for data governance as every digital transaction leaves a footprint in the form of data. Governing this data flow within a borderless world has become a major concern for national governments. Multilateral negotiations are now focusing on how nations can agree to regulate the flow of data since mediums like cryptocurrencies have anonymized the identities of individuals who are transacting across nations. This is perceived as a security concern by national governments who are vulnerable to terror financing, drug trafficking, and belligerent funding by groups who have vested interests in division of societies within the nation.

The Group of 20 (G-20) is a semi-formal grouping of 20 major economies of the world with a rotating presidency. Each nation that holds the presidency sets the agenda for the year and holds multiple ministerial and secretariat level meetings in their nation where a spectrum of discourses is held ranging from business, public administration, economy, policy making, gender equality, etc. The grouping while formed in 1999, initially finance ministers of member states engaged, it received a significant limelight in the aftermath of the 2008 American turned global financial crisis. Subprime mortgage, the flawed financial instrument of trade with hollow fundamentals, fell apart, bringing the majority of western economies to rubble for a substantial period. To evade recurrence of such an event, the Obama administration that held the G-20 presidency of 2008 made governmental oversight on their respective financial markets the centerfold agenda of the grouping. As the world moved on from the financial crisis towards the path of recovery, the significance of G-20 increased since it became a great annually recurring stage where nations, despite their political differences, hold an equivalent amount of voice in the political and economic affairs of the international community.

J. Kirton claims that G-20 governance is important for contemporary globalization. The reason being; given the transnational spread of social, economic, and political forces, the governments of the world need to engage more broadly as the 21st century brings intense connectivity amongst the nations of the world. This also brings mutual vulnerability that renders cooperation a necessity. (Kirton & Kirton -, 2020) The spirit of this observation can be justified by the July 2017 Hamburg Summit declaration that said "Globalization and technological change have contributed significantly to driving economic growth and raising living standards across the globe. (G20 Germany, 2017) However, globalization has created challenges and its benefits have not been shared widely enough. By bringing together developed and emerging market economies, the G-20 is determined to shape globalization to benefit all people."

The grouping is often criticized for its semi-formal structure. However, the purpose of the grouping is to streamline communication amongst the member nations that contemporary global institutions such as (but not limited to) World Trade Organization, BRICS, International Monetary Fund, and United Nations Special Groupings lack. The very reason it works well is the absence of a formal structure, which gives the member nations a level of freedom that they urge for in the abovementioned codified international institutions. This makes G-20 an effective springboard for creating new multilateral conventions that represent the interests of all the members of the international community effectively as well as make the current multilateral institutions accountable to the concerns and values of emerging economies.

The rise of digital public infrastructure in banking and finance by national governments has effectively cracked down the shadow economy that transacted in fiat currencies via hawala networks. India's Unified Payment Interface and Jan Dhan bank accounts have mainstreamed a substantial chunk of the population into the formal economy. Introduction of electoral bonds in 2017 has also decreased the space for cash-based political funding to create a digital trace of fund providers to a plethora of political parties who act as a front for money laundering operations. Such financial mainstreaming has worked wonders for emerging nations with large populations such as India and China. While the western institutions are swinging the pendulum towards regulation when it comes to governing the digital economy and dataflow, emerging economies rely on such Digital Public Infrastructure or DPI because of their overwhelming impact on creating a digital economy. G-20 as a grouping has been vocal on creating a balanced approach on how nations should negotiate in the domain of regulating the flow of data, given the fact that the majority of emerging economies have benefited deeply because of the digital economy as it provides local suppliers an access to the global market.

Data governance focuses on storing, processing, sharing, and protecting the data of citizens and governments of a sovereign state. In many cases the data fiduciaries (either a private or government entity) have their base of operations outside the jurisdiction of the sovereign state whose citizens' and governments' data is getting stored, processed, shared, or protected. Global data governance is a means through which nations of the world will agree upon how the digital infrastructure of their respective nations like data storing centers, cloud servers, ISP hubs, AI-as-a-service servers will be built within the territories and how they will be interpreted from a legal perspective given the fact that they will be storing, processing, sharing and protecting the data of individuals, organizations, governments can be beyond their jurisdiction and national legal framework.

India's G-20 Presidency's Commitment

The Indian presidency of the G-20 was well accepted within the international community because of its spirit of people-centeredness which was termed as "Jan Bhagidari." Plethora of meetings were held all across India where delegates from all around the world witnessed the richness of Indian hospitality and cultural diversity. The summit was held in New Delhi at the grandiose *Bharatmandapam* Convention Center where Prime Minister Modi, in his address, touched upon the issue of 'Global Trust Deficit.'

"The nations of the world also consider how to resolve this problem (of trust deficit). The world is facing various issues of turbulence in trade, inequality between North and South, distance between East and West, food, fuel and fertilizer management, terrorism and cybersecurity, among others. Every nation of the world has to work together to resolve these issues consensually"

- Translated by author from Prime Minister's address

The Indian spirit of "One Earth, One Family" was effectively reflected in the proceedings of digital governance where the focus was on balancing data sovereignty with global efficiency. Indian policymakers hold a conviction that G-20 has acted like a bridge between G-7 and emerging economies, as can be seen from the growing membership of the BRICS grouping, which along with the G-7 is a part of G-20. To quote Dr. S Jaishankar at Munich Security Conference 2024 "If one looks at the G-7 to G-20, I think in a way those additional 13 members who came into this bigger grouping, five of them are BRICS members. The fact that there was another group which was meeting regularly and discussing and debating, I think certainly was an input into the expansion of the G-7 into the G-20. So, I think we (India) did a service to the world."

G-20 grouping has reinforced *Multipolarism* by creating an effective multilateral grouping that represents the median of the national interest of the West and non-Western economies. Keeping the theme of *Multipolarism* at the forefront, the chapter will provide a detailed analysis of major discourses that G-20 engagement groups have initiated in the domain of digital governance from 2014 till India's presidency in 2023.

Duo of New Age Globalization: Data Governance and Digital Economy

Measuring The Global Digital Economy:

Data Governance and Digital Economy for the basis of current age globalization. The estimated gross value addition of five economies surveyed by Moulton et.al. (2022) using Supply-Use Tables stands between the range of 4.4 to 10.2 percent. According to Gajbhiye Dhirendra, et.al., the digital economy can be measured in four tiers:

Core measure includes economic activities that hail from the production and sales of ICT goods and digital services itself. Narrow measure includes elements of the core measure plus economic activity undertaken by firms that rely on the use of elements of the core measure for their sales. Broad measure includes enhancement that digital inputs cause to a business that is involved in the production and sales of non-ICT products and services. And lastly, digital society is formed with is an aggregation of all the abovementioned measures plus the significant enhancement of interactions on the digital space that goes beyond the boundary of domestic economy. (Gajbhiye Dhirendra, 2022)

Community, Profits and State: To Trust or Not to Trust

From a political perspective digital economy enables free flow of money and communication giving a local business to what Naval Ravikant, a tech venture capitalist, 'an infinite amount of leverage' since social media has made community building easy and accessible for a large number of niches where businesses can hedge their brand credibility by representing itself as a brand value ambassador of the community, they belong Hence, businesses who once had to risk a huge amount of financial and social capital to create a market for their products now have globalized communities to do their bidding. This process creates immense value with the nature of data that it creates as it represents the social, economic, and political aspects of every individual who is a part of such a community. Social media has aggregated infinite numbers of such communities who can influence political discourses. This also makes national security vulnerable to the divisive agenda of certain belligerent interest groups and cultural wars. These narratives are commoditized as they are deeply attached to the economic interests of organizations pursuing their specific social, political or economic agenda.

From an economic perspective, such communities also enable businesses to flourish. D. Ciuriak claims that even the definition of national production has shifted as the ability to locate capital anywhere by multinational companies to minimize corporate taxes leads to new state policies that claim jurisdiction beyond its sovereignty and territorial jurisdiction. (Ciuriak, n.d.) For example, Ireland's gross domestic product surged in 2015 as it started reflecting returns to intellectual property that multinational companies claimed by shifting their domicile status to Ireland. Estonia also released an e-residency program where entrepreneurs across the world can set up and run a business on Estonia's business governance platform without having a geographical presence in the country. On paper, any business can be domiciled in Estonia, but the real production of commodity and data occurs somewhere else while the financial value is entitled to a completely different geography. The business outsourcing its production elsewhere also gets access to the data of the factors of production that are outside its jurisdiction of its domicile while the quality of land and labor doesn't improve. This has led to the issue of de-globalization as trade connectivity has divided labor efficiently but at the cost of resentment in the domestic sphere, especially in the big tech projects. American expertise in chip designing is leveraged by Taiwanese and Korean chipmakers who add a significant amount of value on the designs created by American chip and equipment makers. This can be termed as the issue of 'Value Entitlement' as both jurisdictions perceive themselves as entitled to the value of final creation.

Such skewness in the value chain of products and services that digital economy intensifies, furthers the concern of national security, which makes governance significant to contemporary diplomatic engagements. This has led to a comeback of the nation-states who bid to regulate this free flow of data across the porous boundaries of interconnected world making data governance and digital economy a multidimensional agenda with a worldwide scope.

According to Williams (2019) the agenda of 'digitalization' had 28 core commitments and 37 related commitments throughout the G-20 summit since 2008 till 2019. The famous Osaka Track during Japan's G-20 presidency in 2019 deliberated on creating "data free flow with trust." The majority of G-20 leaders, from then US President Donald Trump to Chinese President Xi Jinping, agreed upon the purpose of the process was to enable a rules-based multilateral trade liberation in the e-commerce negotiations at the World Trade Organization. Surprisingly, China and Saudi Arabia, which have historically showcased a restrictive approach to international e-commerce and privacy of sovereign data, were onboard with this. This showcases the political willingness of the nation-states to create an environment of trust, and the G-20 has been a competitive platform to further this global agenda despite the individual differences in approach. While South Africa and India didn't join the negotiation, Prime Minister Narendra Modi privately assured Shinzo Abe not to oppose the launch of the Osaka Track.

The G-20 has stood for channelizing the market forces towards equity in terms of resource sharing using technology as a means to achieve those ends. While the jury is out on deciding how realistic are such prescriptive regulations, in the spirit of it, communiques from various engagement groups within G-20 have a very interesting take on how data governance should be performed for digital public infrastructure, central bank digital currencies, and crypto assets as a medium of exchange and as an instrument for investment Key arrangements within the G-20 framework that are the grounds to these discourses are mentioned below. Each section is in the form of an agreement, conference or a mandate that was an outcome of a G-20 presidency.

(1) G-20 Digital Economy Ministerial Conferences (2007-2020)

The first G-20 Digital Economy Ministerial Meeting was held in 2007 at Düsseldorf during Germany's G-20 presidency. The joint communique acknowledged the opportunities that the digital economy provides to enhance public services, foster innovation and entrepreneurship. The first declaration had an optimistic outlook towards what can be achieved by leveraging the global reach of the digital economy. The narrative slightly shifted towards concern in 2018 during the ministerial meeting during Argentina's presidency. The joint communique called for developing a 'human centric approach' for the governance of digital economy. It also includes the concern of cyberspace security to make the digital economy resilient in the face of threats and risks of cyberattacks. Another significant narrative was upholding the principle of sovereignty, non-intervention and international law. In the context of India, according to the Reserve Bank of India's bulletin, India's digital economy has grown at a compound annual growth rate of 15.62 percent between 2014 and 2019 (Gajbhiye Dhirendra, 2022), which furthers India's concern as well as opportunities in the governance of digital economy.

Another significant joint communique on digital economy governance under the abovementioned conference was in the third ministerial conference in 2020 during Saudi Arabia's presidency. (Group of 20, 2020) The communique took a balanced narrative of the challenges that the global economy poses to the global problems of security as well as opportunities that it provides. Opportunities that the digital economy provided to the world were closely integrated with G-20's objective of "empowering people, safeguarding planet and shaping new frontiers." To mitigate the risks, another clause was added that called for developing a common framework of measuring the digital economy, which is "consistent, comparable and reliable, and which reflects the diversity and dynamism of the digital ecosystem." Since this communique, a new movement has emerged within the ministerial conference on digital economy about the standardization of measurement of digital economy.

The concern of artificial intelligence is deeply integrated with the digital economy as increased automation in digital services calls for regulations in machine learning and deep learning processes as the new AI models are developed on the data that the digital economy creates. Again, the clause of "consistent, comparable, and reliable" measurements of digital economy was upheld in the communique. The latest communique was developed during the G-20 Digital Economy Working Group held in 2023 during India's G-20 presidency. The communique had been more optimistic in its narrative about how the digital economy can be nurtured rather than regulated given the opportunities it creates. The communique mentioned the building of digital public infrastructure for digitized social security processing, digital payments, digitized health records, and provision of education through technology (ed-tech). The communique, like the previous one, mentioned how AI should be harnessed for good as per the G-20 AI principles. (Ministry of Electronics & IT, 2023b)

The textual analysis of the four communiques showcases that the presidencies of the west aligned nations have a more regulatory outlook towards the digital economy given that their national economies are already deeply digitized as compared to emerging economies, non-western presidencies have leaned towards positive regulations by managing the diffusion of digitized products and services into traditional businesses. The emerging economies intend to leverage technology for their economic growth as they intend to leapfrog to a development status that the western nations hold.

From a multilateral perspective, these ministerial engagements have done a great job in balancing the bright and dark side of digital economy regulations, while the approach has differed in different presidencies. From a strategic perspective, these communiques also suggest that the western presidency intends to protect their national digital economies from the security lapses of non-western regulators of DPI as they pose security risk to the critical infrastructure of western nations in the civilian domain. Another interpretation suggests that negotiating positions of the west has always been rooted in the grand strategy of denying the critical technology to outsiders, especially certain members of BRICS who are perceived as the axis powers by the western bloc. Either way, G-20 intends to balance this dynamic by fulfilling the trust deficit between the west and non-western nation-states.

(2) G-20 Digital Economy Development and Cooperation Initiative (2016)

G-20 Digital Economy Development and Cooperation Initiative is a strategic document in 2016 adopted during the Hangzhou Summit. The document outlines basic principles, key facets, and necessary policies for developing digital economy through cooperation among the members of G-20 and beyond. The document is a sacrosanct piece of multilateral cooperation since it defines a broad range of economic activities that use digitized information as a factor of production. It depicts the modern information network as a space and information & communication technology (ICT) as a means to access this space. This is one of the best ways to look at virtual network as a market space where merchandise and services are sold by converting the product into a piece of digital information. The marriage between the real and virtual becomes obvious as the global market is getting digitized. Some key areas identified to achieve the highest potential of digital economy are expanding broadband access, promoting capital investment in the ICT sector, promoting entrepreneurship, and encouraging e-commerce partnership. (Group of 20, 2016)

While the policy support suggested in the document is abstract with no concrete action plan at sight, the optimistic narrative depicts the value that digital economy creates for emerging economies. Since this declaration the global spending on digital technologies and services increased from 0.9 trillion USD in 2017 to 2.4 trillion USD in 2021. The future projections suggest this number to reach 3.4 trillion USD by 2026. Closer to home, India's digital payment index increased from 100 in March 2018 to 270.59 in March 2023, a behemoth 170.59 percent increase in volume of digital transactions in the national economy. The value of the transactions has also shown promising figures. In 2020, the value of digital transactions stood at 25.5 trillion INR to 34.2 trillion INR in 2023, with the estimation of this number reaching 63.2 trillion INR in 2027. (Petroc Taylor, 2024)

Though estimating the impact of this policy suggestion needs further study, the document represents the general will of G-20 members in nurturing global consensus on managing national digital economies which is expanding exponentially with projections showing an upward trend for the next five years.

(3) Ministerial Statement on Trade and Digital Economy (Japan 2019)

Another major contender of nurturing the digital economy was Japan in 2019. The Ministerial Statement on Trade and Digital Economy of 2019 is divided into two parts: trade and digital economy. The part about trade affirms the importance of international trade and investment, which is hindered by the existing trade tensions in the World Trade Organization (WTO). Creating appropriate legislation that calls for changing certain WTO rules and regulations is necessary before prodding regulations for the digital economy. Other aspects of this part of the regulatory suggestion were to consider the scope of e-commerce, industrial subsidies, steel excess capacity, and intellectual property rights vis-à-vis their impact on global trade. (Group of 20, 2019)

Before this, it is necessary to understand that Japan considers digital economy as a means to achieve common prosperity since free flow of data enables trust and communication between trading parties. Keeping that theme at the forefront, the digital economy part of this statement acknowledges the potential of digitization in public administration, national economy, and society as a whole. This part of legislation calls for common principles through which the digital economy should be guided. This includes human-centeredness, synergy, flexibility, ease for businesses to grow and prosper. During the same year the famous Osaka Track was launched in the G-20 summit by Shinzo Abe to promote international cooperation on the digital economy. The centerpiece of this track was the concept called 'Data Free Flow with Trust' (DFFT) proposed by Shinzo Abe in the Davos Meeting in 2019. The idea of this concept is to create common rules and principles for cloud computing, e-commerce, and other trade related aspects of the digital economy.

Given the abstract nature of this document, understanding it in parallel to DFFT clears out what the statement wanted to achieve. To gauge this, between 2019 and 2024 the penetration of e-commerce in China, one of the G-20 member nations, has increased from 50.7 percent in 2019 and is projected to reach 84.57 percent in 2028. (Statista, 2024) In India, the penetration rate is expected to double from 5.5 percent in 2019 to 11 percent in 2024.(Statista, 2023) Cloud services as a market have also increased exponentially. The end user spending for cloud application-software-as-a-service has increased from 102.1 billion USD in 2019 to 232.3 billion USD in 2024. (Catherine Howley, 2023) Such a double down in just five years explains the necessity of regulations of the global digital economy.

(4) AI Principles

The G-20 AI principles are developed based on the OECD Recommendation on AI adopted in May 2019 by 42 countries which also includes G-20 members. The recommendations suggest that policy makers should consider investing in the development of a dynamic and trustworthy AI ecosystem where international collaboration and knowledge sharing is possible. Also, AI should be leveraged to foster a digital ecosystem for which policymakers should increase the access to digital infrastructure, data, and technologies. National policy environment should enable AI, which is human-centered that can address the legal, social, and ethical issues. (Group of 20, 2019)

The pivotal aspect of this declaration of principles is the concept of 'Human-centered Artificial Intelligence (AI)' which recognizes the efforts of stakeholders across governments, academia, civil society, private sector, and international organization; acknowledges that AI technologies can be the means for advancing Sustainable Development Goals (SDG), realize a sustainable and inclusive society and mitigate the risks to wider societal values. The declaration also recognizes that AI, like other emerging technologies, can also present societal challenges such as transitions in the labor market, privacy, ethical issues, and security, which can create new digital divides with some communities having no access to enabling technologies such as AI because of older digital divides.

(5) G-20 Framework for Systems of Digital Public Infrastructure

The G-20 Framework for Systems of Digital Public Infrastructure was declared during the G-20 New Delhi Summit, 2023.(Group of 20, 2023) The declaration proposes common principles to guide and develop cooperation of digital public infrastructure. The 'public' refers to public benefit and access subject to appropriate governance and oversight by public authorities. The common principles on which national laws on digital public infrastructure include inclusivity, innovation, synergy, flexibility, partnership, and trust. The document also called for expanding the potential of digital public infrastructure by widening its access. This can be done by promoting investments in the ICT sector, expanding the broadband access, encouraging e-commerce cooperation, supporting entrepreneurship, and digital transformation.

For an open and secure digital public infrastructure, the document calls for cooperation amongst member nations for the nations who choose to make an independent choice in development path. Also, development and use of international standards in terms of management of radiofrequency spectrum is acknowledged to ensure connectivity and standardization of products and services in the telecommunication sector. The bid for standardization at times contradicts from region to region mainly in telecom. By acknowledging the respect for independent choice along with calling for international standards, while it appears contradictory, requires a deeper understanding of the issue at hand. In 5G spectrum, China developed a 5G spectrum standard that used the 6 GHz frequency band whereas the International Telecommunication Union, a UN specialized body that regulates the common standard mechanisms of telecommunication across the world, functioned on 24.25-86 GHz band for 5G and 6G services.(Nan et al., 2021) India also had a similar issue in 5G spectrum standardization as India developed 5Gi standard for improving rural coverage. India already submitted the 5Gi which was approved by ITU in 2021. However, again industrial groupings, in this case GSMA expressed its concern about interoperability and compatibility of 5Gi with other global standards.

Given that such different standardized metrics have certain political underpinnings. The functional nature of organizations like ITU requires such political dialogues as a leverage since many nations have to develop their own standardized DPI infrastructure which requires further measures to make them internationally operable. Nations need freedom to choose what standard works best for their national functionality rather than following a blanket standardization which may not serve their DPI expansion. Platforms like G-20 can be leveraged by ITU to further discourse on interoperability balanced with national requirements. Such functional organizations can be bid for membership in G-20 to ensure a political outreach stays open that can be done through another multilateral channel.

(6) G-20 Global Digital Public Infrastructure Repository

Launched during the New Delhi Summit 2023, the Global Digital Public Infrastructure Repository (GDPIR) is a comprehensive pool of essential lessons and expertise from G-20 members and guest countries who can provide design, development and deployment of digital public infrastructure (DPI). (Ministry of Electronics & IT, 2023a) The repository aims to increase the knowledge base of G-20 member nations for developing DPI across the board to empower the digital economy. The GDPIR includes DPI components such as technology, governance, and community. It also includes foundational DPI such as payments, data sharing with consent, and identification (The three pillars of India Stack). GDPIR is hosted by Ministry of Electronics and Information Technology (MeitY). It is designed by the National E-Governance Division.

This was one of the greatest achievements of India's G-20 Presidency as India hosted this platform for sourcing its DPI best practices for other emerging economies who intend to develop their own DPI. This can also be considered as India's policy export to the world. India Stack APIs and digital public goods are already provided to Papua New Guinea, Armenia, Suriname, Sierra Leone, etc. These APIs include components of Aadhar, UPI, eKYC, eSign, Digilocker, and Account Aggregator. They are designed to be secure and are interoperable for delivery of various services to citizens. It leverages data and technology for better governance.

Conclusion

Global data governance has garnered attention in multilateral negotiations. Existing functional groupings such as ITU or political groupings such as G7 need to restructure their bureaucratic procedures and regulatory requirements that are more inclusive for new and emerging economies. G-20 grouping for years have evolved as a grouping that has voiced the interests of these economies, forcing the traditional multilateral groupings to change their procedural modus operandi and structural representation.

The narrative analyses of the abovementioned documents state the fact that digital economy has surely opened new avenues of cooperation and new traps of conflicts. The western economies, which have for years integrated ICT in their business operations, have the strategic space to decide the product standards which reflect the realities of their economies and demography, who have sustained a minimum level of living standard. For BRICS nations, the group that represents the emerging economies of the world are new production and consumption bases. The governance of digital economy requires standardization of ICT equipment, regulations of emerging technologies such as artificial intelligence, which needs maximal representation, a need that the G-20 grouping if fulfilling.

Initiatives such as the Global Digital Public Infrastructure Repository, Osaka Track, declaration of principles of AI are the representation of the capability that G-20 holds in terms of aggregation of interest of global economies in the discourses of diplomacy and trade negotiations. While the criticism of how much of the opinions voiced and initiatives taken in G-20 grouping are fructified origins of such criticisms usually lies in conglomerate controlled media, the economic potential of BRICS and diplomatic balancing that India does between the east and the west of which G-20 presidency of 2023 was a critical part, has played a significant role in bringing new and emerging nations to higher table of negotiations. The ironic situation that a multipolar world has created is that the geopolitical vagaries of the world have made emerging economies with a strong political center provide the most policy stability. The negotiating positions of these countries have improved in global diplomatic discourse and the G-20 capability to take initiatives has increased.

REFERENCES

1. Catherine Howley. (2023). Gartner Forecasts Worldwide Public Cloud End-User Spending to Reach $679 Billion in 2024. In *Gartner*. Gartner. https://www.gartner.com/en/newsroom/press-releases/11-13-2023-gartner-forecasts-worldwide-public-cloud-end-user-spending-to-reach-679-billion-in-20240
2. Ciuriak, D. (n.d.). *From Digital Trade Wars to Governance Solutions: The G20 and the Digitally Enabled Economy*. https://ssrn.com/abstract=3239892
3. G20 Germany. (2017). G20 Leaders' Declaration: Shaping an Interconnected World. In *G20 Information Center*. University of Toronto. http://www.g20.utoronto.ca/2017/2017-G20-leaders-declaration.html
4. Gajbhiye Dhirendra, A. R. N. A. Y. R. T. I. (2022). Measuring India's Digital Economy. *RBI Bulletin*.
5. Group of 20. (2016). G20 Digital Economy Development and Cooperation Initiative. University of Toronto. http://www.g20.utoronto.ca/2016/160905-digital.html
6. Group of 20. (2019). G20 Ministerial Statement on Trade and Digital Economy. Ministry of Foreign Affairs, Japan. https://www.mofa.go.jp/files/000486596.pdf
7. Group of 20. (2020). Leaders' Declaration Riyadh Summit. University of Toronto. http://www.g20.utoronto.ca/2020/2020-g20-leaders-declaration-1121.html
8. Group of 20. (2023). G20 FRAMEWORK FOR SYSTEMS OF DIGITAL PUBLIC INFRASTRUCTURE. In *G-20 India*. G-20 India. https://g7g20-documents.org/fileadmin/G7G20_documents/2023/G20/India/Sherpa-Track/Digital%20Economy%20Ministers/2%20Ministers%27%20Annex/G20_Digital%20Economy%20Ministers%20Meeting_Annex1_19082023.pdf
9. Kirton, J., & Kirton -, J. (2020). Globalization's Implications for G20 Governance. *International Organisations Research Journal*, *15*(2), 18–41. https://doi.org/10.17323/1996784520200202
10. Ministry of Electronics & IT. (2023a). Prime Minister announces completion of Global Digital Public Infrastructure Repository and creation of a Social Impact Fund to advance Digital Public Infrastructure in Global South. In *Press Information Bureau*. Press Information Bureau.
11. Ministry of Electronics & IT. (2023b). Third meeting of 'G20 Digital Economy Working Group (DEWG)' concluded on 14 June 2023. In *Press Information Bureau*. Press Information Bureau. https://www.pib.gov.in/PressReleaseIframePage.aspx?PRID=1932370
12. Nan, L., Chunxia, G., & Dapeng, W. (2021). Considerations on 6 GHz Spectrum for 5G-Advanced and 6G. *IEEE Communications Standards Magazine*, *5*(3), 5–7. https://doi.org/10.1109/MCOMSTD.2021.9579392

13. Petroc Taylor. (2024). *Digital transformation - statistics & facts*. https://www.statista.com/topics/6778/digital-transformation/#topicOverview
14. Statista. (2023). Internet penetration rate in India from 2007 to 2022. In *Statista*. Statista. https://www.statista.com/statistics/792074/india-internet-penetration-rate/
15. Statista. (2024). Penetration rate of the e-commerce market in China from 2019 to 2028. In *Statista*. Statista. https://www.statista.com/forecasts/891315/digital-buyer-penetration-in-china#:~:text=The%20penetration%20rate%20in%20the%20E-commerce%20market%20in,percent%20and%20therefore%20a%20new%20peak%20in%202028.

17

Nuclear Energy is a Non-negotiable Choice: A G-20 Approach

– **Reshmi Kazi**

Introduction

Contemporary world affairs are marked by strong centrifugal forces running parallel between rising global economic development goals and intensified risks of climate change, global warming, depletion of carbon space, and heightened geo-political competition/ rivalry. Economic interruptions in 2021 due to the Covid-19 pandemic did slow down the industrialization process and the consequential emission rate. However, a rapid economic rebound in the post-Covid period has accelerated emissions worldwide, particularly among developing countries. Severe weather conditions and decline in nuclear power generation due to maintenance and continued phase-outs further exacerbated dependence of fossil fuels and contributed to the rise in greenhouse gas (GHG) emissions. Rapid industrialization, burgeoning population, and the need to attenuate vulnerability to energy imports constitute important drivers for multiplying human efforts to adopt sustainable and reliable sources of energy. While there is a critical need to power the engine of economic growth and human development, this has to be in balance with climatic and environmental limitations. This is in absolute sync with the realization of Sustainable Development Goals as specified by the United Nations. To ensure consistent economic growth and mitigate climatic risks, the international community needs to explore and invest in energy resources that are decarbonized, safe, cheap, and climate neutral.

There is an urgent need for the international community to collectively develop related energy technologies that are low carbon intensive and cause least social and environmental impacts. Despite the decisiveness of the situation, the recently concluded Group-20 (G-20) Summit 2023 held in India, overlooked nuclear energy as an important carbon-free energy source. This paper explores the global need for a clean energy transition. Why should nuclear energy be regarded as a viable alternative to facilitate energy transition to clean and carbon-free energy resource for sustainable economic development? As a collective community, how can international groupings like the G-20 help expansion of include nuclear energy as part of a globally acceptable governance framework for sustainable energy security and climate neutrality? How can the G-20's deliberations help nuclear energy achieve "equal footing for collaborative action" as part of its agenda?

Global Energy Crisis

In an era marked by rapid industrialization, urbanization and steep economic competition, uninterrupted resource availability is a critical prerequisite for sustainable energy security. Stable resource supply is of key importance to ensure efficiency in electricity generation. Hence, it has become imperative for major economies to take up those sources of energy that are inexpensive, dependable and easily accessible. These factors drove the major economies to increasingly depend upon coal, petroleum, natural gas, making them the leading energy sources globally. Competing market economies, aspirations to lessen vulnerability to energy imports, desire for stabilization of global energy markets, and geo-political trends have rebounded the consumption of fossil fuels worldwide.

However, fossil fuels face several challenges. Despite being affordable and deployable sources of energy, fossil fuels are non-renewables and hence face the risk of depletion. Besides, fuel like coal is the dominant green-house emissions source and is a challenge to climate neutrality. Although petroleum and natural gas lag not very far behind, coal is the largest single source of energy-related carbon dioxide (CO_2) emissions.[1] This has significant implications for several countries, particularly in those where coal consumption is high. "Global energy-related carbon dioxide emissions rose by under 1%

in 2022."[2] Overall, "global energy-related CO_2 emissions grew by 0.9% or 321 Mt in 2022 reaching a new high of over 36.8 Gt."[3] The year 2022 witnessed turbulence in energy systems with energy price shocks, increasing inflation, and interferences in the conventional fuel trade. Though the emissions at a global level were lower, despite gas-to-coal switching in many countries, emissions continue to persist on an unmanageable track. The situation is only a reminder to the collective community of the urgency of their commitment for a clear energy transition at a global level.

The global energy system faced an unprecedented crisis during the Covid-19 period. Worldwide energy security was severely disrupted by the pandemic and the consequential lockdowns. The pandemic years witnessed an extraordinary demand for coal consumption. Evidently, with the rebound of the global economy from prolonged lockdowns due to the pandemic, there has been a dynamic effort to meet lagging energy targets. "Growth in 2023 is strongly dependent on the major Asian emerging market economies, who will account for close to three-quarters of global GDP growth next year, with the United States and Europe decelerating sharply."[4]

For the emerging economies, coal remains a major fuel for purposes of electricity generation and other industrial processes, The demand for coal has multiplied and significantly increased disorder in coal markets. This has resulted in strengthening the phenomenon of peak coal. Increasing demands from developing countries like India and China and several other nations have increased the demand for coal, causing significant overcapacity in coal. "Demand for coal in India has been strong since the start of 2022 and is expected to rise by 7% for the full year as the country's economy grows and the use of electricity expands."[5] India is likely to expand its coal demand further with maintaining efficiency in electricity generation and expanded economic growth. The International Energy Agency (IEA) prognosticates that 'Indian coal demand grows by 3% to 1,160 Mt in 2023."[6]

Relatively, China witnessed a dip in coal consumption "by 3% in the first half of 2022" because of slow economic growth due to prolonged lockdowns during Covid. However, an economic rebound in the second half of the year is likely to have led coal consumption for the full year back to the same levels as 2021.[7] According to the IEA, India and China are the dominant consumers of coal in the world with China solely accounting for more than half of the global demand. The Agency estimates that, though the world coal demand may remain at a plateau in 2023, there is a great degree of ambiguity. China's aggressive pursuits for economic progress, hydropower development and investment in heavy industry are expected to increase Beijing's coal consumption by 1%, or 43 Mt, in 2023.[8] It is worth mentioning that China's economic rebound will determine future coal demands at a global level. The increasing demand of the global energy systems is a reminder that the world is still dependent upon fossil fuels to fulfil its energy needs. However, the stubborn dependence on fossil fuels, particularly coal, will have its push back with rising levels of CO_2 emissions and climate concerns.

In the post-Coronavirus pandemic period, the global energy crisis has raised the bar of anxiety in the face of geopolitical instability. The ongoing Russia-Ukraine crisis has further dealt a "massive energy price shock" to the world economy[9] with the energy markets facing already extraordinary challenges due to the coronavirus pandemic. Russia's crisis escalation has led to unstable food and energy price rise causing food shortages and inflation in parts of the world. The military offense has caused severe financial vulnerabilities and has led to a full-blown energy crisis. The price of natural gas skyrocketed and oil prices were pegged at their highest since 2008. After the disintegration of the Soviet Union, Europe depended heavily on Russia for energy purchases, particularly natural gas. With the Russia-Ukraine crisis continuing, Europe's transition from Russian gas will not be trouble-free. Several European countries have already intensified their dependence on coal-based energy generation, which will come at the cost of delaying the fulfilment of climate change goals. Given the uncertainty of the conflict, it may be prognosticated that supply chains will likely remain disrupted and volatile soon. Russia's military invasion of Ukraine is taking a heavy toll on the world economy and is likely to play a significant role in energy market developments.

Drivers of Nuclear Energy

The risks of severe interference with Earth's climate and the consequential danger of global warming due to greenhouse emissions necessitate the development of new forms of low-emissions, base-load power generating capacity. The grave situation urgently calls for policies and strategies of decarbonization for a clean energy transition process. The contemporary energy mix shows that "over three-quarters of global energy demand is still met by fossil fuels with less than a fifth by non-nuclear renewables, according to energy watchdog the International Energy Agency."[10] If this state of affairs is to continue "global energy consumption and energy-related carbon dioxide emissions will increase through 2050 as a result of population and economic growth."[11]

While renewables would be the dominant source of energy producers, they would be supplemented with fossil fuels like coal and natural gas to meet base-load energy generating capacity. The developing economies in Asia will primarily depend on petroleum and natural gas to meet their energy requirements. This has far-reaching implications for the Asian region. The projected trend of heightened energy consumption to meet economic targets within Asia will be highly carbon intensive with increasing levels of greenhouse gas emissions. The ongoing state of affairs portends a dangerous trend towards global warming and is indicative of how the intense race for development is pushing humanity into an abysmal future. "The Intergovernmental Panel on Climate Change (IPCC) estimated that starting 2020, the total carbon budget remaining, for a 50 per cent chance of temperature rise to remain below 1.5 degrees celsius, as 500 gigatonnes (GT) CO_2 (IPCC 2022)."[12] With the current rate of emissions of ~50 GT observed during 2010-19, the IPCC faces unprecedented challenges of mitigating emissions rate by almost half by 2030 to limit global warming to 1.5°C.[13]

Global warming poses a grave challenge that has urged several countries to look at the threat of climate crisis with a renewed perspective. In line with the Paris Agreement, reduction of CO_2 emissions is already a challenge as projected in the Sustainable Development Scenario. While economic growth and progress goals need to be pursued vigorously, there is also the crucial need to invest in climate resilient development projects. As explained by the IPCC, "there are multiple, feasible and effective options to reduce greenhouse gas emissions and adapt to human-caused climate change that are available now." Nuclear power has acquired a distinctive place in the debate on global climate crisis as the only carbon-free energy source that can facilitate the process of decarbonisation and clean energy transition.

Over the past 50 years, the use of nuclear power has reduced CO_2 emissions by over 60 gigatonnes – nearly two years' worth of global energy-related emissions.[14] Together with hydropower, nuclear energy has already played a significant role in providing low-carbon electricity and generates three-quarters of global low-carbon. However, hydropower has the disadvantage of massive displacement and relocation of affected people who lose their land due to hydel-based infrastructural requirements; nuclear energy, being a low-carbon generating energy source, has wider benefits. Hence, there are more and more countries that are vigorously pursuing it or considering doing so. Within Asia and Eastern Europe, several countries have operating nuclear power generating plants and have announced plans to build more such power plants in the future. Among the leading nations, Russia, Japan, South Korea and India are pursuing nuclear power as a clean transition and efficient energy source.

Presently, there are 410 nuclear power reactors in operation with a total net installed capacity of 368610 $MW_{e.}$[15] The list of countries with active nuclear programmes and proposals is expanding. The list consists of both developed and developing economies like Russia, India, Japan, South Korea, Iran, Czech Republic, and South Africa. The dominant fears surrounding nuclear power due to catastrophic accidents like the Three Mile Island, Chernobyl, and Fukushima are gradually being put behind. A renewed confidence is emerging among emerging economies, which has dramatically shifted the debate in favour of nuclear energy. Sweden has supported nuclear energy and has called upon the state-owned energy company Vattenfall to reconsider possible restart of Ringhals units 1 and 2 "unconditional and quickly" as well as to prepare for the construction of new reactors.[16] In the Tidö Agreement released on 14 October 2022, Sweden unambiguously supports an energy policy that "change[s] from 100% renewable to 100% fossil-free" to achieve an effective climate transition. The Agreement also calls for exploring the possibility for the construction and operation of small modular reactors (SMR) in Sweden for better energy production and environmental protection. The United Kingdom has announced support to a programme of new nuclear projects to boost the confidence of the industry and investors within the energy sector. In a new policy paper, "*Powering Up Britain*" Britain describes nuclear as "the critical baseload of the future energy system."[17]

The policy paper outlines a plan for major projects to expand affordable, clean, indigenous power and build thriving green industries. The aim is to step up energy security and independence, which contributes to achieving net-zero in Britain. The government has launched Great British Nuclear (GBN) which will be propelling new nuclear projects, with the ambition of increasing the nuclear energy share in "the UK's electricity mix from the current 15% to 25% by 2050."[18] The GBN also seeks to prioritise launch of the best SMR technologies for incremental power additions. The USA is a major producer of nuclear energy and accounts for 30% of worldwide nuclear generation of electricity.[19] Although the demand for petroleum and natural gas remains high through 2050, renewable energy is expanding fast. In its Annual Energy Outlook 2022, the US Energy Information Administration's (EIA) reference case shows electricity demand growth averaging 1% per year through to 2050.[20] Almost 20% of Washington's electricity overall and about 55% of its carbon□free electricity are provided by the nuclear plants. Hence, a slight rise in electricity consumption would necessitate new nuclear capacity to sustain this stake. "If today's nuclear plants retire after 60 years of operation, 22 GWe of new nuclear capacity would be needed by 2030, and 55 GWe by 2035 to maintain a 20% nuclear share."[21] Nuclear power will play a significant role in electricity generation across the country.

The Fukushima accident raised several concerns about nuclear energy. Public confidence in nuclear power is recorded at its lowest, particularly in Japan where the authorities shut down 46 of the country's 50 operational power reactors. Nuclear energy was suddenly abandoned even when it was generating almost a third of Japan's electricity for over decades. This impacted upon other countries like Germany, Belgium, Italy, Switzerland and Spain. Post Fukushima, Germany decided to phase out nuclear power completely by 2022 as it was providing nearly 25% of the country's electricity before the accident. With anti-nuclear public sentiments high and obstructive party politics, Germany permanently shut down 17 power reactors. Germany's disparate choice was distinctive in many ways. Nuclear energy was never a favourite among the German public and they had rejected it much before the Fukushima accident. With a stable energy generating market, technological prowess to exploit other renewables and as an exporter of electricity, Germany was able to undertake this transition. Nevertheless, premature shutting down of nuclear power plants has borne a staggering US$3 billion financial cost upon Germany.[22] The geo-political tension in the backdrop of the Russia-Ukraine crisis has further raised the bar for energy insecurity. Germany's expanded dependence on Russia for gas imports and its political position in the ongoing Crisis has put Berlin in a difficult position. Germany's decision for a nuclear phase out would impact its contribution in reducing CO2 emissions.

The Asian region presents a contrasting view with more and more countries pitching for nuclear energy as a sustainable source of energy. Irrespective of the constructive lessons of the Fukushima accident, India and China continue to set massive targets to augment their nuclear capacity. Presently in India, nuclear power currently comprises 3% of its total electricity generation. The Union Minister, Dr Jitendra Singh stated that during 2021-22 nuclear power reactors provided 47112 million Units of electricity, which comprises approximately 3.15% of the total electricity generated in India.[23] According to the Minister, India is likely to get 9 per cent of its electricity from nuclear sources by 2047.[24] This is important to achieve the commitment of the net zero target by 2070. The Department of Atomic Energy also strives towards the target of achieving 20 gigawatts (GW) capacity of nuclear power generation by 2030, which will make India the third-largest producer of atomic energy in the world after the US and France.[25] This will also ensure the country's energy security, a clean energy transition that can contribute to decarbonization for climate justice. In a written reply to a question in Lok Sabha, Dr Jitendra Singh said that during 2020-21, "nuclear power is saving 41 million tonnes of CO2 emissions annually, compared to the emissions that would be generated by equivalent electricity generation from coal based thermal power plants."[26]

China is the fastest expanding nuclear power generator in the world with 38 nuclear power reactors in operation and 19 under construction. China seeks to curb its dependence on coal, which is carbon intensive. Beijing plans to increase energy security from nuclear sources to reduce its dependence of fossil fuels and limit CO2 emissions while expanding its economic growth.

Rationale for Nuclear Energy

Nuclear energy is gradually emerging as a carbon-free alternative to salvage planet Earth from a burning hot destructive world. The question is no longer whether nuclear energy can play a potent role in clean energy transition but rather how soon it can start contributing in this endeavour. There is a purported endeavour both at the global and national levels to raise awareness about the efficacy of nuclear power. A common factor that binds the Intergovernmental Panel on Climate Change (IPCC), International Atomic Energy Agency (IAEA), International Energy Agency (IEA), United Nations Economic and Social Commission for the Asia and the Pacific (UNESCAP), European Research Institute for ASEAN and East Asia (ERIA), Organization of the Petroleum Exporting Countries (OPEC), and International Solar Alliance (ISA) International Energy Agency (IEA), United Nations Economic and Social Commission for the Asia and the Pacific (UNESCAP), European Research Institute for ASEAN and East Asia (ERIA), Organization of the Petroleum Exporting Countries (OPEC), and International Solar Alliance (ISA), World Nuclear Association, several countries including India and supporters have cautioned us about global warming and they believe that nuclear power is a vital part of a clean, affordable, and reliable energy system. In the recently held G-20 Summit under the presidency of India, the 2nd Energy Transitions Working Group (ETWG) meeting emphasized on the necessity to achieve "immediate and pressing solutions to global warming, climate neutrality, and energy security."[27]

In addition, a Ministerial meeting has been planned "to advance global cooperation in clean energy transition and make it central to the agenda of sustainable economic development."[28] Earlier as part of the first ETWG Meeting under India's G-20 Presidency attention was drawn on "six major priority areas such as Energy Transition through Addressing Technology Gaps; Low-cost Financing for Energy Transition; Energy Security and Diversified Supply Chains; Energy Efficiency, Industrial Low Carbon Transitions and Responsible Consumption; Fuels for Future (3F) and Universal Access to Clean Energy and Just, Affordable, and Inclusive Energy Transition Pathways."[29] The importance of clean energy transition transcends beyond the global fight against climate change. It is also directed at benefitting global citizens for a better life through the achievement of net zero and decarbonization of those sectors that emit poisonous greenhouse gases. This is in line with the realization of the Sustainable Development Goals. Nuclear energy produces minimal waste that can be reprocessed and recycled.

In a recently published report, India has emphasized the relevance of fostering resilient renewable energy sources like solar, wind, geothermal, hydropower, biofuel, etc, for the benefit of the global community. The report published under India's G-20 presidency, emphasizes the vast benefits from renewables including zero fuel costs, stable electricity prices, less dependence on fossil fuel imports, and reduced pollution and water usage.[30] The last two ETWG Meetings attached immense importance to the renewable energy sources not only to assist decarbonisation of electricity systems but also promote the realisation of the desired impacts of the SDGs. India has underscored the need for a total $10 trillion till 2070 for energy transition at the first meeting of the G-20 Committee on Energy Transitions in India.[31] Several multilateral financial organizations, such as the Asian Development Bank, United Nations Environment Program, and World Bank, have proposed specific projects like repurposing of power plants and offshore wind to support clean energy transition. While India is in the pursuit of working on a new policy on decarbonization, various countries have also proposed the viability of generating green hydrogen produced from nuclear power.

Nuclear energy is in a decisive time now. Nuclear power plants are currently operational in 32 countries worldwide with about 19,536 reactor years of experience.[32] It provides approximately 10 percent of global electricity from about 440 power reactors and is the world's second largest source of low-carbon power (26% of the total in 2020).[33] Currently, there are fifty-seven reactors under construction in 17 countries, with China surpassing all with 21 reactors under construction.[34] The goal of all these countries is to keep pace with the expanding electricity demands of the growing population and consequential rapid urbanization. According to the UN, the world's population will grow from 7.8 billion in 2020 to about 8.5 billion in 2030 and 9.7 billion by 2050.[35]

It is a crucial moment for the international community to realize that global nuclear power capacity will need to double by 2050 to meet the climate change targets set by the Paris Agreement. According to the IEA, a significant number of developing countries must partake in this clean energy transition process to achieve the purported goal of decarbonizing our electricity sources and fuel economic growth and development. The IAEA and Indonesia co-sponsored a virtual event *Nuclear Potentials in the Energy Transitions* wherein experts deliberated on emerging technologies, such as small modular reactors (SMRs) to add nuclear to the global energy mix.[36] To expand demand for nuclear energy, the "Milestone Approach" under the aegis of the IAEA plays an important role in assisting newcomer countries to plan and develop their first nuclear power plant.[37] Existing civil nuclear energy capable countries can assess for further expansion under the Milestone Approach. To further espouse the initiative, the Milestone Approach is bolstered with the "Integrated Nuclear Infrastructure Review" for developing a safe, secure and sustainable nuclear power programme.[38]

Nuclear Energy is Denied "Equal Footing for Collaborative Action" in G-20 (2023) Deliberations

Despite the relevance of nuclear energy as a clean, reliable and inexpensive energy source, it has not been accorded an equal footing in the current G-20 deliberation held under India's presidency. However, India has stressed that nuclear power remains a non-renewable source of energy.[39] This has taken a backseat to the nuclear energy as a source of clean energy transition and is now out of the ongoing G-20 deliberation agenda. As reasoned by the Power Secretary, Government of India, Alok Kumar, "member countries favoured a people-centric energy transition mechanism."[40] This stands in sharp contrast with the November 2022, G-20 proceedings held under the Indonesia's Presidency in Bali where representatives from the IAEA and other experts as well as South Korea and the United Arab Emirates gathered to discuss the importance of nuclear power in the clean energy transition and its role in achieving net zero and the SDGs.[41]

The G-20 Summit held in 2021 under the presidency of Rome, the Ministers in charge of Energy and Climate faced a sharp energy crisis in the post-COVID-19 situation. The Ministers recognized the devastating economic impact of the pandemic on people's lives. While the world economy strives to rebound from the financial shock, there is a systemic pressure on fossil fuels to accelerate growth and development. This creates challenges for building an "inclusive and sustainable, climate and nature-friendly future." In this context, the G-20 Members emphasized a scientific approach to clean energy transition and reaffirmed the "role of nuclear energy in their energy mix and recognize its contribution to the overall reduction of GHG emissions and reliable supply of affordable energy."[42]

In September 2020, under the presidency of Saudi Arabia, the G-20 Energy Ministers acknowledged the role of nuclear energy in supporting clean energy transition and enhancing energy security. The Director-General, National Energy Agency (NEA), William D. Magwood, IV, in a virtual meeting presented the Agency's analysis of the role of nuclear energy in a circular carbon economy (CCE). The NEA report "Reduce: Nuclear" claimed that "in line with the decarbonisation objectives of the Paris Agreement, nuclear power is expected to play a growing role over the coming decades."[43] The Report that the CCE approach applies the "3Rs" framework of reduce, reuse, and recycle to abate carbon emissions. Nuclear energy is included within the "Reduce" aspect of the CCE framework to lower greenhouse gas emissions through measures such as energy efficiency and low-carbon energy generation. In the G-20 Energy Ministers Communiqué, Members noted that "nuclear plays, in providing clean energy, for those who opt to use it, as well as in enhancing energy security."[44]

In 2019, the same sentiment was echoed in the G-20 Summit held under the Presidency of Japan in 2019. The 2019 Summit encouraged countries that opt to continue utilizing nuclear energy for collaboration on advanced nuclear energy technologies, including small modular reactors, and innovative uses of nuclear energy, including integration with the IAEA, the IEA and other international organizations.[45] Later in October, the same year, Union Minister, Dr Jitendra Singh, while speaking at the inauguration of 11th Nuclear Energy Conclave, New Delhi announced that the Government has diversified the applications of nuclear energy in various social fields, including the field of medicine, especially cancer care. He emphasized that more awareness must be generated about the application of nuclear power as a source of energy to meet the rising energy demands of India.[46] Speaking on the same occasion, on the "Long term vision for Nuclear Energy" the Secretary, Department of Atomic Energy and Chairman, Atomic

Energy Commission, Dr K N Vyas, said that "climate change scenario has gone more grimmer and it is dangerous to the humanity if we continue the business as usual."[47] He emphasized decarbonisation and opined that nuclear energy is an incontestable option to tackle global warming. While speaking on "Nuclear Power India's Development Imperatives," Dr Kakodkar said that given India's enormous energy thorium and solar energy, India can "become a net exporter of clean and safe energy before it is too late."[48] India's G-20 Sherpa Amitabh Kant, while addressing a session at the energy transition working group of G-20 meeting in Mumbai, called for an "unfettered access" to nuclear technology from the US to make advanced small modular reactors (SMRs) in India, that can help drive economic growth.[49]

The G-20 members need to garner crucial support to accelerate technology development and large-scale deployment of nuclear energy worldwide. The G-20 countries must endorse their commitment to exterminate inefficient fossil fuel subsidies so that they can be gradually phased out. The Outcome Document of the recently concluded G-20 Energy Transitions Ministers' Meeting reiterated the significance of accelerating the scale of deployment of nuclear energy for those countries that opt to use it.[50] The idea is to provide clean energy contributing to GHG emissions reduction, achieving energy security to fulfil the goal of SDG 7 related to affordable and clean energy.[51] The Document made a special mention of small modular reactors building resilient nuclear supply chains following the IAEA's high standards of nuclear safety, security and safeguards. However, much more needs to be done to ensure that nuclear energy plays a pivotal role in phasing out fossil fuels, which is indispensable to limit the effect of global warming and to produce more green technology. The G-20 Members must work tirelessly to develop sound and sustainable policies that can act as powerful tools to meet the challenges of achieving climate neutrality.

Nuclear Energy is a Non-negotiable Choice

The world today is undergoing a fluid situation with the aftereffects of a pandemic, the uncertainty over an international crisis over the Russia-Ukraine crisis, an economy struggling to recover with acute challenges for climate change. There is a rising energy demand that threatens the quality of life. It puts enormous pressure on resources and technologies with social and environmental implications. This imbalance only accelerates the inequality among consumers and provokes issues of economic and political stability, leading to competition and armed conflict.

Under the circumstances, there is a crucial need for efficient use of resources for clean and affordable energy generation and consumption while striving for safety, security and sustainability. This is also relevant to increase production, enhance productivity, improve quality of life, mitigate environmental pollution and focus on sustainable growth and developmental goals. With the world increasingly feeling the cost of fossil fuels, nuclear energy comes as a non-negotiable choice to the global energy mix for the betterment of humanity and our environment. Hence, a nuclear investment is a vital element for achieving a people-centric and sustainable energy system. With the G-20 Leaders' Summit, scheduled in New Delhi from September 9 - 10, 2023, the world would be watching upon the G-20 Leaders' commitment towards making the world safe for us and our future generations.

ENDNOTES

1. "Coal Market Update – July 2022," *International Energy Agency* at https://www.iea.org/reports/coal-market-update-july-2022 (accessed on 2 July 2023)
2. Press Release, "Global CO2 emissions rose less than initially feared in 2022 as clean energy growth offset much of the impact of greater coal and oil use," *International Energy Agency*, 2 March 2023 at https://www.iea.org/news/global-co2-emissions-rose-less-than-initially-feared-in-2022-as-clean-energy-growth-offset-much-of-the-impact-of-greater-coal-and-oil-use (accessed on 2 July 2023)
3. "CO2 Emissions in 2022," *International Energy Agency* at https://iea.blob.core.windows.net/assets/3c8fa115-35c4-4474-b237-1b00424c8844/CO2Emissionsin2022.pdf, p.3, (accessed on 2 July 2023)
4. "Russia's war of aggression against Ukraine continues to create serious headwinds for global economy, OECD says," 22/11/2022, OECD at https://www.oecd.org/newsroom/russia-s-war-of-aggression-against-ukraine-continues-to-create-serious-headwinds-for-global-economy.htm (accessed on 2 July 2023)
5 Press release "Global coal demand is set to return to its all-time high in 2022," *International Energy Agency*, 28 July 2022 at https://www.iea.org/news/global-coal-demand-is-set-to-return-to-its-all-time-high-in-2022 (accessed on 30 July 2023)
6. "Coal Market Update – July 2022, *International Energy Agency*, July 2022 at https://www.iea.org/reports/coal-market-update-july-2022/demand (accessed on 30 July 2022)

7. Press release, "Global coal demand is set to return to its all-time high in 2022," *International Energy Agency*, 28 July 2022 at https://www.iea.org/news/global-coal-demand-is-set-to-return-to-its-all-time-high-in-2022 (accessed on 30 July 2022)
8. "Coal Market Update – July 2022," *International Energy Agency*, July 2022 at https://www.iea.org/reports/coal-market-update-july-2022/demand (accessed on 30 July 2022)
9. "Confronting the Crisis OECD Economic Outlook," *Organisation for Economic Co-operation and Development* November 2022 at https://www.oecd.org/economic-outlook/november-2022/ (accessed on 30 July 2022)
10. Noah Browning and Bozorgmehr Sharafedin, "Fossil fuel demand shakes off pandemic in blow to climate fight," *Reuters*, 4 October 2021 at https://www.reuters.com/business/energy/fossil-fuel-demand-shakes-off-pandemic-blow-climate-fight-2021-10-04/ (accessed on 3 August 2022)
11. "International Energy Outlook 2021(IEO2021)," *Energy Information Administration*, 6 October 2021 at https://www.eia.gov/outlooks/ieo/pdf/IEO2021_ReleasePresentation.pdf, p.7.
12. See P.R. Shukla, J. Skea, R. Slade, A. Al Khourdajie (et. al.), IPCC. 2022. Climate Change 2022: Mitigation of Climate Change. Contribution of Working Group III to the Sixth Assessment Report of the Intergovernmental Panel on Climate Change (Cambridge: Cambridge University Press, 2022)
13. "Emissions Gap Report 2022," *United Nations Environment Programme*, 2022 at https://wedocs.unep.org/bitstream/handle/20.500.11822/40874/EGR2022.pdf?sequence=1&isAllowed=y (accessed on 3 August 2022)
14. "Nuclear Power in a Clean Energy System Fuel report," *International Energy Agency*, May 2019 at https://www.iea.org/reports/nuclear-power-in-a-clean-energy-system (accessed on 3 August 2022)
15. "The Database on Nuclear Power Reactors," *IAEA, Power Reactor Information System (PRIS)* at https://pris.iaea.org/PRIS/home.aspx (accessed on 3 August 2022)
16. "New Swedish government seeks expansion of nuclear energy," *World Nuclear News*, 17 October 2022, at https://world-nuclear-news.org/Articles/New-Swedish-government-seeks-expansion of-nuclear (accessed on 3 August 2022)
17. Policy paper, "Powering Up Britain", *Gov.UK*, March 2023 at https://assets.publishing.service.gov.uk/government/uploads/system/uploads/attachment_data/file/1147340/powering-up-britain-joint-overview.pdf, p.19 (accessed on 3 August 2022)
18. "UK looks to nuclear to bolster energy independence," *World Nuclear News*, 30 March 2023 at https://www.world-nuclear-news.org/Articles/UK-looks-to-nuclear-to-bolster-energy-independence (accessed on 3 August 2022)
19. "Nuclear Power in the USA," *World Nuclear Association, June 2023 at* https://www.world-nuclear.org/information-library/country-profiles/countries-t-z/usa-nuclear-power.aspx (accessed on 3 August 2022)

20. Stephen Nalley and Angelina LaRose, "Annual Energy Outlook 2022 (AEO2022), *Annual Energy Outlook*, 2022, March 3, 2022 at https://www.google.com/url?sa=t&rct=j&q=&esrc=s&source=web&cd=&cad=rja&uact=8&ved=2ahUKEwiS7MqIrc2AAxU8zDgGHdrdD-QQFnoECA8QAQ&url=https%3A%2F%2Fwww.eia.gov%2Foutlooks%2Faeo%2Fpdf%2FAEO2022_ReleasePresentation.pdf&usg=AOvVaw23WA66spk0BM-JA9r1JfBu&opi=89978449, p.2 (accessed on 3 August 2022)
21. *Ibid.*
22. R B Grover, "An Examination of the Narratives of the Electricity Sector," Current Science, Vol. 119, No. 12, December 25, 2020.
23. "Dr. Jitendra Singh informs that during 2021-22, nuclear power reactors generated 47,112 Million Units of electricity, which comprises about 3.15% of the total electricity generated in the country," *Department of Atomic Energy, Press India Bureau*, 5 April 2023 at https://pib.gov.in/PressReleaseIframePage.aspx?PRID=1913892
24. Union Minister Dr Jitendra Singh says, nearly 9% share of electricity likely to be contributed from India's nuclear sources by the year 2047," *Department of Atomic Energy, Press India Bureau*, 9 April 2023 at https://pib.gov.in/PressReleaseIframePage.aspx?PRID=1915070 (accessed on 3 August 2022)
25. *Ibid.*
26. "Union Minister Dr Jitendra Singh says, nearly 9% share of electricity likely to be contributed from India's nuclear sources by the year 2047," *Department of Atomic Energy, Press India Bureau*, 9 April 2023 at https://pib.gov.in/PressReleaseIframePage.aspx?PRID=1915070 (accessed on 3 August 2022)
27. "2nd G-20 Energy Transitions Working Group Meeting commences in Gandhinagar India's G-20 Presidency aims to collectively address the immediate and pressing challenges of global warming, climate change and energy security: Dr. Munjpara Mahendrabhai Kalubhai Need for G-20 member countries to collaborate and build a sense of trusteeship to achieve a clean energy transition: Shri Alok Kumar, Power Secretary," *Ministry of Power, Press India Bureau*, 9 April 2023 at https://pib.gov.in/PressReleaseIframePage.aspx?PRID=1913109 (accessed on 3 August 2022)
28. *Ibid.*
29. "Union Minister Shri RK Singh calls upon G-20 partners for united fight against global warming and climate change; First G-20 Energy Transitions Working Group Meet begins in Bengaluru. International seminar on Carbon Capture, Utilisation and Storage (CCUS) held on the sidelines." *Ministry of Power, Press India Bureau*, 5 February 2023 at https://pib.gov.in/PressReleaseIframePage.aspx?PRID=1896439 (accessed on 3 August 2022)
30. Akanksha Tyagi, Dhruv Warrior, Agarwal, Senior Hemant Mallya, Karthik Ganesan, Rishabh Jain, Rishabh Patidar, Sonali Bhaduri, "Developing Resilient Renewable Energy Supply Chains for Global Clean Energy Transition," *Council on Energy, Environment and Water*, April 2023, p. 2

31. Subhayan Chakraborty, "India needs $10 trillion till 2070 for energy transition at G-20 meeting," *Business Standard*, 5 February 2023 at https://www.business-standard.com/article/economy-policy/india-needs-10-trillion-till-2070-for-energy-transition-at-G-20-meeting-123020500740_1.htm (accessed on 3 August 2022)
32. "The Database on Nuclear Power Reactors," *Power Reactor Information System (PRIS), IAEA*, August 7, 2023 at https://pris.iaea.org/PRIS/home.aspx (accessed on 3 August 2022)
33. "Nuclear Power in the World Today," *World Nuclear Association, May 2023 at* https://world-nuclear.org/information-library/current-and-future-generation/nuclear-power-in-the-world-today.aspx (accessed on 3 August 2022)
34. "The Database on Nuclear Power Reactors," *Power Reactor Information System (PRIS), IAEA*, August 7, 2023 at https://pris.iaea.org/PRIS/home.aspx (accessed on 3 August 2022)
35. "World Energy Needs and Nuclear Power," *World Nuclear Association*, October 2022 *at* https://www.world-nuclear.org/information-library/current-and-future-generation/world-energy-needs-and-nuclear-power.aspx (accessed on 3 August 2022)
36. Jeffrey Donovan and Nicholas Watson, "IAEA Joins Indonesia for G-20 Event Highlighting Nuclear Power for Clean Energy Transition," *IAEA*, 13 June 2022 at https://www.iaea.org/newscenter/news/iaea-joins-indonesia-for-G-20-event-highlighting-nuclear-power-for-clean-energy-transition (accessed on 3 August 2022)
37. Approximately 30 newcomer countries including Indonesia and the United Arab Emirates have collaborated with the IAEA to develop nuclear power to help maintain an uninterrupted energy supply system. See "Milestones Approach," *IAEA* at https://www.iaea.org/topics/infrastructure-development/milestones-approach (accessed on 3 August 2022)
38. "Integrated Nuclear Infrastructure Review" *IAEA* at https://www.iaea.org/services/review-missions/integrated-nuclear-infrastructure-review-inir (accessed on 3 August 2022)
39. *Ibid.*
40. "G-20 Energy Transitions Working Group deliberations conclude successfully with shared views and consensus on priority areas," *Ministry of Power, Press India Bureau*, 6 February 2023 at https://pib.gov.in/PressReleaseIframePage.aspx?PRID=1896807 (accessed on 3 August 2023)
41. Jeffrey Donovan and Nicholas Watson, "IAEA Joins Indonesia for G-20 Event Highlighting Nuclear Power for Clean Energy Transition," *IAEA*, 13 June 2023 at https://www.iaea.org/newscenter/news/iaea-joins-indonesia-for-G-20-event-highlighting-nuclear-power-for-clean-energy-transition (accessed on 3 August 2023)
42. "Energy Transition and Climate Sustainability Working Groups. Joint G-20 Energy-Climate Ministerial Communiqué,", *2021 Rome Summit*, 23 July 2021 at www.G-20.utoronto.ca/2021/2021_G-20-Energy-Climate-joint-Ministerial-Communique.pdf, p.6 (accessed on 3 August 2023)

43. "Reduce: Nuclear," *Nuclear Energy Agency*, August 2020 at https://www.cceguide.org/wp-content/uploads/2020/08/03-NEA-Reduce.pdf, p. 7 (accessed on 3 August 2023)
44. "G-20 Energy Ministers Communiqué," *2020 Riyadh Summit*, 28 September 2020 at www.G-20.utoronto.ca/2020/G-20SS_Energy_Ministers_Meeting_Communique.pdf, p. 2 (accessed on 3 August 2023)
45. "G-20 Karuizawa Innovation Action Plan on Energy Transitions and Global Environment for Sustainable Growth," *2019 Osaka Summit*, 16 June 2019 at www.G-20.utoronto.ca/2019/2019-G-20-Karuizawa-Innovation-Action-Plan.pdf, p.6 (accessed on 3 August 2023)
46. 'Dr Jitendra Singh inaugurates 11th Nuclear Energy Conclave. Theme of the Conclave: Economics of Nuclear Power-Innovation towards Safer & Cost Effective Technologies," *Department of Atomic Energy, Press Information Bureau*, 18 October 2019 at https://pib.gov.in/newsite/PrintRelease.aspx? relid=193863 (accessed on 3 August 2023)
47. *Ibid.*
48. *Ibid.*
49. "Kant calls for unfettered access to US nuclear technology to build small modular reactors," *Press Trust of India*, 16 May 2023 at https://www.ptinews.com/news/business/kant-calls-for-unfettered-access-to-us-nuclear-technology-to-build-small-modular-reactors-/571278.html (accessed on 3 August 2023)
50. "G-20 Energy Transition's Ministers' Meeting, Outcome Document and Chair's Summary," *Ministry of Power, Press India Bureau*, 22 July, 2023 at https://www.G-20.org/content/dam/gtwenty/gtwenty_new/document/G-20_Energy_Transitions_Ministers%E2%80%99_Meeting_Outcome_Document_and_Chair%E2%80%99s_Summary.pdf, pp. 7-8 (accessed on 3 August 2023)
51. *Ibid.*

About the Editors

Dr Sitakanta Mishra is currently the Dean of the School of Liberal Studies of Pandit Deendayal Energy University (PDEU, formerly PDPU), Gandhinagar, Gujarat (India). He is also the Managing Editor of the *Liberal Studies* journal published by the School of Liberal Studies (SLS) of PDEU, Gujarat. Previously, he was a Research Fellow at the Centre for Air Power Studies (CAPS), New Delhi, and a Guest Faculty at the Nelson Mandela Centre for Peace and Conflict Resolution, Jamia Millia Islamia, New Delhi. He was the Associate Editor of the *Indian Foreign Affairs Journal* published by the Association of Indian Diplomats, Sapru House, New Delhi.

Dr Mishra received his Ph.D from the Centre for South Asian Studies of Jawaharlal Nehru University (JNU), New Delhi and has authored five books on India's national security, energy security, Cruise Missiles, nuclear safety security, terrorism, etc., besides several book chapters, and research papers related to geopolitics, nuclear energy, missile defence, South Asian and Indo-Pacific affairs. He is also involved in track-2 dialogues in various parts of the world.

Considering his academic contribution and commitment, Dr Mishra has been conferred the prestigious 'Bharat Vikas Award 2018' by the Institute of Self-Reliance (Odisha, India) for outstanding performance in National Security and Nuclear Energy.

Dr Banita Mahanandia is presently working as an Assistant Professor in the School of Political Science, Gangadhar Meher University, Amruta Vihar, Sambalpur, Odisha. She has teaching experience of eight years. She has completed her Ph.D. degree in International Relations from Utkal University Vani Vihar, Bhubaneswar. Her research area covers Climate Change, Gender Issues, Social exclusion and inclusion, Human Security. She has received a Gold Medal from the Chancellor (Governor) of Odisha, for being topper in M.A Political Science Utkal University, Vani Vihar, Bhubaneswar, Odisha. She has published many articles in both national and international journal, co-authored books and also contributed many chapters in the edited books. She has recently completed three important Research Projects funded by ICSSR, World Bank and University Seed Money. She has successfully guided three MPhil Dissertation and has been awarded.

Dr Gyanaranjan Swain did his PhD from University of Delhi. Earlier he was teaching in Aryabhata College, Zakir Hussain College, University of Delhi and Ravenshaw University, Cuttack. At present he is a Professor, Head and PG Council Chairman at School of Political Science, Gangadhar Meher University, Sambalpur, Odisha. Professor Swain has more than 18 years of teaching experience. He has published number of articles in reputed journals like EPW, social change etc. He has specialization in the field of Applied political theory, Odisha politics, Development studies. He is also working as State Coordinator for CSDS Lokniti Survey Team Since 2016.

About the Contributors

1. **Neeraj Singh Manhas** is a Ph.D. candidate at the Department of Political Science at the M.S. University of Baroda, Gujarat, India. He has authored three books and has various research interests covering Sino-Indian border issues, China in the Indian Ocean, India-China foreign policy, water security, defence, and Indo-Pacific studies.
2. **Shankar Chhatria** is a distinguished scholar who earned his Ph.D. from Pondicherry University. His academic expertise lies in the areas of Federalism, Regionalism in India, and the Koshal Movement.
3. **Shreya Das** is a Ph.D Scholar at the Vidyasagar University, Midnapore, West Bengal, India.
4. **Navonil Dey** Assistant Professor, Egra SSB College, Egra, Purba Medinipur, West Bengal, India.
5. **Naresh Kumar Behera,** PhD. Research Scholar, Centre for South Asian Studies, Pondicherry University, Puducherry, India.
6. **Gopika Pavithran** holds a Master degree in Political Science from the Central University of Punjab, India.
7. **Subham Tripathy** is Senior Research Scholar, School of Political Science, Gangadhar Meher University, Sambalpur, Odisha, India.
8. **Singh Subhalaxmi Baidhar** is Assistant Professor in Political Science, Gangadhar Meher University, Sambalpur, Odisha.
9. **Prasanna Kumar Panda** Research Scholar at the Jawaharlal Nehru University, New Delhi, India.
10. **Duryodhan Nahak** is Associate Professor at the Department of Political Science, P.G. D.A.V. College, University of Delhi, New Delhi.

11. **Kalpesh Bag** is Assistant Professor CDOE, Mangalayatan University, Aligarh, India.
12. **Keshab Chandra Ratha**, Assistant Professor, School of Political Science, G.M. University, Sambalpur, Odisha, India.
13. **Priyanka Masant** is an Assistant Professor (Guest Faculty) at Gangadhar Meher University, Sambalpur, Odisha, India.
14. **Mohammed Badrul Alam** is a former Professor at the Department of Political Science, Faculty of Social Sciences, Jamia Millia Islamia University, New Delhi, India.
15. **Nisarg Jani** is a Doctoral Candidate at the Pandit Deendayal Energy University, Gujarat.
16. **Reyaz Ahmad Ganaie** is an Assistant Professor in the Department of Political Science, Maulana Azad National Urdu University, Hyderabad, India.
17. **Rajaram Panda** is a Senior Fellow at the Nehru Memorial Museum and Library, Former Senior Fellow, IDSA, New Delhi, Lok Sabha Research Fellow and ICCR India Chair Professor, Reitaku University, Japan.
18. **Reshmi Kazi** is a Professor at the Department of Political Science of Jamia Millia Islamia, New Delhi, India.